CONCUBINAGE, RACE AND LAW IN EARLY COLONIAL BENGAL

This book analyzes the domestic relations which British men came to establish with native Indian women in early colonial Bengal. It provides a fresh look into the history of imperial expansion and colonial encounters by studying the large number of wills left by the British men who came in an official or economic capacity to India. It closely engages with these wills, considering them as unique personal records. These documents, where the men penned down details of their native mistresses, give a glimpse of what their lives, interpersonal relationships, household objects, and everyday affairs were like. The volume highlights how commonplace such non-marital cohabitation was and constructs the social history of these connections. It looks at issues of theft, violence, rape, bequeathment, and property rights which the women had to contend with, and also studies some of the early experiences of the mixed-race children who were a product of these relationships.

A unique look into the asymmetrical but fascinating history of interracial households in early colonial Bengal, this book will be of interest to students and researchers of history, women's studies, gender studies, colonial law, colonial travel writing, minority studies, colonialism, imperialism, and South Asian studies.

Ruchika Sharma, Assistant Professor, Department of History, Gargi College, University of Delhi, India.

CONCUBINAGE, RACE AND LAW IN EARLY COLONIAL BENGAL

Bequeathing Intimacy, Servicing the Empire

Ruchika Sharma

LONDON AND NEW YORK

First published 2023
by Routledge
4 Park Square, Milton Park, Abingdon, Oxon OX14 4RN

and by Routledge
605 Third Avenue, New York, NY 10158

Routledge is an imprint of the Taylor & Francis Group, an informa business

British Library Cataloguing-in-Publication Data
A catalogue record for this book is available from the British Library

Library of Congress Cataloging-in-Publication Data
A catalog record has been requested for this book

ISBN: 978-1-032-32282-7 (hbk)
ISBN: 978-1-032-32464-7 (pbk)
ISBN: 978-1-003-31518-6 (ebk)

DOI: 10.4324/9781003315186

Typeset in Sabon
by Deanta Global Publishing Services, Chennai, India

FOR MY MOTHER,

RANI SHARMA

FOR BEING THE LOVE, STRENGTH, AND HAPPINESS IN MY LIFE

CONTENTS

FIGURES

PREFACE

This research has taken a long time to turn into a book. I am told first books usually do. I sincerely hope some clichés turn out as promised. I stumbled upon this theme during my early discussions with my supervisor, Professor Rajat Datta, at Jawaharlal Nehru University in 2004. I had just started my M.Phil. dissertation year, and he suggested I look at Peter Robb's work on Richard Blechendyn in the 1790s. One of the highlights of the article was Blechynden's *bibi* or native mistresses. There was no looking back. Then started my long trips to Calcutta, a city second only to Delhi of my affections now. I discovered the wonderful National Library, its various sections, and what historical goldmine I was sitting on.

An interesting turn in my research came when I saw the wills, probates, and other inventories at Calcutta High Court in 2006. I do not think I can ever correctly express my excitement at seeing wills initially at the High Court. Only a historian can understand the feeling of being able to work at a place, that houses your archive, in its most organic 21st-century version. It was a daunting task to work at a functioning High court, which I used to run to, in between my teaching breaks from the University of Delhi.

One of the questions I have been frequently asked is – why did I choose Bengal for research, when I have no connection with the region? The common understanding being that the knowledge of the vernacular is always a useful research tool. The other, of course, is the logistical concern, in finding it easy to stay and manage while you do your field work. After having done my Master's in studying the peripatetic Mughals at the Centre for Historical Studies, at JNU with some of the most amazing teachers, this was not even a concern for me. Just like the Mughals, it was travelling to the unknown that turned out to be where my work was to take a shape. For I was never doing history of a region but looking for the women who were lost behind the term 'native women' in these wills I was looking at.

I have often also wondered if the choice of my theme has been an extension of my own thoughts and ideas, and it has been. The answer occurred to me the day I decided to look for history of women in intimate relationships with British men in early colonial Bengal. Most history writing has forgotten them or has taken them for granted as one of the results of colonial expansion. I was looking for personal histories in early colonial intimacies, without relegating these women to just the private sphere.

This is for me what my research did. It made me ask questions, look for answers wherever they took me and the next thing I knew was, I was writing this book. It is probably not all that I have to say about my inquiry. It is just an attempt to relook at the early colonial Bengal Presidency, beyond the simplistic telling of history, with right interjections. I take analysis of legal language as my tool, with native women at the heart of it. I am glad to have taken that initial step.

ACKNOWLEDGEMENTS

I could only complete the journey of writing this book due to encouragement and continued support from many individuals and institutions. I would like to start by expressing my heartfelt gratitude to Nehru Memorial Museum and Library for the grant of 'NMML Academic Research, Translation and Book Writing Fellowship' to me.

This work would not have been possible without the constant guidance of Professor Rajat Datta, who supervised my research during both my MPhil. and PhD. I am greatly indebted to him not only for shaping up many of my ideas, but also for his valuable insights during numerous discussions over the years, without them, this work would not have come to its summation. I am heartbroken that Prof. Rajat Datta isn't around to see this work reach completetion.

I remain eterenally grateful to Prof. Harbans Mukhia for being such an influence in my understanding of history. Also, for gently nudging me towards writing this book, and painstakingly reading the manuscript and encouraging me to always look beyond the obvious.

I would also like to thank Prof. Yogesh Sharma for diligently reading the book's draft, and offering valuable ideas – both as an academic and as a fabulous teacher. Also extending gratitude to my teachers Prof. Dilbagh Singh, Prof. Joy K. Pachuau, Prof. Arvind Sinha, Prof. Pius Malekandathil, Dr Aditya Pratap Deo, Ms Sangeeta Luthra Sharma, and Ms Anjana Singh for sharing their academic expertise with me, and giving encouragement at various junctures. Thanking Dr Urmimala Sarkar, for being such an inspiring academic, particularly my focus on Nautch girls, Prof. Seema Alavi for her suggestion to consider the aspect of property rights in my work, Dr Charu Gupta for encouraging me to re-look at the question of agency, and Dr Shobhana Warrier and Dr Shalini Grover for their academic inputs as well as for being such supportive friends. I would also like to mention Dr Nitin Sinha and Dr Nitin Varma for their exciting work on Servants' Past and thank them for making me a part of their conferences, both at Delhi and Berlin. The discussions and suggestions during these conferences made me rethink some of my ideas on the notion of service in my own research.

Thanking Kate Allen and Nupur Patel, the organizers of the 'Women and Agency: Transnational Perspectives, c.1450–1790' symposium and raising some pertinent questions that contributed to the way I engage with some of my ideas in this book. I would also like to thank my colleagues and staff at the various colleges I have taught, who have enabled me to take up my research travel and writing.

I would like to particularly thank Prof. Promila Kumar, Principal, Gargi College, for her encouragement, and my colleagues – Dr Alka Michael, Dr Deeksha Bhardwaj, Dr Megha Shukla, Dr Pragati Burman, Mr Piyush Kumar Yadav and Mr Shashi Bhushan, Gupta for being kind and supportive.

I would like to mention Prof. Durba Ghosh, who I chanced upon at the British Library and had an insightful discussion on Wills with. I would express gratitude to Prof. Peter Robb for his valuable time and an interesting discussion on early colonial Bengal during a visit to School of Oriental and Africal Studies. I would also like to thank Mr William Dalrymple for a stimulating conversation on *Bibis* during my early research days.

Special thanks to the High Court, Kolkata, for giving me access to the Old Records Room and the staff of the Old Records Room during my many visits. My work there would not have been possible without the kind help of Mr Imran Sultan Hafesjee, Senior Master and Official Referee, High Court, Original Side, Calcutta, as well as Mr Shibasis Bagchi and Mr Gautam Karamkar, Superintendents, High Court, Original Side, Calcutta. I would like to acknowledge the wonderfully done map, handmade especially for my book, by my old student Ms Aqsa Ashraf.

I am also greatly indebted to the staff of all the libraries and archives for their kind help throughout my research and writing, especially the British Library, London; National Archives of India, New Delhi; National Library, Kolkata; Nehru Memorial Museum & Library, New Delhi; Indian Council for Historical Research library, New Delhi; Sahitya Kala Academy library, New Delhi; Jawaharlal Nehru University library and DSA library, JNU, SGTB Khalsa College, Kamala Nehru College, Sri Venkateswara College, and Gargi College. I also want to acknowledge the Indian Council for Historical Research for the financial assistance they provided me with, enabling me to undertake my field trip to London.

This acknowledgement would remain incomplete without thanking my wonderful family and friends, who have been patient and loving in more ways than I could imagine. I would like to sincerely thank Ravi, for encouraging me to write. Nivedita, Parmita, Shipra and Nupur, for always being ready with their love. My parents-in-law V.B. Singh and Geeta Singh for their affection and support. There are friends with whom I have often discussed my work with and received constant love from – Victoria, Gunjeet, Anila, Gaganjot, Josheen, Sajjan, Pankaj, Uma Shankar Pandey, Anand, Taniya, Jaiti, Robert, Ankush, Aastha, Avanti, Neeraj, Jason, and Vineet – many thanks. Also thanking friends and fellow academics who made Calcutta feel like a home during the first visit itself – Saby, Dharitri, and Ujjayan. I would like to mention Akanksha, Shikha, and Akarsh, for reading different chapters of my manuscript and sharing their perspectives. I want to thank my best friends, Nafisa and Richa for constantly being there for me. I would like to mention R.K. Upadhyay uncle for being such an incredible support.

Heartfelt gratitude to Vijayant, for being my best friend, partner, and my harshest critic. Without his intellectual inputs, emotional support, and love, this book would not have happened. My brother, Rajat for being unfailingly supportive. I am particularly missing my grandparents – Savitri, Baldev, Balram and Sheila, who were there for a lot of my research work. Their lives have been a lesson for me, how large historical events, and churnings like partition, are ultimately personal histories. Finally, I am extremely grateful to my loving parents, Rani Sharma, and Raj Kumar Sharma, who have been relentlessly supportive; particularly my mother, who has always inspired me to map my own path. I dedicate this work to her!

ABBREVIATIONS

H.C.O.S:	High Court Original Side, High Court, Calcutta
O.I.O.C:	Oriental and India Office Collection, British Library, London
IOR:	India Office Record, British Library, London

GLOSSARY

Abdar –	Water bearer
Ayah –	Nursemaid, governess
Chokedar –	Watchman
Cotta/Cottah –	Measurement of land
Cowries –	Currency in shells
Devadasi –	Literally, God's female servant, temple dancers
Dhye/Dhai	Midwife
Ghat –	River bank
Hircarrah –	Messenger
Hookah –	Tobacco smoking instrument
Joomkah –	Earring
Jungal –	Forest area
Kitmuddar (Khidmutgar) –	Male servant
Kunchanee –	A community of dancers and performers
Meerasan –	A community of dancers and performers
Mofussil –	Towns away from Presidencies
Mohur –	Mughal gold coin from North India
Nautch/Naach –	Dance
Pagoda –	Gold coin from southern India
Paan –	Betel leaf eaten with various flavours
Paundanne –	A decorative box to keep prepared pan in
Paunjeb (Pajeb) –	Anklet
Patta –	Measurement of land; contract on land usage
Purdah –	Literally, veil.
Saheb/Sahib –	Master, used for European men
Zenana –	Secluded space for women in a household

1

INTRODUCTION

Reading Wills, Retrieving Native Woman

> I Alexander Watts, Boots and Shoemaker, Inhabitant of Calcutta Fort William, in the Province of Bengal. … I give and bequeath unto a native woman, my servant and housekeeper named Nancy Orphan, Inhabitant of Calcutta, the monthly allowance of Calcutta, the monthly allowance of Calcutta sicca rupees six during her life and bequeath the favour of my executor to be her friend and guardians after my death.[1]

Written in 1821, this was among the earliest wills I came across at the High Court, Calcutta (Figure 1.1). Alexander Watts in this will, along with settling his property matters by leaving money for his widowed mother, brother, and sisters, also mentions a 'native' woman who he fixes up a monthly allowance for. Nancy is mentioned as both his servant as well as a housekeeper, and an inhabitant of Calcutta. Now, what do we understand by his usage of both the terms together, that too for a woman who he wants to take care of, by leaving her a monthly allowance, as some kind of pension for life? She is certainly not just a servant, and yet, if she is servicing him, it would have to be more than mere domestic household work because he does not mention any other servant. We know that domestic servants in the Indian social structure were bound to certain tasks due to caste restrictions and having to employ a host of servants due to the same reason was a usual European complaint.

A large number of wills left by the British men, who came in their official and economic capacity to India during the early colonial times, are catalogued and housed in the Oriental and India Office Collections (O.I.O.C.), British Library, London, as well as placed in the Old Record Room of Calcutta High Court, give a snapshot of what their lives, interpersonal relationships, household objects, and everyday affairs would have been like. This book proposes to study the rich archive of wills from the Bengal Presidency, where the British men penned down legacies as well as details of their 'native' mistresses, domesticity, and its various aspects.

DOI: 10.4324/9781003315186-1

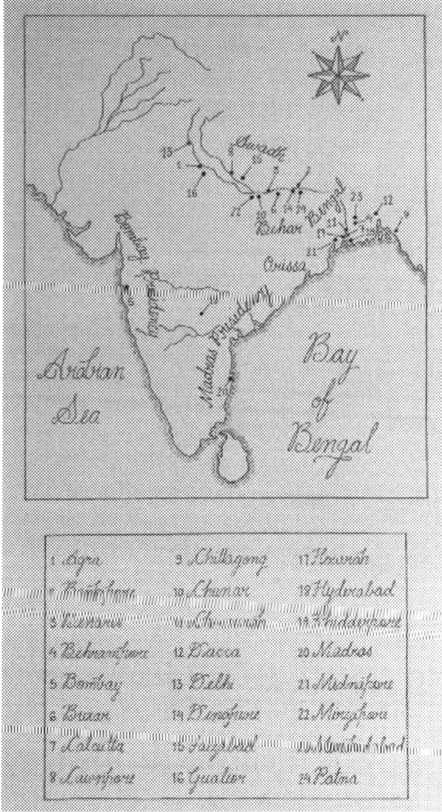

Figure 1.1 Map of places mentioned in the book (Illustration by Ms Aqsa Ashraf).

The wills use different terms of endearment such as housekeeper, faithful servant, my companion, servant girl, female friend, mother of my children, and so on, with the term 'native' used to describe a woman of Indian or mixed-race descent. By the sheer number of their mention, we get to know how commonplace these non-marital cohabitations were, and the various aspects of it as one endeavour to construct the social history of this connection. In my initial research, I came across these wills and realized what an untapped source they can be, to trace the lesser known of these, commonplace mixed-race connections.

It is probably within the same parameters that this research aims to study the various degrees of interpersonal relationships between the native women and the British men in Bengal circa 1750–1830. The term often used for native women in conjugal relationship with a British man around this time is *bibi* or *bebee*, used quite extensively in English sources. This term is used in legal documents as well as in the works of a more personal nature, such as memoirs, diaries, travel writing, articles, and so forth. The term *bibi* in Anglo-Indian parlance of early colonial India, as a prefix or suffix to a name, came to denote the native mistress. The term *bibi*, though commonly used and popularized, was not the only word used to refer to a native concubine. This book intends to look beyond only one meaning of this relationship that of a concubine, as conveyed by this term. There are of course other terms, that allude to the same phenomenon of shared space between native women and the European, particularly British men.

There have been researches on various aspects of sexual connections and domestic establishments pertaining to the early colonial and colonial men with the local women, and not just in early colonial Bengal.[2] There have been case studies in the Indian context too.[3] These were not formalized marriages, and yet, by and large had widespread social acceptance, in almost all instances. A pertinent question that should be asked is how come there came to be a similar set of living arrangements using services of the 'native' women across continents, over centuries of colonial contact? How did the colonial frameworks that differed on the ground in many of their functions be able to establish interpersonal and sexual relations with colonized women in cohabitational, non-marital households everywhere? They were accepted, acknowledged, and connived by both local societies and by the Europeans present in the colony. Terms like 'sleeping dictionary' were used for the local women, and they were expected to provide the white men with the local know-how. As one can imagine, they have been romanticized, where the two civilizations came together, especially in the case of India. It became an ideal setting to understand a political transition, getting out of the shadows of an Indo-Islamic Mughal Empire. This was a cultural space where the elites and the maintenance of harems were viewed as a cultural facet and a part of the socio-familial milieu.

The Oriental gaze of the early European travellers was able to turn that around and make the East as well as the Eastern experience all about the sexualized, hitherto unexplored experience. Even in the case of India, the earliest elaborate description of the Mughal imperial harem comes from the writing of European travellers.[4] The initial depiction of native women in European travel writing over time made way for their presence in various colonial writing. From these early impressions of being domestic partners, servants, etc., in European households led to a shift in their portrayal along with the nature of archives to study and understand early their presence in colonial experience. The Indian experience of the European presence was also going through a transformation during the late 18th century. Following the Battle of Plassey (1757), the European presence in Bengal became increasingly British. However, the British population was overwhelmingly comprised of men, with only a small presence of British women. The early studies of the establishment of the British Empire at the nascent stage, have not paid much attention to considering the role of women – South Asian and European, as an aspect of the study. The early travel literature feminized the entire phenomenon of travel and exploration of the East, but it did not focus on the role women played within the larger structures and processes. It is only in the last quarter of the 20th century that the feminist historiography of gender and empire has brought forth the history of the intimate and 'private' as integral to our understanding of trade, colonization, and the 'arts of discovery.'[5]

Over the past few decades the phases of transition, in Indian history, particularly pertaining to the 18th and early 19th centuries, have received a lot of scholarly attention. This phase, or rather these phases, are now comfortably accepted as 'areas' that need to be studied in their own terms and not constantly compared to their preceding or following period. If one chooses to study this period in Indian history, one of the most important features of this transition would be the expansion of British power, from its primary concern of commercial and trading activities to a position of paramountcy over regional powers. It had not yet taken the form of a full-fledged colonial state, and rather, this period in that sense is early colonial.[6] This was a phase of transition, where 'medieval' did not end as abruptly as believed for a very long time.[7] There were changes, though gradual, that paved way for a more definite structure and it is only by the early 19th century that one can notice formations or trends and patterns that were to acquire a more coherent form in following decades, in the course of the century.

Another development, in terms of history writing, that concerns this research more closely is the way in which relationships between Europeans and Indians have come to receive scholarly attention. There is an attempt to look for a shared space between the two instead of presuming them to be binaries. It is now regarded that the relationship the two shared, evolved, and transformed with changing historical contexts. This book too started as an enquiry into the shared intimate space between British men who came to India, particularly Bengal, where a large British community existed, and the 'native' women. The attempt is to go further back, into the late 18th century, when the British had started to play a prominent role in Bengal. The other European trading companies had begun to fade away in their political and military influence across South Asia. The British population was growing in Bengal. It was not just a homogenous population of Company officials, and army personnel, but also private merchants, persons from the service class, and other civilians were coming to Bengal, in considerable numbers.

The other facet that requires attention is the fact that such an occurrence of an interface of this nature was by no means exclusive to Bengal nor to the timeframe of the late 18th and early 19th centuries. Even other Europeans, who left their homelands to travel to Asia and Africa during the 16th and 17th centuries, developed such alliances with native women in their respective regions. When Europe came face to face with the East, the 'local' women proved to be useful keys to the new language and other mysteries of the local society. Their medical and cultural know-how was credited with keeping many European men alive during their initial, precarious confrontation with tropical life.[8] In fact, the first recorded affair between an Englishman and an Indian girl dates back to 1626 and there were numerous liaisons involving men from other European nations too.[9] But here we focus on the British in Bengal, particularly because of the dominant position they had come to acquire in India by the late 18th and early 19th centuries; and the unique position Bengal had gained in the setup of the English East India Company during the second half of the 18th century.

From the mid-18th century, the character of the English East India Company changed as it overcame the intense European rivalry and exploited the weakening political hold of the Mughals to its benefit. They were also able to obtain privileges from the local rulers, making the Company autonomous in the three most important settlements, i.e., the presidency towns of Madras, Bombay, and Calcutta, which were in due course placed under the rules of the governors and councils appointed by the Company.

It is against this background that we would study the intimate interactions between the native women and the British men. It is also necessary to elaborate upon the term 'native,' which itself is a politically contested term, for who constitutes a native? The term 'native' will be used in this book, to capture as closely as possible, what our archive tried to represent. The attempt is to also understand the meanings the word carried, not today, but in early colonial era. It is indeed a loaded term, but the colonial archive's understanding of the term became a way of addressing a non-European, local, or even a mixed-race person, without going into the details of their identity or parentage. It also became a sort of a presumptive term, where any woman called native would mean a woman whose either or both parents were of South Asian origin. However, it could also mean mixed-race parentage, as many women of Portuguese or French descent also have the term native used for them. The colonial measure of what it took to be classified as 'European' was based not on skin colour alone but on tenuously balanced assessments of who was judged to act with reason, affective appropriateness, and a sense of morality.[10] In the South Asian context too, these classifications were rarely complete or conclusive.[11] It is often used as a contrast to what it meant to be a European, which was as much social as well as a political construct of the times. It is, perhaps, also important to unpack how those who were called natives, were viewed over time.

The research on interracial connections did not exactly start by focusing on just these connections, until quite recently.[12] The anthropological and sociological works have shifted our attention to different research questions. One important change was that even colonial development in different parts of the world began to be studied as evolving structures. The other pertinent change was engaging with the questions of gender alongside the studies of empire formation. The feminist intervention to look for women beyond the roles they were hitherto given in studying colonialism, also underwent change. The study of the role of women started by looking for a gendered impact of imperial interventions on the lives of women on both sides. It also posed questions that were beyond the economic and political control of colonies, but the way women of both the colonized and colonizing nations were participants as well as catalysts of historical processes. Even the questions that often start with victimhood, went on to situate women against the larger imperial structures. The focus on categories such as household, domesticity provided an interdisciplinary approach to look at mixed-race relationships between colonizing men and colonized women. It also led to look at these categories fraught with imbalanced power, making retrieval of the history of the native women extremely important. Such interjections by intent are feminist, that take cognizance of class, race, sexuality, and the bearing they had together on interracial intimacies.

The historiography of the early colonial era has gone on to look for shared spaces between the colonizer and the colonized, which evolved and transformed in view of the expanding role of the colonial rule. The intimate space shared between a 'native' woman and a colonial man, is inherently asymmetrical. However, this work seeks to examine their history, beyond a few, well-known, upper-class mixed-race households, varying from local to mixed race, in the ambit of the larger definition of the term native, by pushing back the historical framework of inquiry to the early colonial. The aim is to start by looking at these women beyond their simplistic identity being reduced to being 'native.' It is a historical construction viewing her existence and depiction in the colonial archive as 'native.' It is this umbrella term, that in a certain sense obscures them. One also finds that these women decidedly existed as personages in the colonial phase. The wills are one such source, which, despite the different ways in which these women were mentioned or merely alluded to, bear testimony that these women were real historical figures. The wills, and a few court cases, are evidence and the only aperture where one catches a glimpse of these mixed-race relationships, making these wills unique as an archival resource. They testify to the fact that this shared interracial space, could be intimate, and functional within the bounds of a household.

Another important aspect that this work proposes to highlight is the numerous references to money, allowances, salary, etc. being paid to these women, to look at how these women were servicing these early colonial men. Not all these men were East India Company officials or high-ranking army officers, they were also merchants, soldiers, and service class British (and other European men too), who took the native women as their sexual and domestic partners. It is these women, who themselves came from a lower social and economic backgrounds, cohabiting with men across the economic hierarchy of the whites in the early colonial era whose histories this work investigates.

Some early scholarly writings in the Indian context have touched upon this theme in their respective works. They have discussed the native *bibi* in various dimensions. She is mentioned as a corollary to the social life of the early colonial male experiencing the exotic.[13] Percival Spear studies the social life of Nabob, in various phases of the settlement life of the British in India in the 18th century, and highlights English men marrying native women, the enthusiasm of the English man for 'Nautch,' along with the various Indian influences on them like the *hookah*, all typical of 'the ideal of a Nabob.' According to him, the custom of establishing a *zenana* by the English was 'too strongly rooted to be affected by new arrivals' and, 'it was in its turn a powerful Indianizing influence.'[14] S.C. Ghosh, in his work, devotes a chapter to 'the development of the Anglo-Indian community,' where he mentions the native mistresses of the British. According to him, 'the British community in Bengal had another kin, however, who deserve attention – their children, born of Indian mothers, who formed the Anglo-Indian community.'[15]

Then there are works that speak about the sexual dynamics between the native Indian sex workers and the British men as an aspect of the imperial structure. However, rather than speaking of these as isolated cases, they highlight the centrality of the Empire in controlling the bodies of the native sex workers in the 19th century. Kenneth Ballhatchet has an entirely different perspective as he discusses the 'official attempts to control sexual relations between English men and Indian women.' He emphasizes that the main concern of the British authorities was to preserve the structure of power. It was so despite the underlying 'contradiction between the care with which the military authorities provided facilities for sexual relations between British soldiers and native women and the care with which other authorities tried to discourage sexual relations between British officials and native women.'[16] Phillipa Levine too highlights 'the existence of approved and registered women, provided specifically and – at least in theory – exclusively for the use of the troops, is critical to understanding the centrality of sexual politics in the maintenance of empire.'[17] Likewise, Sumanta Banerjee mentions a change in the clientele of the prostitutes in 19th-century Bengal, as the 'whites' join in. He goes on to argue that prostitution was carried out in the 'gorgeous' garb of dancing girls, which quite allured the white man and holds that 'the liaisons between the "sahib" and the "native" female' remained within the framework of concubinage.'[18]

For Ronald Hyam, the native woman as *bibi*, forms a part of the discussion on 'The sexual life of the Raj,' covering a large span of time, till about the 20th century. He holds that 'the expansion of Europe was not only a matter of "Christianity" and "commerce"; it was also a matter of copulation and concubinage.[19] Another interesting work by E.M. Collingham, studies the British body in India, as 'it traces the transformation of the early 19th century Nabob, from the flamboyant, effeminate, and wealthy East

India Company servant open to Indian influence and into whose self-identity Indian was incorporated to the Sahib, a sober, bureaucratic representative of the crown.'[20] Here, the Indian mistress is discussed as one of the 'traces of India,' a physical, yet racialized experience of the Nabob, just as his other 'personal habits of eating, clothing, hookah-smoking and cleanliness.'[21]

The historiography that came to focus on these mixed-race sexual connections varies from romanticizing the mixed-race relationships, to emphasizing the 'political and economic contexts of these transactions and transfers, as well as the consequences for the legal, economic and social aspects of the making of colonialism in India.' William Dalrymple's book situates a story of the romantic affair resulting in marriage of the British resident in Hyderabad Major James Achilles Kirkpatrick and Khair-un-Nissa Begum, against the political backdrop of growing racial distancing in early colonial India. For him, crossing cultural barriers was easy and was done frequently till the late 18th century, but this attitude underwent a change once Cornwallis set his foot in India and the changes that were brought in. In his words, 'Two worlds were growing apart … it was largely due to the influence of one man.'[22]

Indrani Chatterjee's article does not differentiate between a female slave and a concubine. She holds that,

> historians of India romanticized her [the female slave's] presence either in terms of nostalgia [the epitome of racial harmony] or in terms of female agency ['consensual cohabitation'] and tended to brush aside the political and economic contexts of these transactions and transfers, as well as the consequences for the legal, economic, and social aspects of the making of colonialism in India.[23]

One of the most extensive works on the theme of the native woman cohabiting with the European men is by Durba Ghosh. Looking at the family in close connection with politics, race, religion, and sexuality in the larger framework of the British Empire, she has looked at interracial relationships as a crucial part of early state formation and governance in British India.[24] Elsewhere, she also writes about the aspects of domestic crimes in colonial Calcutta, and how the 'native women's bodies were domains on which debates over culture, tradition and law were staged,' etching out the idea that the 'European men enjoyed the legal benefits of a marital contract, even when such a contract did not exist, showed the ways in which colonial courts secured and legally rationalized sexual access of the bodies of native women, on behalf of lower ranking European men.'[25] She has also looked at the idea of gender and subjectivity through the namelessness of subaltern women in the colonial archive.[26]

Peter Robb has brought out two volumes based on the voluminous diaries of Richard Blechynden (1791–1822), who was an English surveyor, architect, and builder in Calcutta in the early colonial era. He brings out the more socially acceptable, mixed-race concubinage and its various aspects in Blechynden's life.[27] For him, Blechynden's diaries give out the historical importance of ordinariness and insignificance. His work shows us some extremely personal and emotional details of the mixed race living spaces in early colonial Calcutta.

There have also been some other historical works around the colonial law and the native woman, that touch upon the early invention of law into the mixed-race domestic spheres. Janaki Nair's work, *Women and Law in Colonial India: A Social History*, studies the various ways in which the colonial legislation attempted to transform the status of women in colonial India.[28] Radhika Singha discusses how the colonial governance sought to domesticate patriarchal authority. She contends that colonial officials were hesitant about assuming the functions of moral regulation exercised by earlier rulers, public expectations, and the need to find a normative frame for colonial law pushed them into an interventionist relationship in the household.[29] Elizabeth Kolsky speaks about the experiences of native women, as she argues that physical violence was an intrinsic feature of imperial rule. She also takes the scope of the legal archive beyond the legal, to an understanding of social aspects of early and then, colonial period.[30]

'Wills' as Personal Histories

Bengal wills contain a plethora of information, including several wills of Greek merchants, Armenians, and a few from Frenchmen too. It, of course, calls for a separate body of work, to construct the social composition of the Bengal of the 18th century, just using the wills. What was known as the Bengal Presidency, went beyond today's borders and encompassed areas other than just the Bengali-speaking regions. In that sense, this is not the history of a region, but what the term and space Bengal came to mean in the early colonial era as well as the wills filed in the Bengal Presidency.

The wills written by the British men are a part of colonial archives, but they do cut across sub-regions, class, and other divides as sources. They remain racial and gendered but interspersed with class dimension. In fact, as this book will discuss, the writing and framing of the will itself came with a cultural understanding of property, resources, and their (re)distribution. So, the one who is writing the will must necessarily own the property and material wealth, and at the same time understand how they want to leave it, and to whom. The wills also clearly state that most native concubines got property only for life that came with a precondition of non-ownership, and hence they remain unable to do with it as they pleased. These wills are a testament to women being kept out of the hereditary ownership of property, through marriage and even these interracial live-in partnerships.

The very act of willing property to women, on conditions, with terms laid out, becomes an expression of social structures and boundaries that might not be visible in other sources such as normative texts, political records, official decrees, folk narratives, or even in travel writing of the early colonial era. The political narrative of the preceding Mughal era too, remains a history of elite men where women find mention, as a part of the imperial household structure.[31] So, how does one study the non-elite households, in the early modern era in South Asia? What happens when colonizing men of the non-elite households bequeath goods, clothes, jewellery, and not so much liquid cash or share of their property?

These wills do carry information of material culture and the everyday lived history of non-elite mixed-race connections, and neither of them can be verified from other sources. They are records that are written or filed on a certain day, so one can catch only a glimpse of the life that the person writing it, chose to share in them. The terminology, even what is being written and what is conspicuous, becomes one of the ways to read them. A perusal through them, and one finds that in their specific instructions, they carry a lot of information on the workings of these relationships. Since the native women were almost absent in any other official archive of the early colonial times, the legal archives, especially the court cases and a few wills by women, become rare opportunities to witness their presence. Their silence and resulting erasure from the official archive have always come in the way of writing their history, which is not to say women do not exist in the archives. Contrary to the common perception, some scholars would argue, women are everywhere in the colonial archive, albeit in a fragmented and dispersed way.[32] This haze becomes even more dense in the early colonial archive. With simultaneous and multiple contestants of authority, features like the English law made a foray into South Asia. Bengal as a region, was also transforming into a more active presidency; and we must remember that the interracial connections existed not in the background, but in midst of all these political reconfigurations.

This work adopts a framework to dig deeper through these wills left by British men that mention their native mistresses and natural children, etc. and read them as personal histories and records. These wills are by no means unused source and have been previously looked at by a couple of scholars, but this work uses the wills beyond just enumerating the cases. It looks at wills from the late 18th and early 19th centuries to analyze the details of the living arrangements between these interracial couples – the provisions they make in their legacies and what and how they speak of these domestic intimacies.

As we attempt to retrieve the history of these women, we must be cognizant of the fact that due to transliteration by court officials, the language they spoke during the court case hearings, the expressions they might have used, and their choice of words, are all lost to us. But even then, we get to see some aspects of their multifarious roles in these households. The native women as witnesses, for example, as midwives were susceptible to biases of gender and race that early colonial law claimed it was trying to erase. The wills do give out details from British men's perspective. But often in the act of leaving the native mistress a bequeath, the British men unknowingly, perhaps unintentionally, gave out many details of these connections.

One of the most challenging tasks in introducing this theme of how to study domesticity and intimacies by reading wills, was structuring the sub-themes. Whether one should classify the wills based on the British men – their occupational positions, military, and civil spaces, or divide them by decades or any other way? Each will contains so many aspects that a neat division into simple sub-categories would not have brought out their richness as an archive. Each juxtaposes so many different aspects. However, it is the native woman, who is the focus of this work, and the aim is to retrieve her identity, existence, voice, and roles in the words of her domestic partner, the British man. Therefore, we have formulated sub-themes based on what the wills have spelled out. The details of the wills, what recurs, have become what the chapters delineate.

The wills suggest that these intimacies could crystallize into different kinds of arrangements like polygamous relationships, long-term companionship, or relationships that ended abruptly. The native partner could also be absent in the last will and testament, not get named, or gets a mention with a *given* name which leads to the loss of her history, name, and related identities. There were also cases where she was not left anything. Some wills would go on to describe details of her person, which may have nothing to do with the bequeath as such, but it would help in constructing her history. Incidentally, there was no will, which was *just one of these* and native woman in a conjugal relationship with the British man, remains common to them all. The native woman was servicing the emerging early colonial empire in a myriad of ways, in the confines of a domestic partnership. She was the provider of various kinds of services – sexual, reproductive, housekeeping, personal care, and so on, but all of them were within the bounds of mixed-race domestic relationships.

The idea that history writing as an endeavour remains circumscribed to a particular format of reading of a vast body of sources, is limiting if not perilous. The colonial records, which need to be critiqued for their inherent structuring of hierarchies, their misrepresentations, problems of translations, transliterations, and so on, remain the only corpus and space where we get information about the 'other.' The 'other' being the details, stories, versions, and incidents that the 'regular' archive does not record. The accessibility to education and hence, the actual act of writing remains bound by the parameters of caste, class, and gender in India. In the 18th century, of course, what we see is far more discouraging to find the voices of any kind of 'other.'

The reforms of the 19th century as well as broadening the scope of education were still remote in the 18th century. Where then one should look for history, stories, voices, and even the presence, of 'native' women? How does one think, let alone write about domesticity, household, and interpersonal histories for the 18th century from the 'local' or vernacular archive? So, rather than simply 'hierarchizing' archives, we need to make a foray into all sources possible, critically evaluate them and retrieve the histories of the 'native' women.

Agency or Leverage

Coming to the question of agency, these native women did move out to enter non-marital cohabitations with other white men. This is not to say that they were making choices from a position of power, in fact, far from it. They were certainly in relationships that favoured them in a limited way, not due to race, gender, and class, but by not having much control over the contours of domesticity. However, being outside the formal structure and probably the morality of marital compulsions, these relationships did not bind them to their British 'keepers' and did provide them with a certain leverage. The fact that they were also being paid might have also added to their power to negotiate, although we get evidence of mothers, or other servants acting as intermediaries for them.

The British men, in most cases, took the children away. It probably made it possible for these women to have mobility as far as their domestic boundaries were concerned. Peter Robb's book on Richard Blechynden, also mentions various entanglements that perturbed the early colonial British man, in his intimate spaces with native women. The mention of emoluments, and allowances which were made frequently in these wills, makes one look at domesticity from a more nuanced perspective. Likewise, these wills also bring out the details of the microhistories of the various interracial connections, that show that there were different facets to these intimacies.

One needs to connect the dots and look at the changes that colonial encounter engendered at the micro-level, specifically in the realm of the intimate and domestic. This is not to fall into the trap of keeping the dichotomy of the public and the private alive but to go further into what was interpersonal, sexual, and intimate in these domesticities. These women often moved from one domestic arrangement with a British man to another, for various reasons. Despite the various terms for native women preceding with a 'my,' loaded with control, possession, and the power to define relationship, these women do get out of these relationships. However, some of these associations continued for a long time, also mentioned in the wills, possibly out of affection, as well as legal precision.

The natives, by virtue of residing in or being employed in the British household, do appeal to the colonial law for their wages, and other matters, by coming under its purview. However, there were also instances of the court rejecting the native testimonies, and at times, not even hearing the entire assembly of witnesses. The language, terms, details, and other nuances spelled out in the legal documents hence form the only space where the lesser-known soldiers', merchants', and lower officials' concubines can be researched. The other important set of sources like paintings, official records, diaries, travel accounts, letters, private papers, etc. were confined to the affluent, upper-class personages who narrated their mixed-race connections in them. However, this work endeavours to retrieve the existences, voices, and other finer details of the mixed-race domesticities that existed only in these wills. It attempts to study the bequeaths in early colonial Bengal which certainly establish intimate connections as domestic set-ups, where these women lived with and serviced the British men. Hence, these wills should be studied, keeping in mind various finer aspects of these interracial relationships against the backdrop of the emerging colonial structure.

Arrival and Empire

The 18th century is important for scholars of early modern South Asia, as well as for those working on emerging colonial structures. In the first half, the two-centuries-old regime of the Mughals underwent a political decline, witnessing its various off-shoots in Bengal, Hyderabad, and Awadh as semi-independent 'successor' states.[33] However, the focus of the historiography has shifted to the role of multiple factors in bringing about this change, along with challenging the extent of centralization in these regions even during the Mughal era.[34]

The other important development of the 18th century, particularly in the second half, was the increasing importance of the English East India Company on the political canvas of India beyond a trading body and emerging as an administrative entity.[35] The interpretation of the colonial structure needs to acknowledge this transformation during the early phase of the colonial period and to do so, it must engage with the role of local players and factors. The historical trajectory of colonialism can be understood only if we accept that its making involved various factors beyond just the political and economic ones. The arrival of the Europeans in India was not one drastic event, but a series of events spread across various centuries in early modern South Asia. This implies that one needs to re-look at the 18th-century historiography itself. Rajat Datta points to pertinent changes after 1760 because the Company's regime was aggressively mercantilist and oriented towards Europe, not Asia. State policy was financially driven, and all institutions were to be streamlined to ensure this ultimate objective.[36] Also, the East India Company was able to put an Indian ruler they backed in Bengal by 1760. In 1764, the British defeated the Mughal emperor and his ally, the Nawab of Oudh, at Buxar. This gave the British a chance to gain considerable political leverage over Bengal. The East India Company thereby obtained *diwani* or the revenue administration of Bengal, Bihar, and Orissa. They never denied the authority of the Mughal emperor, but just like any other Mughal 'successor state,' began to manage the administration of these three regions. By 1765, the Company was de facto sovereign in Bengal: it had become the ascendant military power in the region, and it had acquired the *diwani*, the right to collect territorial revenues estimated to be worth between £2 million and £4 million per annum in the provinces of Bengal, Bihar, and Orissa.[37] The English East India Company benefitted from this time of political flux and found an opportunity in 18th-century India, where it could play off one state against the other while it offered its own services in the Indian 'military bazaar.'[38]

During the second half of the 18th century, the approach that the British adopted towards an efficient administration was to study the native traditions, local languages, and ancient laws. Colonialism is often thought of as a change, which it certainly is, but it also purposefully preserved many elements of the old regime. The early period of colonial rule is of course better known for the work of the Orientalists than for that of the 'historians,' though there was not always a strict separation between the two.[39] Here, one can see that the expansion of knowledge was not so much a by-product of the Empire as it was a condition for it.[40] Oriental studies leaning towards the attempts to *know* India, were designed to confer a degree of respectability on the Bengal government. Hastings and his circle of Orientalists also wanted to portray themselves as inheritors of the political knowledge of the previous rulers, particularly Akbar, who they saw as the founder of Mughal rule.[41] It also reflected in the production of art, filled with nostalgia about the Mughal aesthetic. Again, taking cue from Akbar's deployment of art for his personal and political promotion, Hastings and his circle of ambassadors began to construct private art collections focused on this epoch in the Mughal history.[42]

Sir William Jones was a scholar of both Persian and Arabic at Oxford, who later also learned Sanskrit. He published numerous translations and is known as the founder of The Royal Asiatick Society of Bengal. He was an East India Company judge from the years 1783 to 1794. What [Sir William] Jones proposed to do, through the agency of the Asiatick Society of Calcutta, which he founded in 1784, and through the publication of the serial Asiatick Researches (beginning in 1788), was to establish an intellectual and cultural analogue to the extraction of material wealth from the Orient – which was of course the East India Company's main priority – in the discovery and then the translation and circulation of the indigenous cultural, literary, artistic, and scientific productions of the Orient. Therefore, these were not random travel writings, but a planned study of geography, history, economy, people and their religious beliefs, epics, scriptures, etc. The encouragement given to Oriental studies had its own logic, beyond intellectual curiosity. Warren Hasting's own plan of governing India and asserting British Sovereignty did not mean the bringing on English laws and English ways in India.

> 'His idea was to rule the conquered in their own way. ... Thus he wanted to reconcile British rule with Indian institutions'.[43]

This quest to understand and thus administer newly acquired areas was not just what it appeared to be. It seemed that the idea was only to go ahead with continuities in the existing customary practices. It began with a promise to protect the caste and property of its Hindu and Mohammedan subjects under Warren Hastings.[44] Once British officers, in 1772, began not only to supervise Indian administration but to try the cases, Warren Hastings issued a regulation emphasizing,

> in all suits regarding inheritance, marriage and caste, other religious usages and institutions, the laws of the Koran with respect to the Mahomedans, and those of the Shastras with respect to the Gentoos [Hindus], shall be inviolably adhered to.[45]

Thus, the British 'Orientalists' encouraged the studies of ancient Hindu texts and institutions of the Indian past. Without rejecting western cultural and administrative precepts, Anglo-Indian[46] Orientalists were persuaded that, in the main, India's future should be built upon indigenous cultural institutions.[47] Commenting on Jones, Edward Said formulates how he wanted to do both – rule as well as learn and then to make a comparison between the Orient with the Occident. All this 'with an irresistible impulse always to codify, to subdue the infinite variety of the Orient to "a complete digest" of laws, figures, customs, and works, he is believed to have achieved.'[48]

On the face of it, the Orientalist enquiries seem to emerge from a point of non-intervention, but it also meant studying the Indian past the way they wanted to visualize it for themselves. It also reduced the civilizational history of a subcontinent and identities of individuals to religion, the way Jones and his supporters sought to view it. This basically led to viewing Indian history and society largely through religion, without its other nuances. Second, this attempt to understand the Indian social mores through what they termed as 'ancient' (either Sanskrit or Persian) texts reflected the British vision of India rather than the actual practice of the times. There was an attempt to interpret the Indian society in an idealized indigenous form, as seen by British 'Orientalists.' Some have termed this process a combination of a bit of both 'reverse acculturation' and codification or 'recuperation' of Indian manners and institutions.[49] In this entire endeavour, the attempts to show that their authority was indeed virtuous, where looking into the past becomes a justification of colonial (indirect) intervention. The colonizers urged respect for local culture, they did so either to facilitate imperial power, as in the case of Hastings, or to ennoble the idea of the Empire, as in the case of (Edmund) Burke, but both did create the necessary conditions for the use of tradition to justify imperial power.[50]

The Orientalists considered the 18th century as a decadent prelude as well as a justification for the British control, and India had become associated with an image of a rich and opulent space. This, in turn, gave birth to the 'denunciatory' character of the Nabob in Britain, who was the East India Company's employee – soldier, private merchant, or factor, who acted like the Nawabs or the Indian potentates imitating their extravagant lifestyle, etc. (Figure 1.2).

The fortunes of the Nabobs in India had come to play an important role in the domestic politics and economics of Britain. Edward Stephenson, who was the first Nabob to enter the House of Commons, purchased the estate of Lord Dawley from Lord Bolingbroke after he retired from India in 1730.[51] Quite obviously, the British press was critical of the East India Company

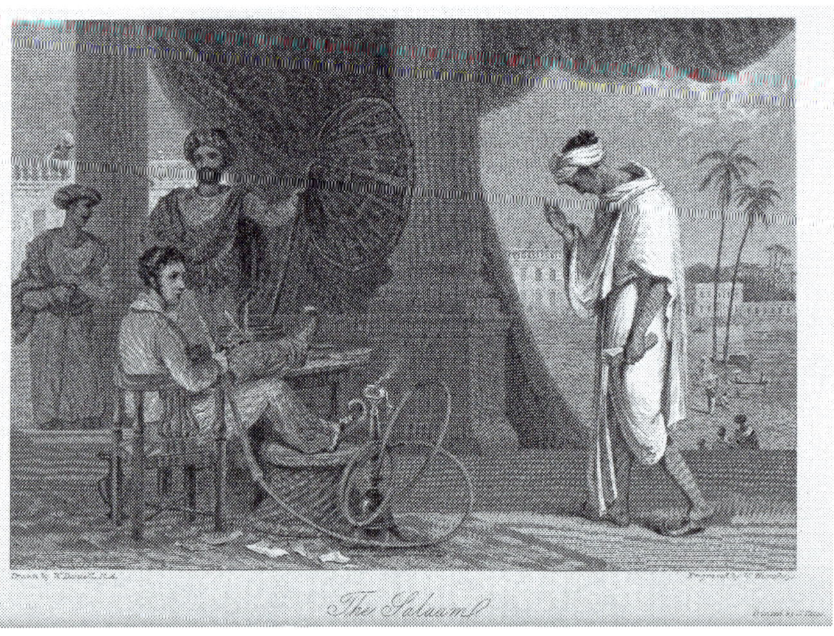

Figure 1.2 Daniell, W., and W. Humphrys. 'An Englishman sits smoking a hookah as an Asian man approaches making a salaam.' Engraving by W. Humphrys, C. 1834, after W. Daniell. Wellcome Collection. Public Domain Mark. 1 print : engraving; image 9.8 × 14.6 cm. London (26 Holles Street, Cavendish Square): Bull & Co., 1834. Reference: Wellcome Library no. 24879i. Link: https://wellcomecollection.org/works/vvhtrpx4.

and its officials at least in 1772, which is when the British were administering only a part of eastern India. The Company was seen to be following the same excesses and extravagance that they had earlier been critical of; they had almost stepped into the Mughal framework of the preceding decades, almost superseding them, without overthrowing their ways.

This was the time of enlightened 'Orientalists' as well as the Nabobs – the former discovering India, and the latter living in that India. This proximity with India is justified by citing enforced separation, which resulted in the 'stranded' officers becoming Indianized.[52] Other reasons could be the physical necessity and continuation of everyday living, apart from the need-to-know India, to govern it. For some, Nabob's 'Indianization' is reflected in the usage of Indian servants, hookah-smoking, palanquins, attending nautches, and so forth.[53] As we will see later, the Indian weather, particularly of Bengal, was presented as a physical and physiological challenge and it will be discussed in the next chapter, because it came to portray the 'natives' in a certain light. Nonetheless, the common idea was that peoples from colder climates had to make up for the lack of external heat and therefore were more vigorous and industrious, but slow-witted; those from hot, tropical areas were more indolent but also of subtler disposition, and much given to sensuality.[54] A medical manual writing about the influence of tropical climates on European constitutions, quotes a Dr Moseley on how there is "in the inhabitants of hot climates … a promptitude and bias to pleasure, and an alienation from serious thought and deep reflection".[55]

There came a major shift when in 1770, the Company asked for a loan from the government, which was given but with an increasing degree of control over the Company. The Regulating Act of 1773 was the first assertion of authority of Parliament over the Company and established the principle that the latter was answerable for its actions to the former.[56] This Act changed the nature of the Governor-General's administrative power, in fact, put limits on them; Hastings was now subject to the supervision of the Company-appointed Council.[57] This move was to not only regulate the East India Company but marked the beginning of a more regulated Empire in India. Some of the changes were deliberated upon within India, but some changes were just imported from back home. The latter was increasingly visible in the form of changing attitudes. As we move closer to the end of the 18th century, more than the actual shared space between the Indians and the British, there were growing apprehensions about what it meant. The cross-cultural references came to be judged not so much by those who did come to India, but by those who did not. The conditions for living in India were being transported from the metropolis, according to the scientific, religious, moral, and political ideas taking shape in Europe at that time.

The arrival of Lord Cornwallis and his experience of administration in the 13 colonies in America, certainly played a role in shaping his policies in India.[58] However, it was Richard Colley Wellesley, 1st Marquess Wellesley

(1760–1842), who brought an uncompromising regal status, visibly augmented by ceremonies and etiquettes and the Palladian mansion to the status of Governor-General. He viewed Indian rulers in the same light as the 'territorial aristocracy' of Great Britain and Ireland and himself as a direct representative of the king and as embodiment (rather than agent) of the Mughal sovereignty.[59] This attitude and policy shift became noticeably clear by the beginning of the 19th century. Its effect looms large over all the different events of the corresponding time – from administrative to societal. The changes were deemed necessary in education, native laws, religions, the land revenue system, etc. This view took another extreme view of Indian culture, bordering on apathy and even hostility. The [previous] atmosphere of mutual tolerance and even admiration was the way East India Company liked it, even if it practised religious toleration more out of pragmatism than principle.[60] As the Company's charter came up for renewal in 1813, things were going to be different. The old Orientalism was about to clash head-on with the new Evangelicalism.[61]

It is not to say that these two phases of colonial development were absolute binaries, in fact, one did lead to the other. The overwhelming European sense of 'otherness,' the sense of chasm had filled travel writings for long. It can be seen in the way Alexander Dow dwells on the extreme climate of India, i.e., the heat and humidity, which he linked to the 'seeds of Despotism.' He thus declared that how the 'languor occasioned by the hot climate of India' (naturally inclined) 'the native to indolence and ease.'[62] The same climate, to which the British attuned themselves, now became a reason to create the stereotype of the 'indolent' Indians. This scornful attitude was also echoed in this statement by Robert Orme, who was the first official historiographer of the English East India Company, witness to their victories of the mid-18th century.[63] In his essay, 'Effeminacy of the Inhabitants of Indostan,' he asserts how the whole make, physiognomy, and muscular strength of men throughout India conveys ideas of effeminacy. Additionally, he compares it to the European efficiency, that how 'two English sawyers have performed in one day the work of thirty-two Indians.'[64]

> Breathing in the softest climates; having so few real wants; and receiving even the luxuries of other nations with so little labour, from the fertility of their own soil; the Indians must be the most effeminate inhabitants of the globe.[65]

These opinions merely flag, what was turning out to be the official policy. The need for reform in India was felt at the political and moral levels too, not only for Indians, but also for the corrupt Nabobs. There were changes in policy, aiming at curbing the corruption, by increasing salaries of the Company employees as well as by imposing discipline on the government expenditure. Thus 'the idea of reform was not only related to the administrative needs of the colonial regime; it was also meant to root out rampant bribery as well as ransom decisions – in short, Oriental despotic rule manifested in arbitrary jurisdiction.'[66] For the subjects of India, now the policy was of intervention and segregation at the same time. Thus, if the emerging Empire was seen as God's will by the evangelicals, the interventionist role of the government was now seen as necessary by those in power.[67]

The British presence in India was going through a transformation; both at the social and the political levels. James Mill recognized despotic rule as the root cause of all degradation and backwardness in India. Also, the emerging policy believed that 'the Empire could be made more permanent if it successfully seized the unlimited opportunities for reform in India.'[68] He believed that since the British were now responsible for governing India, they also needed to ascertain India's civilization and its advancement. Needless to say, India failed on all markers of civilization for him, namely – religion, law, government, manners, arts, science, and literature.[69]

It was as if the task to know the real India, that initial travel writings had attempted, was over. However, from there developed the idea of how all that was held as exotic, became the very thing the British felt the need to topple and change. It was nowhere more felt than in discussions on sati. Abolition of sati in 1829 was the first major legislation of the East India Company's administration in India.[70] The fact that gender and race intersect with such imposing power dynamics is why the history of colonialism cannot be studied without wondering how the private is always brought into the public.

The ideas of differences in race, which became obvious by the last decade of the 18th and early decades of the 19th centuries, did not come in one go. The process of othering started with the earliest travel writing, even the Orientalists chose to see India through a prism of what they came to 'discover' about India's past. But with the emergence of utilitarian and evangelical ideas, increasing emphasis on the purity of blood and the fear of 'mixed' blood resulted in racial differences, that manifested into physical distancing or racial segregation. The Oriental gaze had come a full circle, continuing to see India as the other, which had more to do with the way Europe wanted to place itself. The Empire had arrived, and by the first half of the 19th century, all its aspects became clear – political, commercial, administrative, jurisdictional, and social. The men who had carried forward the British Empire, connected with India and the Indians in various ways. As Dirk succinctly puts it, 'where once scandal referred to the exploits of the colonizers, scandal now began to refer to the lives of the colonized.'[71]

Chapter Scheme

The first chapter, 'Beyond the Purdah – "Constructing" the Native Woman,' will conjure the native woman as seen by the Europeans travelling to India using travelogues, Indo-European paintings, memoirs, etc. As soon as the Europeans started coming to India, the details about what and who they witnessed began to fill the pages of travel literature. By the 18th century, Europe was overflowing with travellers' tales, adventure stories, picturesque paintings, etc. These men (and a few women) now travelled to India with a certain image, and the impression of India provided to them in Europe itself. So, these men stepped onto Indian shores with a certain broad overview and some perceptions, which took the shape of attitudes here. This chapter underlines the prevailing views back in Europe, where the wave of enlightenment thought had narrowed down the social boundaries of sexual laxity, around the late 18th century. The 18th-century drive for moral reforms slowly evolved not only to feed further into patriarchy and sentimentality but also into paranoia, prudery, and sexual repression.

Keeping the European background in mind, this chapter would try to look at the stereotypes of India put in place by the abundantly available travel writing and what shaped their gaze. We will look at various ways in which Indian social mores, and physical presence of Indian women – behind the veil and beyond it, were captured. Clearly, these were not merely knowledge production, or an attempt at capturing the picturesque, but had a political impact on shaping the Empire in the 19th century. It is against these perceptions that we place the 'construct' of these Indian women, also termed as native in contemporary sources, where it was her identity that was seen as being diametrically opposite from those who were writing about it. She then went on to also become an intimate part of the British household in the early colonial Bengal and elsewhere in India. The existing historiography has also focused on how at the level of everyday existence, the 'local' women's being 'useful' for learning the new language and other aspects of the local society, made them crucial, in the Indo-European interface.

Studying the construct as a background to establishing an intimate space between the British man and his native live-in partner, we will explore the connection between initial impressions of the travel literature and the emerging colonial rule. The colonial control that becomes visible in the 19th century stood upon a different and hierarchical reading of the knowledge of these travel writings.

The chapter, 'Forging Intimacies' talks about the complexities of the mixed-race intimacies and the different ways in which these domesticities played out. We must remember the fact that most of these native concubines only exist in these wills, and in no other source. Even in Baptism records of the mixed-race children, as their mother, she is not named.[72] She and her name are simply omitted.

Among the young British men who reached India, only a few were already married. We get a variety of reasons in their letters and travelogues, etc. as to why the other men took on Indian mistresses. The contemporary sources mention different reasons from the sultry climate to the high expense of maintaining an English wife, the presence of only a few unmarried British women, and so on. An increasing number of British men, who were getting comfortable with the local lifestyle and customs, found themselves partners among the 'native' women. Going beyond the idea of native women cohabiting with the English man as a part of his social experience or him going 'native,' this chapter engages with the various aspects of these mixed-race intimacies in early colonial Bengal.

We will also establish wills as records to delineate the different terms of cohabitation that the wills often spill out in various details, become a way in which we retrieve the native women. Wills, last testaments, and court cases take us to the histories of every day, which is where we find these women to spell out the details of these relationships, especially regarding emoluments, ways of acquiring mistresses, conditions and considerations of bequeaths, and other contentions (that led them to court cases). There has been some research on some well-known, and better-documented interracial households. However, here we look at the wills of the ordinary British men in India, who left bequeaths for their native concubines. Highlighting their histories, this chapter will ponder over issues such as name, identity, and narratives about these women. Wills, as documents, put emphasis on the correct details, but despite that the women are often mentioned by given names, mostly in English, rather than their actual names. A practice that renders the native women nameless, and without the correct identity often.

With a careful reading of wills, this chapter would bring out the myriad ways these conjugal relationships could go – short-term concubinage, long-term domesticity, polygamy, and so on. Here we, of course, will have to think of a dimension of class variation, even among the British population of the Bengal Presidency. It also means going beyond the simplistic monolithic understanding of the idea of domesticity itself. There are layers and nuances in these relationships that will be lost if we continue to read them from one simplistic perspective. Additionally, we would try to understand the various ways in which these native women were mentioned in these wills, and whether it reflected their work, position, and kind of domesticity they were a part of. What were the different roles that they were expected to fulfil, what were the services they were providing, for there is the mention of money, monthly allowance, wages, pensions, and so on? This brings us to the terms like 'my faithful servant' or her being mentioned 'for her care and services,' and to read these relationships, as well as their details beyond glamorizing them.

How to locate instances of intimacies in sources such as wills and last testaments of these interracial early colonial households? While engaging with intimacies, one also stumbles upon the question of love. Can we find instances of those in these legal records? Linking love as an emotion and intimacy as an experience is not what this work is going to do but perhaps we would stumble upon intersections by carefully picking and reading the wills. As this chapter would discuss, the Wills often carry expression of care and attention to her comfort while making the bequeaths. However, they also mention certain conditions for her to receive the legacy. Conditions to remain unattached, a good 'moral' character, and so on, which can sometimes trigger as controlling to a feminist endeavour such as this. Any attempt at retrieving voices of women, marginalized in the sole archive they exist in, is by nature feminist, but with intersections of race, and class. In a scenario, where the colonizing men control the resources, and there are so many ways a domestic and intimate connection could develop, we look for certain themes that run through most of them. The everydayness of native women's history through the wills, may not be as dramatic as a revolt, a bill, or a law changing the course of events. But the very notion that history must be drastic, is one of the reasons why it has taken so long for personal and private spaces to be historicized.

Different wills bring out different details of lives of individuals. There was no one 'right' kind of domesticity, and to view domesticity as one-dimensional would be an extremely shallow way to understand its complexities. It would continue the glaring lacuna in reading intimacies as historical and contextual. There are wills that express a great deal of affection, as well as those that do not mention the native mistress but do talk about children by her. There are wills that tell us that some of the British men had natal as well as families from marriage back home, who we get to hear a great deal about in these wills. At the same time, there are wills where only the native mistress and the child/children from her are mentioned. How do we read these details? How do we read distortions, affections, and even erasures of native women's identities together? This chapter would attempt to pick up common themes from these wills to write microhistories, that provide a glimpse of the social reality of the time, in a larger historical context.

Chapter 3, 'Legality – Property, Violence, and Discord' delves specifically into the legal aspects of these mixed-race intimacies. The wills written by native women, the actual bequeath of property to her, court cases concerning theft and rape as well as the contentious aspects that will give out are some of the concerns this chapter covers. Legal sources remain one such archive that gives us access to these native women, and their histories. The wills of the British men, who often left them bequeaths, have an interesting pattern. Most often, the money that these women inherited was given to them, as interest on a sum or a kind of monthly pension, and not the principal sum. Hence the issue of bequeaths is not just limited to what is being left but also if it is in complete control. And in this case, it was usually only for the natural life of these women. They did not enjoy complete rights over property such as land most of the time. The men would often make the provisions for the principal sum or a house (which she could live in during her life), to go to his children from her or from his married wife in Britain, or to the members of his natal family after her decease. Here, it would be relevant to understand the laws pertaining to women's property rights in Britain, and where do we place the property rights of native women living with the British men in early colonial Bengal, against that backdrop. There were also wills that did not leave anything to the concubines and mistresses, nor was their mention despite a reference to natural child/children.

The advent of early modern law did not consider the existence of these relationships, as a separate category. These relationships were quite common; nonetheless, the law turned a blind eye to these connections in an almost conniving manner. Incidentally, the mixed-race children became a grave concern, who were acknowledged more often than their mothers. The English East India Company had initially encouraged their men to marry the native women briefly in the 17th century, to suit their purpose as it were during the early days of their presence and the number of such men was not too many, although the focus was on marriage.

This chapter also considers the issue of property rights of women in England and in English law around the same time. Along with that, the concept of writing wills in South Asia will be discussed. Wills, where women do get complete rights over the property bequeathed to them, are also discussed in this chapter. There were a few women writing their wills, who certainly disposed of their property themselves. Like in the will of Bebee Zenut of Calcutta, who 'spoke her will in Hindostanee,' we get the details of her bequeath and what property she owned. She left part of her house to her son and granddaughter.[73]

Issues such as discord, or contention over money, come out rarely in wills, although such issues are mentioned there. However, issues of violence, theft, and rape involving native women in mixed-race localities come under the purview of the court. The discussion of the court proceedings also brings out the details as well as the voices of these native women. For example, in one of the cases of violence by a British man and his native mistress, questions are raised about her and even the purview of the court's jurisdiction, given that she was only his concubine and therefore not under his service for any work.[74] Discussions like these make the work of the native woman, in the personal and the intimate spaces, a central concern for their presence in the legal arena. It also brings the conversation back to whether concubinage was a form of employment in England. The attorneys argue over it as to how it was considered different from prostitution. It was a difficult question to answer since there were no fixed emoluments nor did the early colonial state make any official policy despite the regularity of these arrangements.

What we come across in this archive, are the native women, speaking as witnesses, victims, or perpetrators of violence, negotiating with the early colonial law. Their serviceability to men who established the colonial empire is accepted quietly at best, but never formally recognized. They are the most intimate point of contact, for they provide economic, sexual, reproductive, and emotional services, and are often paid, in cash or kind as the wills suggest.

Hence, this chapter will largely concentrate on the aspects such as property, complete control, bequeaths left to these women, violence, rape, and the ways in which the mixed-race interpersonal relationships were presented in the legal space. It will analyze the aspects of these intimate relationships, that are laid threadbare in some of the cases. For example, we will look at the relationship between different native women, in different roles, in a household in a particular court case. The natives in the court cases come out as witnesses, midwives, servants, and those who could have played a role in the crime itself.

One can notice that the 'irregular' companionship between a British man and his native woman counterpart was commonplace, readily accepted and arbitrated upon. They did come under the purview of 'rule of law' just like any other mixed-race space, and the native woman was also tried for being 'under the walls of a British man.' It was around the last decade of the 18th century when there is a shift in attitude towards the increasing number of mixed-race children signalled a major shift, which brings us to the next chapter.

The fourth chapter, 'Interracial Progeny' talks about the children of these relationships – the mixed-race children. Not just the material goods, money, and property, they had also inherited the racial, physical, cultural, and emotional legacies of this connection. These children were referred to, in the legal and official sources as half-castes, Eurasian, East Indians, mixed race, and so on. The term Anglo-Indian came to be used much later in the 19th century, until then, it stood for the life of the British living in India.

The change in the atmosphere towards mixed-race households was reflected in the treatment and policy towards the mixed-race children in the last quarter of the 18th century. Eurasians could no longer be appointed to the Company's civil, military, or marine services, and they were recruited for clerical posts or non-combatant posts in the rank and file of the army. More than the interracial connections, it was the children born of these cohabitations who came to be frowned upon in official policies. They were conceived as a dangerous source of subversion, a threat to white prestige, an embodiment of European degeneration and moral decay.[75] As we proceed further on to the 19th century, the native connections stop getting mentioned in the wills, as the political role of the East India Company was changing by then.

This chapter will look at one of the most obvious connects, the coming in of the Memsahib, or the white women to India in greater numbers. They were often blamed for creating a wedge between the perfectly harmonious mixed-race social connect of the Indians and the British. However, this chapter seeks to study the advent of the English woman, her role, racial expectations from her, and her gendered self against the potent political changes of that time.

It becomes clear that the native women were often referred to and valued in the wills, as the mother of the British man's child/children. In fact, at times, her only identity in the will was as the mother of the mixed-race child/children, who almost always, belonged to the father. In cases where she got interest on a sum, or a house for her life, the principal and the house, usually went to the children. Obviously, it is not to say that all men who had offspring from a native woman, left a will. But when they did, and a child is mentioned, there were still chances that the native woman's identity was withheld from being recorded or that she would not get anything at all.

Major Thomas Naylor left his 'female friend' Muckmul Khanum, a native woman of 'Hindostan' not only large sums of money but also his bungalow and garden at Bishanpore, along with other household goods including all his male and female slaves too. He mentioned her being pregnant and that it was 'indispensably necessary to provide for the unborn child.' So, he left a handsome amount along with it in writing that he would like a certain sum to be spent on the education of the unborn child. This is one of the wills that mentions both legitimate children as well as the child from his mistress and treats them with a comfortable equality.[76]

Harry Palmer, in the service of Honourable East India Company at Bengal, in 1772, left £2,500, for his 'dearly beloved son Charles Palmer.'[77] He even specifies his date of birth as November 5, 1772. He kept the money for his son at interest till the said son was sent to England. He appointed his friend Walter Ewer Junior, as the guardian, and appeals to him in the will with regard to Charles Palmer, 'I hope he will have him educated in the best manner possible and place the said sum . out at interest as he the said guardian deems most beneficial to ... Charles Palmer.' The residue money was to be paid to Charles Palmer when he came of age. He also mentions 'Joany Camem, mother of the aforesaid Charles Palmer the sum of *sonat*[78] rupees four thousand to be paid to her immediately after my decease.'

Some of these wills were extremely detailed, and also served as evidence in the case of the hereditary transfer of the property the children's education, future financial endeavours, and even their going to Britain. This is another issue this chapter will take up. Many mixed-race children were sent back to Britain. Who were these children being sent back to? Also, as more low-ranking army officials start coming to India, fewer Eurasian children were being sent back home. The issue of race should not be divorced from that of class. So, who could and who could not send the children back? This was generally so with the well-off Britons, 'but the children of ordinary soldiers were placed in orphanages where they were trained for menial jobs or married off to soldiers who attended the regular match-making dances at the orphanages.'[79] There were also such children who managed to get accepted in the British circles, but most of them were seen with deep distrust by both the sides. The children usually retained the last names of their fathers and were taken away from their mothers.

Over time, more orphanages and institutions were opened for the growing numbers of mixed-race children. And the employability of the mixed-race youth became a concern for many members of the British community. However, this was a valid concern, especially as the racial bias against them became obvious in the economic as well as the social space. The writings of travellers as well as memorandums and other petitions that raise concerns about the British outlook towards the increasing Eurasian community have also been examined. These changing perceptions about the children of mixed race were also visible in the policies being drafted for them. The mixed-race community had flourished initially because they were not treated differently, and they had opportunities to go to England for studies without any stigma. In 1786, the first of three orders issued by the Court of Directors stated that 'wards of Upper Orphanage School at Calcutta, which had been established by the Company for orphans of British military officers, were prohibited from proceeding to England to complete their education.'[80] This was the first official step towards discrimination against the mixed-race individuals and paved way for more.

As the British rule in India prospered, the posts in covenanted services and higher grades of civil services became more desirable; the Court of Directors became more eager to exert their rights to this patronage.[81] In April 1791, they resolved that Eurasians could no longer be appointed to the Company's civil, military, or marine services. They were recruited for clerical posts or non-combatant posts in the rank and file of the army. This attitude towards mixed-race persons got worse in the 19th century. The 'Anglo-Indian Codes,' which reviewed the civil and criminal law of India in the 1830s, mentions the children of mixed race under the title 'bastards' in its index. This speaks loudly of how these relations of cohabitation and its subsequent offspring came to be frowned upon.

Notes

1 'High Court Calcutta – Original Side: Bengal Wills,' 9381.

2 D. Ghosh, *Sex and Family in Colonial India: The Making of Empire* (Cambridge: Cambridge University Press, 2008); A. McClintock, *Imperial Leather: Race, Gender and Sexuality in the Colonial Contest* (London: Routledge, 1995); A.L. Stoler, 'Rethinking Colonial Categories: European Communities and the Boundaries of Rule,' *Comparative Studies in Society and History* 31, no. 1 (Jan., 1989); *Carnal Knowledge and Imperial Power: Race and the Intimate in Colonial Rule* (Berkeley: University of California Press, 2002).

3 W. Dalrymple, *White Mughals: Love and Betrayal in Eighteenth Century India* (New Delhi: Penguin Books, 2002).

4 R. Lal, *Domesticity and Power in the Early Mughal World* (Cambridge: Cambridge University Press, 2005).

5 K. Wilson, ed., *A New Imperial History: Culture, Identity and Modernity in Britain and the Empire, 1660–1840* (Cambridge: Cambridge University Press, 2004).

6 C.A. Bayly, *Rulers, Townsmen and Bazaars: North Indian Society in the Age of British Expansion, 1770–1870*, 3rd ed. (Oxford: Oxford University Press, 1983; repr., 2012); R. Datta, 'Commercialisation, Tribute, and the Transition from

Late Mughal to Early Colonial in India,' *The Medieval History Journal* 6, no. 2 (2003); P.J. Marshall, *Bengal – the British Bridgehead – Eastern India, 1740–1828*, The New Cambridge History of India (Cambridge: Cambridge University Press, 1987).

7 M. Alam and S. Subrahmanyam, eds., *The Mughal State, 1526–1750* (New Delhi: Oxford University Press, 1998); S. Alavi, ed., *The Eighteenth Century in India* (New Delhi: Oxford University Press, 2002); P.J. Marshall, ed., *The Eighteenth Century*, The Oxford History of the British Empire (Oxford: Oxford University Press, 1998).

8 Stoler, *Carnal Knowledge and Imperial Power: Race and the Intimate in Colonial Rule*, 49.

9 Dalrymple, *White Mughals: Love and Betrayal in Eighteenth Century India*, 22.

10 Stoler, *Carnal Knowledge and Imperial Power: Race and the Intimate in Colonial Rule*, 2–6.

11 D. Ghosh, 'Who Counts as "Native?": Gender, Race, and Subjectivity in Colonial India,' *Journal of Colonialism and Colonial History* 6, no. 3 (2005).

12 C.R. Boxer, *Race Relations in the Portuguese Colonial Empire, 1415–1825* (Oxford: Clarendon Press, 1963).

13 D. Kincaid, *British Social Life in India Upto 1938*, 1939 (London); P. Spear, *The Nabobs: A Study of the Social Life of the English in the Eighteenth Century* (Cambridge: Cambridge University Press, 1963).

14 P. Spear, *The Nabobs: A Study of the Social Life of the English in the Eighteenth Century* (Cambridge: Cambridge University Press, 1963), 36–37.

15 S.C. Ghosh, *The Social Condition of the British Community in Bengal: 1757–1800* (Lieden: BRILL, 1970), 57.

16 K. Ballhatchet, *Race, Sex and Class under the Raj: Imperial Attitudes and Policies and Their Critics 1793–1905* (London: Weidenfeld and Nicolson, 1980), 1.

17 P. Levine, 'Venereal Disease, Prostitution, and the Politics of Empire: The Case of British India,' *Journal of the History of Sexuality* 4, no. 4 (1994): 596.

18 S. Banerjee, *Dangerous Outcast: The Prostitute in Nineteenth Century Bengal* (Calcutta: Seagull Books, 1998), 44.

19 R. Hyam, *Empire and Sexuality: The British Experience* (Manchester: Manchester University Press, 2017), 2.

20 E.M. Collingham, *Imperial Bodies: The Physical Experience of the Raj, C. 1800–1947* (Cambridge: Polity Press, 2001), 3.

21 Ibid.

22 Dalrymple, *White Mughals: Love and Betrayal in Eighteenth Century India*, 54.

23 I. Chatterjee, 'Colouring Subalternity: Slaves, Concubines and Social Orphans in Early Colonial India,' in *Subaltern Studies*, ed. G. Bhadra, G. Prakash, and S. Tharu (Delhi: 1999), 52.

24 Ghosh, *Sex and Family in Colonial India: The Making of Empire*.

25 D. Ghosh, 'Household Crimes and Domestic Order: Keeping the Peace in Colonial Calcutta, C. 1770–C. 1840,' *Modern Asian Studies* 38, no. 3 (2004).

26 D. Ghosh, 'Decoding the Nameless: Gender, Subjectivity, and Historical Methodologies in Reading the Archives of Colonial India,' in *A New Imperial History: Culture, Identity and Modernity in Britain and the Empire*, ed. Kathleen Wilson (Cambridge: Cambridge University Press, 2004), 297–316.

27 P. Robb, *Sentiment and Self: Richard Blechynden's Calcutta Diaries, 1791–1822* (Oxford: Oxford University Press, 2011); *Sex and Sensibility: Richard Blechynden's Calcutta Diaries, 1791–1822* (New Delhi: Oxford University Press, 2011).

28 J. Nair, *Women and Law in Colonial India: A Social History* (Bangalore: Kali for Women, 1996).

29 R. Singha, *Despotism of Law: Crime and Justice in Early Colonial India* (Delhi: Oxford University Press, 1998).
30 E. Kolsky, *Colonial Justice in British India: White Violence and the Rule of Law* (Cambridge: Cambridge University Press, 2010).
31 S.P. Blake, 'The Patrimonial-Bureaucratic Empire of the Mughals,' *The Journal of Asian Studies* 39, no. 1 (1979); 'Courtly Culture under Babur and the Early Mughals,' *Journal of Asian History* 20, no. 2 (1986); 'Returning the Household to the Patrimonial-Bureaucratic Empire – Gender, Succession, and Ritual in the Mughal, Safavid and Ottoman Empires,' in *Tributary Empires in World History*, ed. P.F. Bang and C.A. Bayly (New York: Palgrave Macmillan, 2011). However, F. Hasan, *State and Locality in Mughal India: Power Relations in Western India, C. 1572–1730* (Cambridge: Cambridge University Press, 2006), speaks of ordinary womenfolk and their day-to-day engagement and interface with Sharia law in various aspects in 17th-century Gujrat.
32 B. Joseph, *Reading the East India Company, 1720–1840: Colonial Currencies of Gender* (Chicago: University of Chicago Press, 2004), 3.
33 M. Alam, *The Crisis of Empire in Mughal North India* (Delhi: Oxford University Press, 1986); Bayly, *Rulers, Townsmen and Bazaars: North Indian Society in the Age of British Expansion, 1770–1870*; K. Leonard, 'Indigenous Banking Firms in Mughal India: A Reply,' *Comparative Studies in Society and History* 23, no. 2 (1981); Karen Leonard, 'The "Great Firm" Theory of the Decline of the Mughal Empire,' *Comparative Studies in Society and History* 21 (1979); P.J. Marshall, *The New Cambridge History of India, Bengal: The British Bridgehead, Eastern India, 1740–1828* (Cambridge: Cambridge University Press, 1987).
34 Alam and Subrahmanyam, *The Mughal State, 1526–1750*, 1–71.
35 W. Dalrymple, *The Anarchy: The East India Company, Corporate Violence, and the Pillage of an Empire* (New York: Bloomsbury Publishing USA, 2019).
36 R. Datta, 'The Making of the Eighteenth Century in India: Some Reflections on Its Political and Economic Processes,' in *Sir J. N. Sarkar Memorial Lecture* (Kolkata: Bangiya Itihas Samiti, 2019).
37 H.V. Bowen, 'Investment and Empire in the Later Eighteenth Century: East India Stockholding, 1756–1791,' *Economic History Review, 2nd Series* 42, no. 2 (1989): 187.
38 C.A. Bayly, *Indian Society and the Making of the British Empire*, The New Cambridge History of India (Cambridge: Cambridge University Press, 1990), 48.
39 N.B. Dirks, 'Castes of Mind,' *Representations* 37: Special Issue: Imperial Fantasies and Postcolonial Histories (1992): 61.
40 C.A. Bayly, *Empire and Information: Intelligence Gathering and Social Communication in India, 1780–1870*, Cambridge Studies in Indian History and Society (Cambridge: Cambridge University Press, 1996), 56.
41 Ibid., 52.
42 N. Eaton, 'Nostagia for the Exotic: Creating an Imperial Art in London, 1750–1793,' *Eighteenth-Century Studies* 39, no. 2 (2006): 238.
43 S.N. Mukherjee, *Sir William Jones: A Study in 18th Century British Attitudes to India* (Cambridge: Cambridge University Press, 1968), 79.
44 N.G. Cassels, 'Social Legislation under the Company Raj: The Abolition of Slavery Act V 1843*,' *South Asia: Journal of South Asian Studies* 11, no. 1 (1988): 63.
45 G.W. Forrest, ed., *The State Papers of the Governor General of India, Vol. 2: Warren Hastings Documents* (Oxford: B.H. Blackwell, Broad Street, 1910), 295–96.
46 In contemporary British parlance the term 'Anglo-Indian' in eighteenth and sometimes even in nineteenth centuries meant the Britons living in India. Although later it came to mean persons of Indian and British mixed parentage.

47 W.A. Green and J.P. Deasy Jr, 'Unifying Themes in the History of British India, 1757–1857: An Historiographical Analysis,' *Albion: A Quarterly Journal Concerned with British Studies* 17, no. 1 (1985): 27.
48 E.W. Said, *Orientalism* (New York: Vintage Books, 1979), 78.
49 N. Leask, *British Romantic Writers and the East. Anxieties of Empire* (Cambridge: Cambridge University Press, 1992), 9.
50 N.B. Dirks, *The Scandal of Empire – India and the Creation of Imperial Britain* (Cambridge, Massachusetts: The Belknap Press of Harvard University Press, 2008), 296.
51 N. Dirks, *The Scandal of Empire – India and the Creation of Imperial Britain*, 39.
52 T. Wilkinson, *Two Monsoons* (London: Duckworth, 1976), 46.
53 Spear, *The Nabobs: A Study of the Social Life of the English in the Eighteenth Century*.
54 S. Stuurman, 'François Bernier and the Invention of Racial Classification,' *History Workshop Journal* 50 (2000): 53–78.
55 J. Johnson, *Influence of Tropical Climates on European Constitutions: Being a Treatise on the Principal Diseases Incidental to Europeans in the East and West Indies, Mediterranean, and Coast of Africa* (New York: W.E. Dean, Printer, No. 3 Wall Street, 1826), 420.
56 K.K. Dyson, *A Various Universe: A Study of the Journals and Memoirs of British Men and Women in the Indian Subcontinent, 1765–1856* (Oxford: Oxford University Press, 2002), 14.
57 B. Harlow and M. Carter, eds., *Imperialism and Orientalism. A Documentary Sourcebook* (Oxford: 1999), 25.
58 C.M. Rosenberg, *Losing America, Conquering India: Lord Cornwallis and the Remaking of the British Empire* (Jefferson, North Carolina: McFarland & Company, Inc., Publishers, 2017).
59 C.A. Bayly, "The British Military Fiscal State and Indigenous Resistance, India. 1750–1820," in *An Imperial State at War: Britain From 1689–1815*, ed. Lawrence Stone (London: Routledge, 1994), 341.
60 N. Ferguson, *Empire. How Britain Made the Modern World* (New Delhi: Allen Lane, 2004), 134.
61 Ibid., 135.
62 A. Dow, *The History of Hindostan from the Death of Akbar to the Complete Settlement of the Empire under Aurangzebe, to Which Are Prefixed; I. A Dissertation on the Origin and Nature of Despotism in Hindostan; Ii. An Enquiry into the State of Bengal; with a Plan for Restoring That Kingdom to Its Former Prosperity and Splendor*, 3 vols., vol. 3 (London: Printed for John Murray, No. 32, Fleet-Street, 1792), i. Vol. 3.
63 S.T. Delgoda, '"Nabob, Historian and Orientalist." Robert Orme: The Life and Career of an East India Company Servant (1728–1801),' *Journal of the Royal Asiatic Society* 2, no. 3 (1992): 363.
64 R. Orme, *Historical Fragments of the Mogul Empire, of the Morattoes, and of the Concerns in Indostant; from the Year 1659* (London: Printed for F. Wingrave, 1805), 463.
65 Ibid., 472.
66 H. Fischer-Tine and M. Mann, *Colonialism and Civilizing Mission: Cultural Ideology in British India* (London: Anthem Press, 2004), 32.
67 R.W. Winks, *Historiography*, The Oxford History of the British Empire (Oxford, 2001), 54–55.
68 F.G. Hutchins, *The Illusion of Permanence: British Imperialism in India* (Princeton: Princeton University Press, 1967); Nair, *Women and Law in Colonial India: A Social History*.

69 A. Loizides, *James Mill's Utilitarian Logic and Politics* (New York: Routledge, 2019).
70 R.S. Rajan, *Real and Imagined Women: Gender, Culture and Postcolonialism* (New Yotk: Routledge, 1995), 40–63.
71 Dirks, *The Scandal of Empire – India and the Creation of Imperial Britain*, 297.
72 Ghosh, *The Social Condition of the British Community in Bengal: 1757–1800*, 77; *Sex and Family in Colonial India: The Making of Empire*.
73 'High Court Calcutta – Original Side: Bengal Wills,' 9901.
74 'The Hyde Papers and Hyde Reports' (Calcutta: National Library Calcutta). reel 17, 23 Dec. 1796.
75 A.L. Stoler, 'Sexual Affronts and Racial Frontiers: European Identities and the Cultural Politics of Exclusion in Colonial Southeast Asia,' *Comparative Studies in Society and History* 34, no. 3 (1992): 515.
76 'High Court Calcutta – Original Side: Bengal Wills,' 3172.
77 'Bengal Proceedings,' in *India Office Records* (London: British Library), IOR/P/154/56.
78 For details of different currencies mentioned in the book, see: S. Garg, *Monetary Foundations of the Raj* (New York: Routledge, 2019); J.L. Laughlin, 'Indian Monetary History,' *Journal of Political Economy* 1, no. 4 (1893); R.M. Martin, *History of the Colonies of the British Empire in the West Indies, South America, North America, Austral-Asia, Africa and Europe: From the Official Records of the Colonial Office* (London: W. H. Allen, 1843), 141.
79 Capt. T. Williamson, *The East India Vade-Mecum; or Complete Guide to Gentlemen Intended for the Civil, Military or Naval Service of the East India Company*, 2 vols. (London: Printed for Black, Parry, and Kingsbury, 1810), 216.
80 C. Younger, *Anglo-Indians: Neglected Children of the Raj* (Delhi: B.R. Publishing Corp., 1987), 11.
81 Ballhatchet, *Race, Sex and Class under the Raj: Imperial Attitudes and Policies and Their Critics 1793–1905*, 97.

2

BEYOND THE PURDAH

'Constructing' the Native Woman

> I humbly request that the Hon'ble the court of directors, India Affairs and the Hon'ble Governor-General and supreme council of Bengal, will so far look into & superintend my affairs, that a true state of my estate may be laid before them, also my length of the service and the large family of children I have left to be brought up, both legitimate and illegitimate (the latter arising from the vigour of youth, under the influence of hot climate, distant from my country & cut-off from every possibility of forming a more creditable & honourable connection at an earlier period. I therefore trust they will be considered as deserving of protection and meet with indulgence from my Hon'ble employers, for they are essentially the children of necessity, & alas the law proves a cruel stepmother to them).[1]

The famous poem by English poet Lord Byron that equates 'gallantry' with 'adultery', conveys the often-repeated concern where 'adultery' and 'sultry' do not just rhyme but denote the way the Indian weather was viewed by the European travellers to the East.[2] Such expression for tropical weather not just presented it as strange or inconvenient, but often romanticized and corresponded it to the colonized women's bodies. An early colonial imagination marked the native topographies and peoples as feminine spaces to be violated and thereby instantiated a sexual/racial hierarchy between the colonizer and the colonized.[3] The geographical and sexological homologies between the females of the tropics with its warm climate and lush vegetation fantasize an early puberty for the tropical woman (as fruits/vegetables mature quickly in the heat) and an eager sexual readiness.[4] This very easily qualified the notion that the Oriental woman 'ripened' very early. It could over-qualify her as an offender, as for instance in cases of homicide, and under-qualify her as a victim, such as in crimes such as rape.[5] Not just sexual maturity, but other 'vices' are also attributed to the weather. Johan Splinter Stavorinus, writing about his voyages to the East Indies in the third quarter of the 18th century, blames the 'warmth of the climate' as he goes on to explain the Indian woman's jealousy

DOI: 10.4324/9781003315186-2

to his readers. In his words, it 'influences strongly upon their (Indians') constitutions, together with dissolute lives of men before marriage, are the causes of much wantonness and dissipation among the women.'[6]

Apart from letters and other personal writing emphasizing the sultriness of the weather, nowhere is it more blatantly mentioned as in the cases of rape of the 'native' girl by the European men. How the European men were often acquitted in such rape cases stating that the girl was not a 'virgin' or her physical presence in the European residential area made her a potential candidate for concubinage.[7] Despite the native *dhye*, or mid-wife's testimony of the victim being 'underage' or pre-puberty, it was not taken under consideration. It was probably for the 'given' reason, that Indian women matured early.

The quote at the beginning of the chapter is taken from the will of Major Andrew Wilson Hearsey, Captain in the Military Service of the East India Company – Bengal Establishment, who echoes similar sentiments in 1798. He mentions a wife Charlotte Maria Hearsey, and four children from her in the will, along with his natural children. He leaves both his legitimate and illegitimate children, well taken care of. For the illegitimate children, he apologetically justifies them 'arising from the vigour of youth, under the influence of a hot climate distant from my country and cut off from every possibility of forming a more credible and honourable connection at an earlier period.'[8] His will is one of those detailed ones that carry an expression of his sense of family, and hence, the responsibility that he feels towards them.

The legal archive, which is the space for bequeaths, contentions, and other matters of the law, cannot remain untouched from the mundane lived experiences and the impressions of the 'other' that the European community was forming in its early days in South Asia – even more so in travel writing. The words would have also been chosen carefully, for they added to the representations of the 'Orient' for the readers back home. These travelogues also meant the emergence of the discourse on race, gender, and sexuality, which laid the ground for colonial constructions later. I would like to argue that it was these early interactions, even when fully awed by the India that they write about, still manufacture the later acceptance of the colonizer and colonized, as far, distant and different from each other. The Indian women became the ultimate 'other,' for the earliest European travellers to the East were indeed men. Philippa Levine also shows that sexuality and sexual behaviour of the colonial women of colour were already prominent in the accounts of the travellers.[9]

Travel Literature

> To write a literature of travel cannot but imply a colonial relationship. The claim is that one travels to learn, but really, one travels to

> exercise power over land, women, peoples. It is a commonplace of Orientalism that the west knows more about the East than the East knows about itself.[10]

As we study the portrayal of the native Indian woman put across by European officials, their wives, travellers, painters, etc., we realize that their stereotyp ing exists in the form of letters, memoirs, travelogues, diaries, paintings, etchings, and even in the legal archive. This depiction of the Indian woman, in black and white or on a canvas is not exclusive to the 18th and 19th centuries but began as soon as the Europeans landed on the Indian shores. The dialogue between the Indian subcontinent and the West gained momentum once the travels and explorations from the West increased in number. As more and more Europeans reached the Indian coast, they wasted no time in filling pages with what they thought was different and, in some senses, the 'other.'

> A very short sojourn in any foreign country will generally suffice to dissipate that sense of novelty for a time is ever present with the travellers infusing into all his ideas and imparting a fanciful and dreamlike want of reality even to his action. Englishmen who visit the East ... find this effect protracted much beyond its ordinary duration, by a very striking contrast existing between Asia and Europe, both in the climate, scenery and people.[11]

What becomes clear is that this 'striking contrast' which provides the stimuli to capture the details of the 'other' to the Western travellers, was also invented by these travellers. Edward Said's work on Orientalism has led to numerous enquiries into the creation of such binaries, creating a more dynamic picture of the interaction itself. Such binaries were not just limited to the colonizer and the colonized, but were deeply racialized, and gendered as well. Even though neither of them was a homogenous category, the European presence was empowered by writing, hence creating the colonized bodies in that process. Such imagery, spread across travelogues, diaries, paintings, and even legal documents, gives the sense of chasm that went beyond the previous century's attempt to just 'know' India.

Firstly, the points of difference in the two cultures were so numerous and so obvious that a cultural cleavage was unavoidable from the moment that Englishmen (and other Europeans), first touched foot on Indian soil.[12] Secondly, it would be wrong to assume that the interaction between India and Europe was restricted to the economic, commercial, and political arena; it certainly extended to the social and interpersonal levels. This multifarious interaction also gave rise to a divergent impression of the images of India as the 'other.' So, there is no monolithic image of India, Indians, and subsequently of Indian women but an array of them. Though stereotypes formed over time, they were easier tropes. It is also interesting to observe the classifications invented and used by the Europeans. What they witnessed during their early travels as exotic and alluring, by the end of the 18th century overwhelmingly became a reason of emphatic and hierarchical 'otherness'; and was to further transform into a tool of control by the need to civilize India and the Indians. European travel writings up to the 17th century do present paradoxical observations of the East, from fascination to creating strange categorizations, but they do not automatically translate into the inferiority of the East. However, at some point in the 18th and 19th centuries, a different kind of statement began to emerge, one that was to become a part of the standard British image of India.[13]

Among the early impressions, the famous Venetian 'adventurer'[14] Nicolao Manucci (1656–1712) wrote, 'never are they (Indians) ready to listen to reason; they are very troublesome, high and low, without shame, neither having the fear of God.'[15] Whereas Dr Ives, writing in the 18th century, observed that Indians were extremely quiet and inoffensive people. He extends his argument about their honesty, which turned to dishonesty on the coast as a result of the tricky Europeans.[16]

These are contradictory accounts too, probably due to a variety of experiences. Jemima or Mrs Nathenial Kindersley came to India in the mid-1760s with her husband and wrote detailed letters about her travels. For her, Indians were gentle, patient, temperate, regular in their lives, charitable, and strict observers of their religious customs. At the same time, she confessed that she also finds them, 'superstitious, effeminate, avaricious and crafty, deceitful and dishonest in their dealings and void of every principle of honour and gratitude.'[17] The effortlessly contradictory and judgemental portrayals were also complemented by another kind of observation. William Hodges, one of the first British painters to come to India wrote,

> but why should we admire it in an exclusive manner, or blind it to the majesty, boldness and magnificence of the Egyptian and, Hindu, Moorish and Gothic, as admirable wonders of architecture, unmercifully blame and despise them because they are more various in their forms, and not reducible to the precise rules of the Greek hut, prototype, and columns?[18]

We hear similar views in his description of 'Hindus' and 'Mussulman gentlemen' when he talks about their simplicity, cleanliness and courtesy, and the grand manners, respectively. Likewise, Lieutenant Colonel Briggs, writing letters to two young men entering public life in India wonders, if the darker skin colour of the people in the tropics than those situated more remotely from the equator should be a matter of reproach to them? He reminds them, 'you must endeavour to get over this antipathy to their colour, if it really exits, though I blush to think that it does.'[19]

The views on India and the Indians range from fascination to condemnation, from surprise to understanding and empathy. Many of these were preconceived notions, thanks to previously written travel accounts. Therefore, there is no single set of opinions, but a variety of views put together which remain true to the idea of informing Europe about the East, especially about the native women. Soon enough, Europe was flooded with travellers' tales, adventure stories, picturesque paintings; and the heterogeneous Indian culture with its range of uncommon customs found a large public with a keen interest in India. Travellers and adventurers filled their journals with stories of sati, child marriage, untouchability, and the caste system, and stereotypes began to be formed.[20] The idea of excessive sexuality undergirded the Anglo-Indian perception of Hinduism, which was constructed in the colonial discourse as arcane, ritualistic, and vile, with erotic underpinnings.[21] In the words of J.S. Stavornius, 'Here and there, were representations of a divinity, to whom they pay adoration, under the appellation of lingam. This is the most scandalous worship of all the numerous abominations.'[22]

The Indian outlook on sexuality came to be seen as different, with descriptions of harem, polygamy, public bathing, phallus-worship, *devadasi*'s artistic presence in a place of worship, nautch girl as a part of socio-cultural life, etc., fascinating the travellers. What they considered aberrant in terms of sexual behaviour, was taken as the breakdown of natural laws. Such concerns with deviant sexuality, articulated almost always through descriptions of women, are a constant theme in the travel of explorers and other travellers of early modern Europe for Africa and the Americas. Indeed, Columbus used the metaphor of the female body to articulate the colonial venture when he wrote that the earth was shaped like a breast with the Indies composing the nipple.[23]

So, a lot of what was written about the Indians and the Indian women has certain pre-conceived ideas about their social and sexual selves. Particularly the British, who 'had an ultra-squeamishness and hyper-prudery peculiar to itself': narrow, blinkered, defective, and intolerant attitudes towards sex which it all too successively imposed on the rest of the world.[24] Was the confinement of elite women a plea for chastity or was it a guard against their promiscuity? But it surely provided the ground for speculation and fantasy. The Indian woman behind the *purdah* thus came to be viewed as 'the hidden beauty' ... the object of the white man's sexual fantasy, projecting the gendered 'other' as excitingly sensual.[25]

A quick look at the attitudes towards sex in Europe, the Medieval Church frowned upon sex and assigned an upper place to the soul over the body. The dichotomy between the soul and the body went a step further as the Church also associated the soul, i.e., the spiritual, with the man, while the body, the sensual, with the woman. However, many medieval writers feared that women were more lustful than men, the stereotypical understanding of Medieval European sexuality remained gendered.[26] If this was the view of the men of conscience, the renewed proliferation of pornography in the mid-17th century may well have been a part of the larger movement against authority of any kind, a revolt that progressed from religion to politics to sexual mores.[27] This 17th-century pornography, centred on the permissive female or the whore, which not only provided men with an escape from responsibility, but this satirical myth of the whore again confirmed male superiority and patriarchal attitudes putting the responsibility for carnality on woman's 'provocative' shoulders.

The wave of enlightened thought narrowed these social boundaries of sexual laxity down to around the late 18th and early 19th centuries. There was a massive transformation from 1700 to 1850 due to an increased understanding of the human bodies in the works of medicine. Despite the contemporary erotica representing the female sexual desire in positive terms, women's sexuality was once again relegated as passive.[28] The 18th-century drive for moral reform slowly evolved not only into patriarchy and sentimentality but also into paranoia, prudery, and sexual repression.[29] This trend was observed in the literary genre too. In the 18th century, John Cleland's[30] *Fanny Hill. Memoirs of a Woman of Pleasure*, who had an exuberant appetite for sexual pleasure, turned out to be a winner, but the next century saw Samuel Richardson's *Pamela Or, Virtue Rewarded* and it was her rarefied sense of feminine delicacy that held sway.[31] Such an increasingly suspicious attitude to sexuality also found expression in beliefs that held sexual activity as being a dangerous waste of energy for men. A marriage manual as late as 1839 went on to state that any female who displayed excessive ardour and desire caused sterility.[32] It is hardly surprising that the size of the profession of prostitution as well as that of pornographic literature grew by leaps and bounds.

The way women and the female body find representation, both in the metropole as well as in the colony, needs to be juxtaposed. The masculine, mercantilist, and later colonial, enterprise was shaped by their perspectives on gender and gendered experiences too. The way 'their own' women were portrayed in the writings of ecclesiastical or medical men, also influenced the way they viewed and then, constructed the 'other' women. The native women's bodies, the spaces they inhabited, their visibility – were all reduced to a homogenized production. Especially when they were presented in contrast to the women in Europe. The white woman shown in various travel writings as morally superior, chaste, educated, and so on, was also a trope to control the narrative of the native woman as the constant 'other.' However, the two simultaneously construct and get constructed in the process. The act of observing the Indian woman in her habitat was shaping up to be a perfect setting for the writing of a political discourse. The discourse, however, changed with an increase in the number of Europeans travelling to India by the 18th century, including many white women. For they could enter the 'scandalous' spaces of the *zenana* or harem and actually interact with the women, and write about them.

Harem

The 16th-century encounter with the people of darker skin colour created in the European mind the picture of 'semi-humans driven by bestial passion.'[33] The tropics thus came to mean something different that could be exoticized as the 'other.' It was, again, a by-product of the travel and exploration enterprise that Europe undertook much before the colonial quest. The tropics became a site for European pornographic fantasies highlighting lucid details of sexual license, promiscuity, and excess – all creating otherness for textual and pictorial presentation to sell in the metropole.[34] These writings witness intersections of race, femininity, and representation, actively evolving throughout, in many ways constituting one another.[35] These categories also cannot be looked at in isolation, for they were part of the larger historical framework as the early colonial encounters shaped up. It is only by engaging with these ideas that we come across the finer aspects of how the shared experiences between the colonizers and the colonized were formed initially.

The feminizing of the land represents a ritualistic moment in imperial discourse, as male intruders ward off fears of narcissistic disorder by re-inscribing, as natural, an excess of gender hierarchy.[36] Part of the Orient's charm for Europe lay in the fact that it promised a sexual space, a voyage away from the self, an escape from the dictates of the bourgeois morality of the metropole.[37] The 'rigid sexual protocols of Europe' are often cited as one of the reasons that led the Indian women to being reduced to prototypes of the sexual and were coveted as the permissible expression of the topic as taboo at home. If relaxed and culturally different attitudes to the body were a reason, so were the titillation observers associated with more visible bodies.[38] By juxtaposing the scene back in Europe with an image of hitherto unknown territories of the East, Europe came to explain as to why the 'Oriental,' and in this case, specifically Indian, woman presented a reverse image of the 'chaste' European woman.

Even the invisible bodies of the upper class and upper caste women living in seclusion provided space for mythmaking, and stimulating versions of the harem in print. It was not writing their history. Rather, it was de-historicizing and presenting the harem as a fantastical idea. As we start looking into the lives of early modern South Asian imperial women and the harem, we must remember that most of what we know, comes from these European travelogues. We either have the word of official court chroniclers, who relegate imperial women into a respectable veil of invisibility, or the early European travellers, who pick up the bazaar gossip about the 'frozen-in-frame,' idle women behind the *purdah* and sexualize them. The early travellers, not so many in number, had this unique power of portrayal, for only the European readership. Their language, metaphors, and presentation of these travelogues were in no way meant for the people being portrayed. The harem remains marginalized albeit the 'scandalous' space in the early Mughal European travelogues.[39] The Ottoman Empire had been similarly sexualized previously. Beginning with the earliest encounters of the West with the Islamic world during the Middle Ages, European writers characterized Islam as licentious and the Muslim women as potential sexual temptresses of the hapless Christian men.[40] The writings on the harem, cross-culturally largely emerge around the 17th century. However, the shifts are clearly noticeable as the European presence was undergoing a transformation in India. The political dynamics of the British stepping into the Mughal bureaucratic framework discussed earlier needs to be considered.

The harem was restricted to male outsiders, which gave rise to a lot of curiosity. Reverend William Tennant while talking of the strict vigilance over the secluded Indian women at the close of the 18th century, blamed the Indian man who he thought was 'conscious of habitual frailty in himself, and cannot easily give credit to another for continence and self-denial, virtues almost beyond his conception.'[41] This focus on strictly guarded seclusion, was not just the portrayal of the native woman but also of the native Indian men and experience of the 'other.' Reverend Tennant's observations also go on to provide us with the justification for the seclusion:

> Perhaps neither the Hindoo nor the Mussulman forms a wrong estimate of female virtue in the east. Whatever virtue obtains there must be either constitutional, or the effect of restraint. What virtue regulated by principles of duty, can be expected from persons almost without education, who have been excluded from their infancy from every active scene of life, where alone there can be self-government, and where either virtue or temptation can alone exist? The women in Hindostan seem actually possess but few ideas, and but little chastity.[42]

This emphasis on lack of chastity was not new. It was a typical religious, gendered tool, only here it is used regarding women of the other culture and continent too. The forbidden entry into the harem and the invisibility of imperial women placed the European man on an unequal footing. The elite Indian man could see, meet, and freely mix with white women, unlike the European man, who could not interact with the Indian women of elite households. It left scope for fantasizing and mythmaking about the women behind the *purdah*, either about her 'virtue' or her as 'temptation.' The seclusion of women seems to have made them possess 'few ideas' and 'lesser chastity,' as the passage above would suggest. To the voyeuristic gaze of an outsider, the 'respectable' Indian woman was a silent unseen creature for the European man, who then chose to see her only in sexual terms. The enclosed space that the harem was, it continued to be presented by the European travellers as 'a lascivious world of idle women that lie adorned as if ready for unending festivities, the harem is deeply fascinating and equally disturbing.'[43]

The women of the harem, similarly, were projected mostly in physical terms, using various kinds of sexual metaphors, even if the description took on various forms of admiration, curiosity, disapproval, comparison, and so on. Although it was not just men travelling to the East, by the 18th and 19th centuries, a lot of white women were also stepping into the largely male domain of travel as well as travel writing. Dúnlaith Bird's investigations into the vagabonding gender identities raise some pertinent questions about Oriental writing being an escape for these women.[44] These women, encountering alternative cultural and social zones, were introducing a gendered gaze to this genre of knowledge production.

The book will discuss Memsahibs (white women) later, but it's pertinent to remember here that they have been long critiqued for creating physical distance and heightened racial tensions between the 'respectable' British presence in India and the natives. They were mostly bound by their role, which was reduced to racialized and gendered dimensions. Though it would be unfair to expect their experiences and writing to be homogenous; however, women travellers did have access to the enclosed spaces of the *zenana*. Jemima Kindersley's letter 53 is dedicated entirely to the 'Oriental Ladies' in Calcutta. She writes,

> Even the handsomest of the Mahomedan women have very disagreeable complexions; and the fairest among them may rather be called more yellow than more white but they are admired in proportion as they are distant from black: a beauty much esteemed in them is the long-cut eye, and long eye-brows, which most of them have naturally; but the female infants have sometimes the skin at the corner of their eyes cut, to increase their length, and give them more room to play.[45]

The description reads like a fantasy that could induce awe and horror in the readers, especially by mentioning practices like cutting the skin at the corner of the eyes of female infants. She said it provided 'their eyes more room to play.' It juxtaposes the idea of the native excess, with the latent sexuality of the women of the harem. The entire letter gives a descriptive physical account of the secluded elite women and their socio-cultural space. She does acknowledge the 'beauty in their fine long black eyes, eyebrows and long black eye lashes' but with a rider that 'if they were set off by a fine red and white complexion, they would have been incomparable.'[46]

Fanny Parke narrates her visit to the house of an 'opulent Hindu in Calcutta' for a Nautch, who then asks her if she would like to visit his wife and female relatives. She finds two of them very pretty and adds that as a reason why other men weren't allowed in the zenana.

> Two of the ladies were pretty; on beholding their attire I was no longer surprised that no other men than their husbands were permitted to enter the zenana. The dress consisted of one long strip of Benares gauze of thin texture, with a gold border, passing twice round the limbs, with the end thrown over the shoulder. The dress was rather transparent, almost useless as a veil.[47]

Bishop Reginald Heber of Calcutta, writing in the first half of the 19th century, on the other hand, was greatly attracted by the Indian woman's skin colour and pointed out that how the 'bronze tint was more naturally agreeable to the human eye than the fair skins of Europe.'[48] He also justifies how habit and association can lead one to adapt. An indigo planter in Bengal, William Huggins was quite taken in by the Indian woman's soft expressions, which 'made us forget the difference of complexions or rather convince us that complexion does not constitute the desirable in a woman.'[49] Planters by and large lived in close physical proximity to Indians and often separated from other Britons in India. Hence, they were often Indianized to a great extent, especially in the mofussil area away from Presidency towns, till much later.[50]

Major General Charles Stuart, famously known as 'Hindoo Stuart,' anonymously published, 'A Ladies' Monitor' as a series of letters first published in Bengal about the female apparel.[51] As the title would give away, he attributed the beauty and proportion of Indian woman's forms to the fact that they allowed nature to take its own course, only aiding it by frequent ablutions and constant exposure to the air. He goes on to suggest that the European woman should 'throw away their whale bone and iron and adopt the Indian corset.'[52] From calling the long waist disproportionate to declaring European women as masculine, Charles Stuart constantly pits the Indian women against their European counterparts. The moralistic tone of the writing certainly intends to preach, but it conversely constructs the 'native' Indian woman as the idealized 'other,' to be emulated by the European woman.

The views of Philip Dormer Stanhope, who came to India in 1774, seem in sync with Charles Stuart's. He went ahead to appreciate the 'dazzling brightness of a copper-coloured face' over the 'pallid and sickly hue which banishes the roses from the cheeks of the European fair.'[53] He exoticized the Indian women by telling European men, 'you would think even this (harem) extravagance in some degrees pardonable, had you once experienced the attractive charms of an Asiatic beauty.'[54] Mrs Mary Martha Sherwood, who came to India with her husband Captain Henry Sherwood, expressed the evangelical beliefs in her fictional work with the Indian character of *Ayah* (mid-wife or nanny). Mrs Sherwood questions the emphasis on modesty that Indian women seem to portray. According to her, it was all merely outward, taking pride only in covering the face, putting down the eyes, and pretending to be ashamed to look at a man. In contrast, it was the Christian women, who were taught to refrain from filthy conversation and to hate even filthy thoughts. Carefully hierarchizing the body and heart, she declares, 'Christian modesty is from the heart.'[55] Mrs Eliza Fay, who accompanied her husband Anthony Fay to India in the last quarter of the 18th century, wrote in her letter,

> I once saw two apparently very beautiful women; they use so much art however, as renders it difficult to judge what claim they really have to that appellation – Their whole time is taken up in decorating their persons: – the hair, eye-lids-eye-brows-teeth, – hands and nails, all undergo certain processes to render them more completely fascinating; nor can one seriously blame their having recourse to these, or the like artifices – the motive being to secure the affections of a husband, or to counteract the plans of a rival.[56]

Lieutenant Colonel John Briggs also echoes the 'incomparable superiority in every respect of our ladies to the Eastern females,' but also held that 'their (Indian women's) state of ignorance does not debase their minds or even stop them from possessing great influence over their husbands.'[57] Fanny Parkes similarly held Indian women to exert more influence over men in India than in any other country.[58] This view unintentionally gave Indian women little more agency than just being their physical selves and their toilette.

J.S. Stavorinus, who came to India in the second half of the 18th century, does not think of Indian women merely as what they appear but goes on to describe how they are not deficient in the powers of understanding. He reasons by blaming the lack of education and closeness to their servants since infancy for Indian women to become 'useful' members of society. But, as discussed earlier, he narrated the description of excessive jealousy cherished by the women of India regarding the 'smallest familiarity' between their husbands and female slaves and the cruelty they could show in punishing the female slave.[59] Thus, rendering an active life to the women behind the *purdah*, who, he said, were capable of intrigues and cruelty due to jealousies, without problematizing it beyond the usual misogynist explanations.

Such descriptions of intrigue and movement behind the curtains of the *zenana* are not unprecedented. If a 17th-century record by John Fryer fantasized about the 'incontinent' desires of the harem women,[60] sensuality reigns in the work of another contemporary writer and traveller Niccolao Manucci while describing the Mughal seraglio.[61] Abbe Carre, again a 17th-century traveller, considered 'hundreds of wives of Oriental Kings as King's flock,' but did not see them as dutiful wives but rather as sensual beings, as 'wives for pleasure.'[62]

These travellers, most of the time, picked up on bazaar gossip and thus presented a vastly different picture of 'respectable' women than what the official court chronicles wanted us to believe. Harbans Mukhia says, among the travellers, Edward Terry, Pelsaert, John Fryer, Careri, and of course, Manucci and Bernier are the most loquacious; they engage in some salacious gossip about the goings-on in the imperial harem.[63] The picture of the women of the harem we get from some of these travellers, portrayed them as far from meek creatures. The travellers were denied the sight of these women, who in turn had the power to gaze at these men, even mock them. The seclusion of Indian women denied the European man of 'his customary masculine prerogative of visual (and implied) sexual possession.'[64] Sir Thomas Roe, the ambassador to the Mughal Emperor Jahangir's court, mentioned catching a glimpse of two of the Emperor's wives,

> whose curiosity made them breake litle holes in a grate of reede that hung before yt to gaze on mee. I saw first their fingers, and after laying their faces close now one eye, now another; sometyme I could discern the full proportion … When I looked at up they retyred and were so merry, that I supposed they laughed at me.[65]

Even as late as the first quarter of the 19th century, the *zenana* was still seen as 'a place of intrigue and those who live within four walls cannot pursue a straight path.'[66] This was the life in the harem, as perceived, presumed, and presented, mostly by European men restricted from entering the secluded space. They chose to fantasize as to what lay behind the *purdah*, and it was to some extent confirmed, and more vividly presented by European women, who could enter that space. It was not only the veiled Indian woman who was associated with idle sensuality but even the public woman, who was not a part of the zenana, got noticed for she was visible.

Gendering Native Bodies – Bathing, Ghats, and Saree

In the native woman's representations, both in words or through paintings, her body remains central, and even the most mundane aspect of her physical experience, could be captured, as exotic. It is especially true in the 17th century, when the French traveller François de La Boullaye-Le Gouz, chose to point out the bathing rituals of the Indian women. He chose to disparage the Mughal women by describing the sweet-smelling oil, with which they 'anoint themselves,' but tried to show the contrast by showing a Hindu woman bathing, covered with 'a cloth so fine that her body is almost revealed.'[67] But surprisingly, both descriptions only give glimpses of sensuality, be it the sweet-smelling ointment or a woman bathing. The women are presented, unveiled for the reader's gaze.

The portrayal of Indian women in a harem or at public bathing spaces alludes to an idle world of voluptuousness. If the harem was fantasized by the virtue of being in the invisible space, the public bathing *ghats* become visible spaces to witness the spectre of Indian women bathing. It was not just the novelty of it, but the public spectacle of the native woman's body, that could be exoticized as well as eroticized. While the sight of women bathing at the public *ghats* seemed to have enamoured many European male viewers, it also added to their understanding of the tropical sultriness of India that they wanted to convey. John Briggs, in his way of presenting native customs and practices, justifies the act of bathing to Hindoo ordinances as well as to its climate. He is struck by both men and women bathing at the same *ghats*, 'decently dressed' with such propriety that one does not even notice them changing clothes, underneath loose garments. He contrasts them with European men bathing in Indian rivers, without any shame. Such portrayals are not being written in isolation and often echoed the thoughts that the travellers were constructing about the social mores of the time. Briggs, however, is instructing the new officers joining India, and seems to be underlining the appropriate behaviour for them.

Fanny Parkes, who wrote about women of the *zenana*, was struck by the way the Indian women 'wade into the stream, wash their dresses, and put them on again all wet, as they stand in the water; wash their hair and their bodies, retaining all the time some part of their drapery, which assumes the most classical appearance.'[68]

General G.C. Mundy, touring through India in the first half of the 19th century, drawing sketches as he wrote, went on to describe a bathing scene in a manner, quite common to the European travelogues. To him, the Indian women carried their modesty to a ridiculous extent. He could not fathom the reason for these women turning their backs or covering their faces upon looking. In his words, he found the practice, 'very provoking and curiosity-exciting.'[69] A little later, through his journey around Mirzapore, he went on to describe the well-poised and common scenario of graceful Indian women, with their still more graceful garments, carrying water vessels. The native Indian woman in the public arena, was being described in her everyday role. He put forth the image of the Indian woman 'performing her domestic offices and rendering even labour graceful' quite paternalistically. He elaborated for his readers on the scene of the Indian woman alone or in groups going down to the river 'to bathe their fervent limbs in the refreshing flood.'[70]

Similarly, the simple act of ablution is described by P.D. Stanhope as the 'Indian damsel' rising 'from the limpid bath, in all the native charms of cleanliness and artless beauty.'[71] On the one hand, his theme of an Indian woman walking out of a pond gracefully was what the Europeans termed as 'picturesque,' on the other, it went on to construct the very visible Indian woman. Interestingly, Mundy's write up draws a parallel between the Indian woman's walk from the river with the French woman's walk, which might be pretty, but he asks, is it natural? Stanhope too, critiques the English woman's fondness for dancing in the unsuitable Bengal weather, and juxtaposes it with the limpid bath of the Indian woman which to him is more likely to 'inspire you with sentiments of desire and love.' There is a construct of the native woman in her natural habitat, being compared to her European counterpart, both are being constructed in this early colonial, masculine discourse. How one of them is being defined, in the process, creates a definition for the other.

William Hodges was one of the earliest and most famous painters to travel to India in the 1780s who gained the patronage of the Governor-General Warren Hastings. He travelled and painted the terrain of Bengal, Agra, Banaras, Murshidabad, and other cities as well as maintained a diary. His writing, in part, was a record of an official tour by his patron, Warren Hastings, through British-controlled Bengal.[72] Hodges described certain social customs of the time like sati which left an impact on him.[73] These paintings and portraits thus become important not because of their artistic merit but by the depiction of the theme that was chosen. He also painted small figures of women in and around the rivers. They are not the focus of his paintings but can be seen as a part of the 'picturesque' surroundings he was to portray. Similarly, he noted in his diary about these women bathing in the river in the mornings, highlighting the younger ones who 'in particular, continue a considerable time in the water, sporting and playing like Naiads or Syrens.'[74] In his mind, as a painter,

> the fine antique figures never fail to present themselves, when he observes a beautiful female form ascending these steps from the river, with wet drapery, which perfectly displays the whole person, and with vases on their heads, carrying water to the temples.[75] (Figure 2.1).

In all these images, in words or otherwise, there is an almost simultaneous reference to the garment – the saree. It is sensualized to such an extent that it is always described extremely minutely along with the image of Indian women bathing in public spaces. Mundy describes it as a dress that consists of only one piece of cloth (Figure 2.2).

> It is fastened round the waist and thrown over the head and across the bosom. Simple though it be, this attire is infinitely more graceful, and even more decent than the evening costume of the belles of the more sophisticated regions.[76]

Figure 2.1 The Marmalong Bridge, ca. 1783, William Hodges, 1744–1797, British, Oil on canvas,. Yale Center for British Art, Paul Mellon Collection, B1974.3.8. http://collections.britishart.yale.edu/vufind/Record/1666698

Figure 2.2 Indian girl, 1793, by George Morland, 1763–1804, Oil on canvas mounted on panel, Yale Center for British Art, Paul Mellon Collection, B1981.25.455. http://collections.britishart.yale.edu/vufind/Record/1671670.

Figure 2.3 Grinding corn, between 1792 and 1795, by Arthur William Devis, 1762–1822, Oil on canvas, Yale Center for British Art, Paul Mellon Collection, B1981.25.747. http://collections.britishart.yale.edu/vufind/Record/1665746.

Although Mrs Kindersley, in letter 57, did talk about various aspects of weaving and embroidery in various parts like Dacca, Benares, etc., most of the references about the knowledge of women's clothes retained their sensual descriptions.[77] Fanny Parkes describes the women of an 'opulent' Hindoo household's zenana, and carefully mentions the transparent *Banarasi* gauze of thin texture, that was almost 'useless as a veil,' and how the body's contours and even the tint of skin could be traced through it.[78]

The saree came to be more than a mere garment. There is a constant denigration of the saree for its transparency, that was additionally invoked as a signifier of 'native' female libidinousness as well as the moorings of Indian culture.[79] Fanny Parkes carries the description of women's clothes, namely the saree, for readers by defining how 'no other garment is worn beneath the sari'[80] (Figure 2.3).

Nautch Girl – the Public Performer

The nautch girl, the performer of the elite socio-cultural space in the early colonial as well as the colonial era, is perhaps the most obsessively documented native Indian woman in travel writing. Her representation, like the description of other native categories, evolved along with the changing nature of European involvement in the subcontinent. The sight of the nautch, anglicized from the word *Naach* (to dance), was a part of the Indian aesthetic where the female dancers and singers along with their troupe, often performed at private and public gatherings of elite households. In stark contrast to the seclusion of the zenana, the nautch woman was at the visible centre of an eroticized performance that the Europeans were also becoming a part of. On the one hand, it presented a resistance to patriarchal walls by establishing their own economic and residential spaces, and on the other, patronized by the same elite.[81] These dancing women were certainly not a homogenous group. Margaret Walker brings forth their shared inherited occupation of music and dance as well as their involvement, to some extent, with the sex trade, but their audiences, genres, status, and reputations ranged widely.[82] Her mere presence as an eroticized body in the shape of a native dancer forms a huge corpus of literature and is also visually depicted (Figure 2.4).

As a public woman, the category of a nautch girl often presented overlaps with a courtesan, a prostitute, or even a *devadasi* in a different set of writings. The category of public performer, a woman who was not veiled, was titillatingly sexualized for the readers of these travelogues. Stanhope

Figure 2.4 Dancing girl, 1772, Tilly Kettle (1769–1776), Oil on canvas, Yale Center for British Art, Paul Mellon Collection, B1981.25.385. http://collections.britishart.yale.edu/vufind/Record/1671353.

refers to the *devdasi*, as a prostitute both by religion and profession, emphasizing the preference European men show for them. However, even these women were very ready to oblige them, 'as they find them so much more generous than their own countrymen.'[83] This fantasy of a European male traveller being preferred over the Indian man or having access to an indigenous man's wife as a common custom in parts of Asia, persisted as medieval travel writing, and later travelogues depict.[84] The early 16th-century traveller Ludovico di Varthema, mentioned the King of Calicut selecting an honourable brahmin to deflower his wife. He also claimed that he was also impounded by a merchant to sleep with his 15-year-old bride on their wedding night, and how the lady would have truly desired that her night with the European man, had lasted a month.[85] These early writings hint at the sexual prowess of the European man while adding a lascivious disposition to their fantasy of the native woman.

By the 18th century, as the British stepped into the Mughal political network, there were early representations of the Nabob having gone native, showing him as being served by a retinue of Indian servants, smoking a hookah, dressed in Indian elite attire and fineries, and enjoying a nautch. The British man got accustomed to the Indian climate which was the gradual result of two factors – the need-to-know India (to govern it) and secondly, physically encountering the Indian ways of life. In fact, it took (them) two generations of sudden deaths and illness to adapt their food, drink, clothing, and habits to the climate.[86] There are plenty of visual depictions, like the painting of Colonel Antione Louis-Polier, dressed in Indian elite fineries, with a hookah enjoying a nautch. Or the famous nautch painting with David Ochterlony, the British resident at Delhi, enjoying the ultimate Indian experience, that became a marker that those European men enjoying nautch, had indeed 'gone native.' However, reducing the nautch woman to just a physical experience without considering its representation to start with, robs it of its gendered and racial dimension. Nautch remains one of the few shared spaces besides mixed-race intimacy, where colonial men came into proximity with native women.

During the early interactions, Europeans took to nautch with a lot of enthusiasm, which is clear by the way it is mentioned in their writing. Some Europeans did try to understand the nuances of the distinction between a common prostitute and a courtesan, but not always. This made Edward Terry announce with concern, how 'there is a toleration for impudent harlots, who are as little ashamed to entertayne [entertain] as others openly to frequent their houses.'[87] John Ovington, in the 17th century considered, 'the Dancing Wenches, or the Quenchenies [*kanchanis*] (who) entertain you … with their sprightly motions and soft charming Aspects, with such amorous Glances and so taking irresistible a Mien, that … they … gain an admiration from all.'[88] All here probably included the European gentlemen. And it usually comes as a surprise that they too who, had taken up the nautch as a regular part of their entertainment, while it was also a proclamation of joining the opulent Oriental political and social elite of South Asia.

Different travellers experienced nautch differently, though mostly in the house of an Indian noble or landlord. Jemima Kindersley chose to call nautch, 'the favourite and most constant amusement of the great.' She went on to explain further as to why this 'entertainment' is delightful to the eyes of European men,

> There are many proofs that Europeans do not think them (the Nautch girls) altogether intolerable; time and custom reconciles them to the yellow and the black, which at first sight appears frightful ... it is their (Nautch girl's) languishing glances, wanton smiles and attitudes not quite consistent with decency, which are so much admired.[89]

At times, these ideas are presented as gendered, by highlighting the attraction that the early male colonizers must have felt for these bodies versus the threat that the European woman perceived them as.[90] The whole sight of the nautch is seen as merely sensual by both men and women. As Jemima Kindersley decides, it was 'not quite consistent with decency,' and she put the blames on the deliberate 'wanton' gestures of the nautch girl, John Ovington speaks of the 'amorous' gestures. However, writings by both men and women retain the male gaze, as they construct the European woman in the process of viewing the native woman. The nautch woman remains a visible, native body, who was mentioned for her clothes, jewellery, and not so much for the musical or artistic talent. In the words of Reverend William Tennant,

> Part of the ceremony (of Nautch) consists in listening to music of the singing girls, who drawl out their monotonous ditties with a nonchalance and dullness, which can only be equalled by the sluggish dance, and inanimate gestures, with which they are accompanied. Of all entertainments an Hindostanee notch is probably the most insipid: they are sometimes accompanied with pantomimical performance of no delicate nature.[91]

Elsewhere, he simply describes the dancing women as votaries of pleasure, who 'are taught every qualification, which they can imagine, or may tend to captivate and entertain the other sex.'[92] Here again, instead of their performance, which Reverend Tennant found 'dull' and 'sluggish,' while the dancing women are seen 'votaries of pleasure,' as their capacity to captivate men comes forth in his writing. He thus pointed out the sexual aspect of the 'pantomimical' here.

In the first decade of the 19th century, there is more than one engraving of a nautch scene by Charles D'Oyly. He was born in India, and later became a part of the Bengal Civil Service. He went on to talk about 'the beauty of the individuals and the grace with which they dance or accompany their songs.' Speaking of nautch women, he added in haste, 'we must not ... estimate reputation on same scale by which it is valued among us.'[93] He was surely addressing the likes of Richard Carr, who reported, 'I was much diverted by the singing and dancing of the dancing girls, which is truly ridiculous to our ideas and taste.'[94]

There were a few who did try to present the details of various performing communities like Captain Williamson, writing in the first decade of the 19th century.[95] Katherine Schofield also differentiates between the performing female artists and placed them in three groups. This division, she argued, had primarily to do with their musico-cultural role and their sexual status, which were arguably linked.[96] Captain Williamson of the Bengal Army, in his East India Vade-Mecum; or Complete Guide to Gentlemen intended for the civil, military, or naval service of the Honourable East India Company, attempted to demystify dancing girls to his readers, by mentioning different sub-divisions. He mentions how the '*meeraseen*' are modest and chaste, whereas '*kunchanee*' are of an opposite stamp. He tried, in his words to 'correct some prejudices respecting the fair sex in Eastern countries.'

> They (kunchanees) do not consider any part of their profession as either disgraceful or criminal; and are not therefore liable to those pangs of conscience which, at some period or other are supposed to oppress females of this description in other countries.[97]

James Forbes, who travelled to India in the second half of the 18th century, in his Oriental Memoirs, described the nautch girls as extremely delicate in their person, soft and regular in their features, with forms of perfect symmetry and although dedicated from infancy to this profession, they in general, preserve decency and modesty in their demeanour, which is more likely to allure than the shameless effrontery of similar characters in other countries.[98] References to ideas of modesty, decency, and conscience do place a judgement on the profession of these public women, but it was often juxtaposed with another set of adjectives, rendering the entire space of nautch into an exoticized one.

Nautch women, seldom alone, most of the time with their troupe and musicians, often turned into an ultimate Indian experience. Until the 18th century, along with other physical details like an Indian attire worn by a British man, sitting on an Indian throne or carpet, with hookah, Indian servants, were all symbols of a typical Nabob. These were the early colonial times when Indian social experiences were still not frowned upon. Gradually, over the 19th century, the nautch women were disassociated from the British life in the colony. Although she continued to be portrayed in European gatherings, the Europeans were often sitting on a chair, sofa or even standing. Instead of the 'Indianized' Nabob, here the European men were dressed in western clothes. These representations were, in fact, trying to explain the nautch girl in the context in which she belonged. Though just like other descriptions of the native woman, descriptions like Forbes' also cannot help comparing her to 'similar characters' in Europe.

If nautch was a favourite form of entertainment, the nautch girl had won rounds of applause from the European men, and at times was also patronized by them. Captain Williamson also gives us a vivid description about the nautch girl or the nautch *taffahs* (nautch troupe). According to him, where these nautch girls are found in the vicinity of army encampment or civil area, it was common for them to

> attach themselves to some particular European gentleman, of whose friendship they make much boast: the profits of such a speculation cannot be wholly reserved by any one of the party; they are supposed to be surrendered, without diminution, to the proprietor, for the general benefit of the set.[99]

The establishment of Lal Bazars around the mid-19th century – places designated for sex workers who were to serve only the European military clientele – were there for precisely the same reasons.[100] On the one hand, racial segregation seemed to be the motive, it also became a regulated way to provide sexual services to an increasing number of men in the British army in India.

It was the 'sway' that she held, especially over the men of Europe that vexed many. Writings such as Mrs Sherwood's also echoes a deep-rooted fear of the nautch woman's 'influence' over the well-bred Christian men

> The influence of the Neuich girls over the other sex, even our men who have been bred up in England and who have known, admired and respected their own countrywomen, is not to be accounted for; it is not only obtained in a peculiar way, but often kept up even when beauty is past.[101]

Mrs Sherwood's words echo a strange fear for she leaves to one's imagination as to what was 'the peculiar way.' According to her, the influence of the nautch girls also affected the senses of those who came within its charmed circle, comparing them to an intoxicating drug, or using a European memory and trope of the 'wiles of witchcraft.'[102]

George Hadley reported,

> When a gentleman gives an entertainment, he often gives a dance performance by dancing girls ... the entertainer generally

> compliments his guests with the liberty of chusing [choosing] their partners for the night.[103]

According to Emma Roberts, writing in the first half of the 19th century, nautch 'when addressed to male eyes alone, is said to be not particularly decorous.'[104] Others held that encouraged by their (European men's) applause of 'wah wah,' the nautch girls would shed their stiff and cool propriety to captivate the audience through their alluring charm and grace.[105] It was due to the undertones of sensuality, at times very apparent but mostly subtle, that the nautch girl came to be seen as 'alluring.'

What was noticeable was how the nautch girl hardly, got any merit for her performative prowess but often came across in European records as an overt sexual being. It was her beautification, grace, glances, and smiles that were portrayed time and again. It is also interesting to note how the European men were antagonized by her allure, yet simultaneously enticed by her, and even attracted to her. Contrarily, the white female writers found the nautch girl enigmatic. When we look at the writings of white women, their views certainly reflect a gendered perspective, where the nautch girl becomes the most obvious sexual threat. Some of their writing certainly was more nuanced than that, as it also viewed the nautch girl with a racialized gaze, for the sway she held over 'their' men. Considering so many European men writing about, as well as attending nautches, it did become a concern where the white woman's expected racial and moral roles are often reflected in their writing.

Taken together, we see that the nautch gave rise to gendered as well as racial anxieties because we often read about (the fear) of entering a mixed-race connection with the European men. I have argued elsewhere that she was 'exotic' enough to fill pages and drawing books with, but all that happens within the political framework where the physical distance between the colonizer and the colonized was widening. There was growing anxiety about purity and increasing fear of moral degeneration. The Indian dancing girl becomes the most visible symbol of all that, and so does her dance.[106] The nautch girl had become a part of the European cross-cultural social life in India by the late 18th century. She was the 'public' woman in the European gaze who embodied institutionalized sensuality and continued to fascinate the Europeans and was considered to have held a 'peculiar' power over the European imagination.

At Your Service – Ayah, Nursemaid, and Female Servant

As more British women started coming to the colonies to join their male relatives, their numbers, hitherto limited, went up. The white woman or the Memsahib is often blamed for the shifting attitude towards the natives as well as creating racial anxieties. The Memsahibs do get positioned as bearers of English morality, for their racial exclusiveness. The Memsahib behaved the way she was supposed to due to the requirements of the Raj expecting aloofness between the ruler and the ruled. Thus, 'her limitations were largely imposed upon her.'[107] As discussed in earlier sections, more women had begun to travel towards the east from the 19th century and had access to the women-only spaces, the zenana. They ended up interacting and writing about the veiled women, which so far was based just on male fantasy. One of the results of more white women in what was shaping up to be a colony, was the increasing number of children and the need for an *Ayah* (Figure 2.5), nursemaid as well as a personal female attendant for them. The growing prominence of a new kind of a household with reformed domesticity (the 19th-century Anglo-Indian household) offered one possibility of finding work in exchange for wages – without these women being attached as long-term dependents or incorporated as kin or quasi-kin.[108]

The female servant has been quite talked about and is quite visible in the writings and portraits of Europeans travelling to India. The female servant had an ambiguous role in these documents, she often blurred the lines between a sexual partner and a nursemaid of the British children. Given how common concubinary relations were between the European men and those native women in their domestic (and sexual) service, the person of the

Figure 2.5 Ayah, or female attendant for European and Indian women, Calcutta, West Bengal. Coloured etching by François Balthazar Solvyns, ca. 1808–1812. Wellcome Collection, London. https://wellcomecollection.org/works/t5edz8r3

mother and the accused was often one and the same. Western writing has a certain mistrust of the native servants, even Captain Williamson who wrote of the native mistress albeit with a better understanding of his first-hand experience of a native *bibi* in the cantonment, talks about the female native servant serving as *Ayah* in quite another tone. For him, native *bibi* was a 'necessity,' but he turned the figure of the Ayah into a 'crafty' attendant in his writing,

> this generality of those remaining ... under the care of ayahs become crafty, proud, and unmannerly; which has occasioned several ladies to engage as few as possible of those attendants, and to give their little ones in charge to bearers, or other male servants; under whose care they found to be less vitiated, and in general far more healthy. Unless great attention be paid, ayahs will initiate their younger charges in many practices, and especially in language such as must require infinite assiduity to subdue; and after all, may not be completely suppressed. Besides they are usually very slovenly, and offensive in their persons.[109]

Although, when we read Captain Williamson alongside his contemporaries, his views echo the sentiment of quite a few. Discussed earlier, Mrs Martha Sherwood, expressed a similar sentiment in her fictional work *Ayah and the Lady* as she points to the various vices of the native Ayah.[110] Written in the first quarter of the 19th century, her book stereotypes the character of the Ayah, labelling her habits such as chewing *paan*, sleeping, gossiping, and using foul language as detrimental. However, the cautious and devout British female protagonist keeps catching the wrongdoings in the Ayah's work and brings in the Christian religious teachings. This clearly places the native women as a distinct character, immersed in the art of 'intrigue,' which is easy to associate with the women who could be a part of a harem, or a nautch girl with wanton gestures, or the Ayah who was a necessary evil. Such bias is also carried to the legal sphere. We shall be looking at it in other chapters that as the testimonies given by the native *dhye* or mid-wife often did not hold much merit.

The figure of a female servant, however, did become an integral part of living in India, reflected in the visual representation too. For example, in a painting by Charles D'Oyly, a British woman is shown getting ready, as two native female servants wait on her (Figure 2.6). One can see the face of the white woman in the mirror, who is putting on jewellery and looks pleased with the result. She is wearing an elegant gown and has a feathered Victorian hat on. The two Indian women of different ages are carrying a necklace and jewellery box for the Memsahib to choose from. They are standing physically close to her, and almost match her expression of pleasure. The room

Figure 2.6 Female Attendants, undated, by Sir Charles D'Oyly, 1781–1845, Printed by the Behar Amateur Lithographic Press, 1781–1845, Yale Center for British Art, Paul Mellon Collection, B1977.14.1251. http://collections.britishart.yale.edu/vufind/Record/3623224.

has many European paintings, quite visible on the wall. Both native women are wearing lower garments of extremely rich colours.

We also have a painting, where Warren Hastings poses with his wife in full English regalia, by Johann Zoffany, where there is a sense of a full circle.[111] The landscape looks English, and Hastings and his wife almost belong there. They appear in control, standing at a relative height, in their visible Englishness, except for the dark native servant, holding Mrs Hastings's hat. She comes into the frame, as the servicing Indian, almost as a reminder of the scene being Indian, but in a sense of a cultural encounter as well. She just happens to be in the frame, for her 'otherness' and the service she is providing of looking 'native' along with holding her hat.

Many conversation pieces, or family portrayals feature servants as a part of the larger early modern household, not only in India but in colonies elsewhere too. It is not the specific ethnicity of the servants that is relevant, but the fact that they 'originate in tropical, fertile, and remote land.'[112] Johann Zoffany's 1786's portrayal of Colonel Blair's family with their Ayah, where the young Ayah as big as their daughter, is seen holding a cat.[113] The two young girls standing in physical proximity as if caught while playing with that cat. Their clothing, and complexion set them apart, but the young Ayah seems a part of their household, unlike Mrs Sherwood's description.

There are various portrayals by François Balthazar Solvyns (1790s), Charles D'Oyly (first quarter of the 19th century), Mrs Belnos (1830s), mostly situating her in her work. These paintings, often a collection of life of certain sections, communities, and occupation, categorized women and men in those classifications. However, in fiction, travel writing as well as the newly emerging photography, the *Ayah* continued to figure as important. Also, many *Ayahs* continued to travel to Europe along with their families because the children got attached to them.

The native Indian woman, who was to become the intimate partner of the British man was not just seen, but also constructed for the European readership in such ways. She was already an established figure in the European travelogue, in multiple versions before she entered a mixed-race relationship with the early colonial British man. Even in the wills, she was presented in her diverse roles – an intimate caregiver, sexual partner, mother of his children, housekeeper, and so on. This work focuses on legal archives; however, the native women had already caught the fancy of European travel writing, much before the establishment of the Calcutta Supreme Court. What started as curious and diverse portrayal of what travellers were witnessing, progressed largely into a gendered, racialized experiences that were essential for fashioning a masculine, colonial enterprise. The initial portrayal was in line with what the travellers were witnessing in central Asia on their way, as the quintessential 'other,' formulating the 'Orient' for the consumption of the Western readership. It was a construct that was to be used when the spirit to civilize gained momentum under the Utilitarians, in the early- to the mid-19th century. The aspects that were exoticized as the contours of the 'other' during the 17th and 18th centuries, were the same ones that were debated, discussed, and controlled in strong moral terms as the 19th century progressed.

Notes

1 'High Court Calcutta – Original Side: Bengal Wills,' 5426.
2 T. Moore et al., *The Poetical Works of Lord Byron, Complete in One Volume, Collected and Arranged with Illustrated Notes* (John Murray, Albemarle Street, 1866), 597.
3 S. Sawyer and A. Agarwal, 'Environmental Orientalisms,' *Cultural Critique* 45, no. Spring (2000): 72.
4 H. Banerji, *Inventing Subjects: Studies in Hegemony, Patriarchy and Colonialism* (New Delhi: Tulika, 2001), 87.
5 R. Singha, 'Making the Domestic More Domestic: Criminal Law and the Head of the Household, 1772–1843,' *Indian Economic & Social History Review* 33, no. 3 (1996).
6 J.S. Stavornius, *Voyages to the East Indies, Translated from the Original Dutch by Samuel Hull Wilcocke, with Notes and Additions by the Translator*, 3 vols. (London: Printed for G.G. & J.Robinson, Paternoster-Row, 1798), 320. Vol. 1.
7 'The Hyde Papers and Hyde Reports' (Calcutta: National Library Calcutta).
8 'High Court Calcutta – Original Side: Bengal Wills,' 5426.

9 Catherine Hall and Sonya O. Rose, *At Home with the Empire – Metropolitan Culture and the Imperial World* (Cambridge: Cambridge University Press, 2006), 127.
10 R. Kabbani, *Europe's Myth of Orient: Devise and Rule* (London: Macmillan, 1986), 10.
11 W. Daniell and Rev. H. Caunter, *The Oriental Annual or Scenes in India Comprising Twenty Two Engravings from Original Drawings by William Daniell and a Descriptive Account by the Rev. Hobart Caunter* (London: Charles Tilt, 86, Fleet Street, 1838), 32.
12 J.M. Mickelson, *British Women in India, 1757–1857* (Michigan: University of Michigan Press, 1978).
13 R. Lal, *Domesticity and Power in the Early Mughal World* (Cambridge: Cambridge University Press, 2005), 25.
14 For a detailed account of Nicolao Manucci's work, and his life in India, see Sanjay Subrahmanyam, Further thoughts on an enigma: The tortuous life of Nicolò Manucci, 1638–c. 1720.
15 W. Irvine, ed., *Storio Do Mogor or Mogul India, 1653–1708 by Niccalao Manucci Venetian*, 4 vols., Indian Texts Series (London: 1907), 452. Vol. 2.
16 Quoted by P. Spear, *The Nabobs: A Study of the Social Life of the English in the Eighteenth Century* (Cambridge: Cambridge University Press, 1963), 195.
17 N. Kindersley, *Letters from the Island of Teneriffe, Brazil, the Cape of Good Hope, and the East Indies* (London: Printed for J. Nourse, in *the Strand*, 1777), 132.
18 W. Hodges, *Travels in India During the Years 1780, 1781, 1782, & 1783* (London: J. Edwards, Pall-Mall, 1793), 33.
19 Lieut Col. J. Briggs, *Letters Addressed to a Young Person in India Calculated to Afford Instructions for His Conduct in General and More Especially in His Intercourse with the Natives* (London: John Murray, Albemarle Street, 1828), 14.
20 S.N. Mukherjee, *Sir William Jones: A Study in 18th Century British Attitudes to India* (Cambridge: Cambridge University Press, 1968), 8.
21 I. Sen, *Women and Empire, Representations in the Writings of British India (1858–1900)* (New Delhi: Orient Longman, 2002), 42.
22 Stavornius, *Voyages to the East Indies, Translated from the Original Dutch by Samuel Hull Wilcocke, with Notes and Additions by the Translator*, Vol. 1, 420.
23 J. Morgan, '"Some Could Suckle over Their Shoulder": Male Travelers, Female Bodies, and the Gendering of Racial Ideology, 1500–1770,' *William and Mary Quarterly* 54, no. 1 (1997): 170.
24 R. Hyam, *Empire and Sexuality: The British Experience* (Manchester: Manchester University Press, 2017), 3.
25 Sen, *Women and Empire, Representations in the Writings of British India (1858–1900)*, 56.
26 R.M. Karras, *Sexuality in Medieval Europe: Doing Unto Others* (London: Routledge, 2017).
27 F.A. Nussbaum, *The Brink of All We Hate: English Satires on Women, 1660–1750* (Kentucky: The University Press of Kentucky, 1984), 15.
28 K. Harvey, 'Sexuality and the Body,' in *Women's History in Britain, 1700–1850: An Introduction*, ed. Hannah Barker and Elaine Chalus, Women's and Gender History (London: Routledge, 2005).
29 L. Stone, *The Family, Sex and Marriage: England, 1500–1800* (London: Harper & Row, 1977), 647.
30 For an interesting detail on the author John Cleland's early Indian stint, as an English E.I.C. employee, see S. Subrahmanyam, *Europe's India: Words, People,*

Empires, 1500–1800 (Cambridge, Massachusetts: Harvard University Press, 2017), 160–162.
31 Nussbaum, *The Brink of All We Hate: English Satires on Women, 1660–1750*, 675.
32 Ibid.
33 H. Ridley, *Images of Imperial Rule*, Routledge Library Editions: World Empires (London: Routledge, 2018), 74.
34 A.L. Stoler, *Carnal Knowledge and Imperial Power: Race and the Intimate in Colonial Rule* (Berkeley: University of California Press, 2002), 43–44.
35 R. Lewis, *Gendering Orientalism: Race, Femininity and Representation*, ed. Kum-Kum Bhamani, Gender, Racism, Ethnicity (London: Routledge, 1996).
36 A. McClintock, *Imperial Leather: Race, Gender and Sexuality in the Colonial Contest* (London: Routledge, 1995), 24.
37 Kabbani, *Europe's Myth of Orient: Devise and Rule*, 67.
38 Hall and Rose, *At Home with the Empire – Metropolitan Culture and the Imperial World*, 127.
39 Lal, *Domesticity and Power in the Early Mughal World*, 24–49.
40 H. Madar, 'Before the Odalisque: Renaissance Representations of Elite Ottoman Women,' *Early Modern Women: An Interdisciplinary Journal* 6 (2011): 2.
41 Rev. W. Tennant, *India Recreations: Consisting of Thoughts on the Effects of the British Government on the State of India, Accompanied with Hints Concerning the Means of Improving the Condition of the Natives of That Country*, 2nd ed., 3 vols., vol. 3 (Edinburgh: University Press, 1808), 188.
42 Ibid.
43 M. Alloula, *Colonial Harem*, ed. W. Godzich, trans. M. Godzich (Manchester: Manchester University Press, 1986), 35. Malek Alloula's study of the postcards of Algerian women from as late as the 20th century, produced and sent by the French, reveals an intense preoccupation with the veiled bodies of these women. It shows how they wanted to capture women in the interiors of their closed quarters.
44 D. Bird, *Travelling in Different Skins: Gender Identity in European Women's Oriental Travelogues, 1850–1950*, Oxford Modern Languages and Literature Monographs (Oxford: Oxford University Press, 2012).
45 Kindersley, *Letters from the Island of Teneriffe, Brazil, the Cape of Good Hope, and the East Indies*, 221.
46 Ibid.
47 F. Parkes, *Wanderings of a Pilgrim in Search of the Picturesque, During Four and Twenty Years in the East with Revelations of Life in the Zenana, Illustrated with Sketches from Nature* (London: Pelham Richardson, 23, Cornhill, 1850), 59. Vol. 1.
48 R. Heber, *A Narrative of a Journey from the Upper Provinces of India from Calcutta to Bombay, 1824–1835*, 3 vols., Vol. 1 (London: John Murray, Albemarle Street, 1827), 4.
49 W. Huggins, *Sketches in India, Treating on Subjects Connected with the Government Civil and Military Establishments; Characters of the European, and Customs of the Native Inhabitants* (London: John Letts, Cornhill, 1824), 207.
50 B.S. Cohn, 'The British in Benares: A Nineteenth Century Colonial Society,' *Comparative Studies in Society and History* 4, no. 2 (1962): 198. Bernard Cohn in fact goes on to talk about a certain Christie Sahib, in a village in Jaunpur district who he heard about in 1952–1953 during his fieldwork. His name probably is a reference to his religion and was used by the villagers. The village memory of him, recalls him living a semi-regal life of early Europeans, with two

Indian mistresses – one Pasi (pig-herder) and one Chamar (skinner and tanner). He had a large family with both.

51 C. Stuart, *The Ladies Monitor, Being a Series of Letters, First Published in Bengal, on the Subject of Female Apparel, Tending to Favour a Regulated Adoption of Indian Costume; and a Rejection of Superfluous Vesture by the Ladies of This Country* (London; J. Bodwell, 344, near Catherine Street, Strand, 1809).

52 E.M. Collingham, *Imperial Bodies: The Physical Experience of the Raj, C. 1800–1947* (Cambridge: Polity Press, 2001), 27, 38.

53 P.D. Stanhope, *Genuine Memoirs of Asiaticus, in a Series of Letters to a Friend, During Five Year Residence in Different Parts of India ... In the Service of the Nawab of Arcot* (London: J. Debrett, opposite Burlington House, Piccadilly, 1785), 34.

54 Ibid.

55 M.M. Sherwood, *The Ayah and Lady: An Indian Story* (New York: John P. Haven, 1822), 63–64.

56 E. Fay, *Original Letters from India Containing a Narrative of a Journey Through Egypt and the Author's Imprisonment at Calicut by Hyder Ally. To Which Is Added an Abstract of Three Subsequent Voyages to India* (Calcutta: Messrs. Thacker, Spink & Co., 1789), 302.

57 Briggs, *Letters Addressed to a Young Person in India Calculated to Afford Instructions for His Conduct in General and More Especially in His Intercourse with the Natives*, 102–103.

58 Parkes, *Wanderings of a Pilgrim in Search of the Picturesque, During Four and Twenty Years in the East with Revelations of Life in the Zenana, Illustrated with Sketches from Nature*, 88–89.

59 Stavornius, *Voyages to the East Indies, Translated from the Original Dutch by Samuel Hull Wilcocke, with Notes and Additions by the Translator*, Vol. 1, 318–319.

60 J. Fryer, *A New Account of East India and Persia, Being Nine Years' Travels, 1672–1681*, 3 vols. (London, 1910), Vol. 1, 328.

61 Irvine, *Storio Do Mogor or Mogul India, 1653–1708 by Niccalao Manucci Venetian*, Vol. 1, 218.

62 C. Fawcett, *The Travels of Abbe Carre in India and the near East, 1672–1674*, trans. Lady Fawcett, 2 vols., Works Issued by Hakluyt Society (London: The Hakluyt Society, 1947), Vol. 1, 247.

63 H. Mukhia, *The Mughals of India* (Oxford: Blackwell Publishing, 2004), 125.

64 K. Teltscher, *India Inscribed: European and British Writing on India, 1600–1800* (New York: Oxford University Press, 1995), 38.

65 W. Foster, ed., *The Embassy of Sir Thomas Roe to India, 1615–1619, as Narrated in His Journal and Correspondence*, 2 vols. (London: Printed for Hakluyt Society, 1899), Vol. 2, 282–83.

66 Parkes, *Wanderings of a Pilgrim in Search of the Picturesque, During Four and Twenty Years in the East with Revelations of Life in the Zenana, Illustrated with Sketches from Nature*, 391.

67 Teltscher, *India Inscribed: European and British Writing on India, 1600–1800*, 39.

68 Parkes, *Wanderings of a Pilgrim in Search of the Picturesque, During Four and Twenty Years in the East with Revelations of Life in the Zenana, Illustrated with Sketches from Nature*, 97–98.

69 G.C. Mundy, *Pen and Pencil Sketches in India. Journal of a Tour in India*, 2 vols. (London: John Murray, Albemarle Street, 1832), Vol. 1, 157–158.

70 Ibid., Vol. 1, 152–153.

71 Stanhope, *Genuine Memoirs of Asiaticus, in a Series of Letters to a Friend, During Five Year Residence in Different Parts of India ... In the Service of the Nawab of Arcot*, 48.
72 Teltscher, *India Inscribed: European and British Writing on India, 1600–1800*, 131.
73 Hodges, *Travels in India During the Years 1780, 1781, 1782, & 1783*, 79.
74 Ibid., 33.
75 Ibid.
76 Mundy, *Pen and Pencil Sketches in India. Journal of a Tour in India*, Vol. 1, 154.
77 Kindersley, *Letters from the Island of Teneriffe, Brazil, the Cape of Good Hope, and the East Indies*
78 Parkes, *Wanderings of a Pilgrim in Search of the Picturesque, During Four and Twenty Years in the East with Revelations of Life in the Zenana, Illustrated with Sketches from Nature*, 59–60.
79 Sen, *Women and Empire, Representations in the Writings of British India (1858–1900)*, 57.
80 Parkes, *Wanderings of a Pilgrim in Search of the Picturesque, During Four and Twenty Years in the East with Revelations of Life in the Zenana, Illustrated with Sketches from Nature*, 60.
81 S. Shah, 'In the Business of Kāma: Prostitution in Classical Sanskrit Literature from the Seventh to the Thirteenth Centuries,' *Medieval History Journal* 5, no. 1 (2002); V.T. Oldenburg, 'Lifestyle as Resistance: The Case of the Courtesans of Lucknow,' *India Feminist Studies* 16, no. 2 (1990).
82 M.E. Walker, 'The "Nautch" Reclaimed: Women's Performance Practice in Nineteenth-Century North India,' *South Asia: Journal of South Asia Studies* 37, no. 4 (2014): 553.
83 Stanhope, *Genuine Memoirs of Asiaticus, in a Series of Letters to a Friend, During Five Year Residence in Different Parts of India ... In the Service of the Nawab of Arcot*, 39.
84 Teltscher, *India Inscribed: European and British Writing on India, 1600–1800*, 47.
85 K.M. Phillips, *Before Orientalism: Asian Peoples and Cultures in European Travel Writing, 1245–1510* (Philadelphia: University of Pennsylvania Press, 2014), 133.
86 T. Wilkinson, *Two Monsoons* (London: Duckworth, 1976).
87 W. Foster, *Early Travels in India, 1583–1690* (London: Humphrey Milford, 1921), 320.
88 J. Ovington, *A Voyage to Surat in the Year 1689*. Ed. H.G. Rawlinson. (London, Oxford University Press ,1929), 153.
89 Kindersley, *Letters from the Island of Teneriffe, Brazil, the Cape of Good Hope, and the East Indies*, 229–231.
90 N. Bhattacharya, *Reading the Splendid Body: Gender and Consumerism in Eighteenth Century British Writings on India* (Newark: University of Delaware Press, 1998), 135–136.
91 Tennant, *India Recreations: Consisting of Thoughts on the Effects of the British Government on the State of India, Accompanied with Hints Concerning the Means of Improving the Condition of the Natives of That Country*, 3, 55–56.
92 Ibid., 204.
93 Capt T. Williamson and F.W. Blagdon, *The Europeans in India; from a Collecction of Drawings by Charles Doyley Esq ... Accompanied by a Brief History of Ancient and Modern India from the Earliest Periods of Antiquity*

to the Termination of the Late Maharatta War (London: Edward Orme, Bond Street, 1813).

94 Bhattacharya, *Reading the Splendid Body: Gender and Consumerism in Eighteenth Century British Writings on India*, 127.

95 S.P. Verma and A.J. Qaiser, *Art and Culture: Painting and Perspective*, vol. 2 (New Delhi: Abhinav Publications, 2002); S.M. Chenoy, *The Mughal Capital in Time of Muhammad Shah or Murraqqa-I-Dehli of Dargah Quli Khan* (New Delhi: Deputy Publication, 1989).

96 K.B. Schofield, 'The Courtesan Tale: Female Musicians and Dancers in Mughal Historical Chronicles, C. 1556–1748,' *Gender & History* 24, no. 1 (2012).

97 Capt T. Williamson, *The East India Vade-Mecum; or Complete Guide to Gentlemen Intended for the Civil, Military or Naval Service of the East India Company*, 2 vols. (London: Printed for Black, Parry, and Kingsbury, 1810), Vol. 2, 386.

98 J. Forbes, *Oriental Memoirs: Selected and Abridged from a Series of Familiar Letters Written During Seventeen Years Residence in India ... And Narrative of Occurances in Four India Voyages. In 4 Volumes* (London: Printed for the author by T. Bensley, Bolt Court, 1813), 61.

99 Williamson, *The East India Vade-Mecum; or Complete Guide to Gentlemen Intended for the Civil, Military or Naval Service of the East India Company*, Vol. 2, 422.

100 P. Levine, 'Venereal Disease, Prostitution, and the Politics of Empire: The Case of British India,' *Journal of the History of Sexuality* 4, no. 4 (1994).

101 S. Kelly, *The Life of Mrs. Sherwood, Chiefly Autobiographical, with Extracts from Mr. Sherwood's Journal During His Imprisonment in France and Residence in India* (London: Darton & Co., 1857), 148.

102 Ibid.

103 Cited by Collingham, *Imperial Bodies. The Physical Experience of the Raj, C. 1800–1947*, 32.

104 I. Ghose, *Travels, Explorations and Empires: Writings from the Era of Imperial Expansion, 1770–1835* (London: Pickering & Chatto, 2001), 320.

105 P. Nevile, *Beyond the Veil: Indian Women in the Raj* (New Delhi: Nevile Books, 2000), 86.

106 R. Sharma, 'The Indian Nautch Girl in Early Colonial Travel Writing,' ed. Mythili Anoop and Varun Gulati (Lanham. Lexington Books, Rowman and Littlefield, 2016), 22.

107 Hyam, *Empire and Sexuality: The British Experience*, 120.

108 N. Verma, 'The Many Lives of Ayah: Life Trajectories of Female Servants in Early Nineteenth-Century India,' in *Servants' Pasts: Late Eighteenth to Twentieth Century South Asia*, ed. Nitin Sinha and Nitin Verma (New Delhi: Orient Blackswan, 2019), 105.

109 Williamson, *The East India Vade-Mecum; or Complete Guide to Gentlemen Intended for the Civil, Military or Naval Service of the East India Company*, Vol. 1, 341.

110 Sherwood, *The Ayah and Lady: An Indian Story*.

111 To see the painting, refer to http://www.museumsofindia.gov.in/repository/record/vmh_kol-R1432-C1311-587.

112 B.F. Tobin, *Picturing Imperial Power: Colonial Subjects in 18th Century British Paintings* (Durham: Duke University Press, 1999), 27.

113 To see the painting, refer to https://artuk.org/discover/artworks/colonel-blair-with-his-family-and-an-indian-ayah-203039

3

FORGING INTIMACIES

> The men in Company's service the moment they arrive in India seem at once to reconcile themselves to the country as a home; they appear to settle to it; they get Native women, who soon obtain over them as much influence, particularly where there are children, as any European wife; they keep the men in order and make them most comfortable and have authority sufficient to take from him his pay the moment he receives it, giving him a small portion back for his personal pleasures. But with the daily mite they cannot do this, the man will not part with it; he says, "what's the use of such a trifle?" so away he goes and gets daily drunk, instead of once a month.... To the European woman, who cannot so well manage as the country – born (as they are called), the distress is greater.[1]

Lieutenant Colonel Hopkinson of the Madras Establishment, wrote this, thus making a case for monthly wages for the men in the Company's service. He wrote about mixed-race cohabitation and the influence of the native partner with candour. His juxtaposition of the European wife and the country-born partner intersected at the point of native women providing the men in the Company's service with a sense of home as well as for keeping them in order and making them most comfortable. The phenomenon of a native woman cohabiting with the colonizing man, however, was common to almost the entire colonized territory. In India too, British men entered conjugal and domestic arrangements with women of native origins and a veritable historical treasure trove can be found in the plethora of wills stored in Calcutta's High Court.

Such mixed-race set-ups were not limited to urban areas and towns of the Bengal Presidency, they were even recorded in the *mofussil* and other remote areas too. There were large numbers of women with Portuguese and (often given) English names as well as those with names of just South Asian origin. As the passage above points out, the native women were not just temporary sexual partners, but they often managed the British man's household. One

DOI: 10.4324/9781003315186-3

of the most used terms for a native concubine was 'housekeeper,' which was certainly more than a mere euphemism because it encompassed the various roles these women took on. A romanticized view of these domesticities or even 'the focus on "management of the intimate" leads to a "tenderized" study of colonialism if it ignores the violence and inequities lodged in privatized space and turns away from the uses and abuses that unsolicited and even desired intimacies may entail.'[2] Especially in the early colonial era, when the racial boundaries and colonial identities were still shaping up, the domestic space shared by the native women and the British men needed to be unearthed keeping various aspects in mind.

For the more elite sections of the British military and civilian officers, there are letters, private papers, diaries, memoirs, and even paintings (Figure 3.1) etc. that attest to their details and history in early colonial Bengal. But in case of most of the middle as well as lower level and class of British men in India, such detailed records do not exist. Hence, we turn to the legal archive, more specifically the wills. Joan Thirsk mentions wills as one of the unexplored local records, especially to study different aspects of a family in the case of early modern England.[3] In case of early colonial India, wills left by the British men have been studied, but mostly, only the more well-known cases. In trying to use wills as more than enumeration, there is a need to go beyond a cursory glance and analyse the language of the bequeaths and other details they spell out.

Figure 3.1 Muslim lady reclining, 1789 (Probably a *bibi* of a British man, in Dacca), by Francesco Renaldi, 1755–after 1798, oil on canvas, Yale Center for British Art, Paul Mellon Collection, B1981.25.519. Link: http://collections.britishart.yale.edu/vufind/Record/1665157.

These wills were almost always written by the British men, though there were a few native women who left bequeaths too. Either way, they bring out interracial relationships that were not monolithic. On the one hand, they fall into the larger category of interracial domesticities that existed wherever colonial control was wielded, but they also bring us closer to understanding specifically the intimate space shared by the British men who travelled to India before the English East India Company had become a full-fledged colonial enterprise.

In recent times, early colonial history writing has begun to discuss the shared space between the colonizer and the colonized. However, a chapter on the working of these intimacies should start by stating the obvious – the native women and the British men who established a relationship, were by no means on an equal footing. If not binaries, even in the spectrum of race, gender, economic station, and status, they were on vastly different planes. Their shared space, which could also be intimate and within the bounds of a household, had almost always had some sort of remuneration as a medium of exchange without any laws concerning this version of conjugality. Hence, one needs to problematize these connections and the idea of intimacy itself here. Should one view these women as servants, providing sexual as well as reproductive labour, or consider them merely as concubines cohabiting with the colonizers? The intimacy of this connection, and the resultant class of mixed-race children, both became contentious with increasing racial distancing. Ann Laura Stoler speaks of the political discourse and a politics that made a racially coded notion of who could be intimate with whom – and in what way – being a primary concern in colonial policy.[4]

This study attempts to bring forth the complexity of the mixed-race households, where the life and history of the native concubine will be constructed using legal documents. Very few of these relationships were formalized through marriage but were a socially accepted norm. Therefore, except for the few elite mixed-race families, the histories of the lesser-known British men and their domestic set-ups are practically non-existent. Wills occupy a unique position as archival sources as they offer a glimpse into the shared personal space of mixed-race conjugality. By the sheer number of mentions, it becomes apparent how commonplace these non-marital cohabitations were. Thus, they become the only source that even mentions a native concubine's existence and the various aspects of the space she shared with the British man as her 'keeper.' Hence, legal documents such as wills must be carefully read, which is unlike a private diary or personal memoir, but can carry many personal details. The language, terms of endearment, details of bequests and material goods, limits on control, etc. can all be called on to understand the workings of these interpersonal relationships.

This chapter will analyze how the interpersonal relationships between the British men and the native women in early colonial Bengal existed within the parameters of domesticity and conjugality. This will bring to light a host of ways in which such living arrangements functioned – from monogamous to polygamous, from long companionships to termination of such arrangements after contention, and so on. There was a clear class difference, where a concubine entered a complete household-like structure, and in numerous wills, her status was described as her having been bought or as a servant, or by her other services and roles.

These wills remain specific to the day they were written and filed (with changes through codicils at times). The terminology, even what is being written and what is not, is how they provide an insight into these relationships. Considering that early colonial women are almost absent or silent in other official archives, legal archives, especially court cases, became a rare opportunity, to see them.

The ways in which the language of the wills defines the concubine's role in the British man's writing becomes an aspect of her history. Among other terms of endearment, the terms like 'my faithful servant,' or her mention for her services during illness, payments, etc. challenge a unidimensional idea of mixed-race domesticities. This being the most intimate contact for the colonized British man, these native women often end up being mentioned for the different kinds of services they provided. We also need to remember that care discourse can sometimes function ideologically, to justify or conceal relationships of power and domination.[5] The power to bequeath interest on a particular sum, sometimes even a loving declaration of letting her keep all that has been given to her, it is the British man, who always gets to write of their relationship, which is certainly an incomplete picture of their household.

Domesticity

In these wills written by the British men, one catches a glimpse of the relationships and the sphere of domesticity from strictly their perspective. The wills give us an insight as to how the British men perceived this relationship vis-à-vis the native women, her body, and the progeny. Language remains an important tool to read a legal document such as will as well as to look for minute details. For example, the various ways native women are addressed in these sources is how we determine the kind of conjugal set-up that it was or may be how the relationship came to be established. We can also read into wills the everyday aspects of their relationship. Perhaps it calls for a separate body of work, but the exhaustive details of material remains of a shared domestic space are often listed in these wills as well.

Regarding the usage of the term 'domestic,' it can be taken to mean the setting up of a household, but it also indicates different things with respect to the time and place where it is used. Nineteenth- and early 20th-century works have usually treated medieval domestic life as being linked to 'home,' and focussed on everyday activities, the structure of houses, and the objects found therein.[6] What is clear is that domestic is certainly a private sphere and it denotes the confines and comforts of a home, not necessarily linked to a family as we understand it today. Felicity Riddy argues that 'domesticity' – even in its 19th-century form of a 'state of mind' is defined by privacy and comfort within the physical structure of a house wherein the occupation of a domestic space by members of the family evolved into the concept of home.[7]

The concept of domesticity can be imagined as a 'state of mind,' may be due to the comfort it offers and stands opposite to the sphere of what was considered 'public.' While discussing domestic discourses over imperial space, home should not be reduced to being static and confining, but is understood in terms of being more mobile and productive.[8] In the wills too, families both back at home and the ones established in India are mentioned. The married and unmarried status of women and children born into and outside wedlocks are also termed as such. Likewise, in the context of explorations and travel eastwards, even the actual sense of intimacy and family did not remain static and, in fact, extended beyond one's natal family. The fluidity that the early colonial era offered in these mixed-race cohabitations was in fact their marked feature. This social acceptability by Indians of such conjugal arrangements without marriage was often pointed out by the European travellers with wonder and surprise. However, the truth is that the Europeans not only adjusted to it quickly but that such mixed race conjugality was common to almost all imperial state structures in the early modern era.

The ease with which these mixed-race cohabitations of various kinds translated into domesticity in India was most close to the familial connect many European men created especially during the late 18th century. These mixed-race families often also socialized with other similar set-ups and not so much with other kinds of families, pointing to a set of socialization as an unspoken code of conduct. As the legal archive points out, the mixed-race domesticity certainly meant co-residence, and at times was also used in terms of a family that may not have been 'legitimate' but was surely an acceptable social unit in the late 18th to the early 19th centuries in Bengal (and in other parts of India too).

Popular Names, Unknown Identities

The commonly used term for a native 'kept' woman used in contemporary sources was *bibi*. The term meant different things in South Asian common parlance, but it had come to mean the native mistress in the late 18th to early 19th centuries in Indo-British society, both in legal as well as other personal documents. Though there were other terms with similar connotations too, the word *bibi* appeared most often, with different spellings and versions – like *bibee*, *beebee*, *bebee*, *bubu*, and so on.

The native mistress could be 'acquired' (as the sources would say) through various means and was referred to differently in different cases. She could be part of a lifelong conjugal relation with a complete hold over the household, even over the slaves or be in a polygamous set-up or may have even been taken as a servant and so on. This, therefore, calls for going beyond the umbrella term of *bibi* to study the various terms denoting the native mistress. So, one would have to come back to the term *bibi*, where required, but the idea would be to go beyond and capture the variations of the conjugal set-up. These interpersonal relationships clearly had the element of conjugality and came under the confines of domestic, as reflected in various records of that period.

A serious problem faced while studying the nature of these intimacies is the relative absence of the voices of the native women, who are often not even mentioned by their original names. It becomes almost impossible to find their presence, let alone to know their views as they are silent and absent by the virtue of being addressed by European names like Polly, Betty, Mary, Sarah, Nancy, etc. along with other terms emphasizing her role like 'my girl,' 'my housekeeper,' 'the mother of my children,' 'my female companion,' 'female friend,' 'slave girl,' and so on. As it is these women belonged to the wills as the second person, but this namelessness makes them invisible. Sometimes, only the children borne out by these native women are referred to in the wills, with no reference to the woman or their mother; and some wills that mention both, do not establish the relationship between the woman/women and the natural children mentioned in the will.

Lieutenant Pierce Cassady of the Bengal Establishment, in his will from 1797, tells us the 'country name' and the name he gave his *bibi*.

> Secondly, I will and bequeath all my property whether in lands, money, Houses or any other kind of effects, to and for the sole use of my natural daughter Mary Cassady with the following instructions that immediately after my decease or as soon as it can be possibly done, the mother of my aforesaid Mary Cassady now living with me, shall have paid to her, by the commanding officer who shall have taken charge of my effects agreeable to the articles of war, the sum of one thousand rupees besides all the clothes and toys or jewels of any kind which I, at any time gave her, this woman I call Polly, but her real or country name is Saib Jaun, should the amount of the sale of any effects and arrears of pay not amount to the above sum it is to be made up to that sum by my executors.[9]

Lieutenant William Cresswell of the Bengal Establishment, in his will written in 1794, bequeathed all his property to a natural daughter by a 'native Portuguese woman,' who he had once lived with without any reference to her name or any other details about their relationship. He also mentions 'the native woman now living with me and who has lived with me for five years,' being pregnant now.[10] However, the sense of affinity is lacking in his tone nor is there any reference to the names of either of these women. He did leave money for both the women. The woman he was cohabiting with him while he was writing the will was given preferential treatment. She was also the one carrying his child.

In another will from 1785 of James Hunter, a surgeon with the East India Company, there is a detailed description for the benefit of his 'natural' daughter, Sarah Hunter.[11] He specified the date of birth of his daughter in his will so that she could get her claims as soon as she turned 21, but her mother is simply referred to as 'a Bengal Woman.' He did not leave anything to her, and she gets mentioned only once in the will as the mother of his daughter. In both these wills that both women were 'native' gets established, one as being of Portuguese origin and other being from Bengal, thereafter they are rendered nameless. Another will of a merchant from Calcutta, Anthony Lambert, in 1799, stated that he had a natural daughter by 'a Mogul woman, a native of Delhi, Jaun Bhegum [*sic*].' He also went on to mention two natural sons born to him by a native woman named Nancy. His legacy to them both also differed. Jaun Bhegum got the interest from 10,000 sicca rupees, and Nancy, received 6,000 sicca rupees.[12]

Isaac Golledge, a Mariner from Calcutta in his will only refers to 'my friend and companion' who is the mother of his adopted daughter, whom he left 32 rupees per month, but there is no name or indication about the status of their relationship. Then in the codicil to the will, he refers to a 'companion and housekeeper' who he described to be pregnant and 'as I firmly believe by me.'[13] He then made provisions for the unborn child. This woman mentioned in the codicil is probably the same woman as mentioned in the will, but this remains unclear since no name was provided. In the will, she is the mother of his two adopted children and in the codicil (the same or different woman), is mentioned as the mother of the unborn child.

Edward Eyer Burges, in his elaborate will, written in 1800, made provisions for the education of his 'illegitimate daughter Frances Burges,' whom he has already sent to England. But there is no mention of the woman who bore the child for him.[14]

Major John Williams of the Bengal Establishment, in the year 1797, wrote his will where he talked about his two natural children, leaving them provided for. He then added that if more children were born to him, during his life or '10 months after his decease' the child/children should also be taken care of. But there is no reference to his mistress or the mother of children, and she remains unnamed, and even unmentioned, only existing in her role as the mother of his children.[15]

There are many more wills like these where the native women exist only as mothers of the children borne by them, at times not getting anything out of the men's property. It is, therefore, an uphill task to read these women who are conspicuous not only due to the lack of any written records by them, but also by their namelessness in the sources they exist in. By their very absence, it was apparent that local women were the grounds on which boundaries of colonial communities were formed, as even the most well-known mixed-race men were known through their European fathers, and not their indigenous mothers.[16]

The English names by which these women were referred to, may have been easy to pronounce or even easy to remember for these men, owing to their familiarity with the language. But what this phenomenon certainly did was that it made it rather difficult to discover the origins, social backgrounds, and histories of these women in these relationships. By renaming, and un-naming them, or even categorizing them as a group, rather than as an individual, it becomes imperative to understand that they were valued for their care, service, reproduction, and not for their historical pasts, for they remained simply as native women in many wills. Although there are few wills in which these women bequeath their property as property owners, which we will discuss in the next chapter. They surely were an exception and not the rule because most of these women were never given absolute control over the property. Most of them did get clothes, jewellery, household furniture, etc. At times, the control over jewellery became the bone of contention as one shall see later. But in most cases, women were not given absolute proprietary rights.

'Acquiring' a Bibi

It is interesting to see how these relationships came about; there were various ways in which the British men could let a native companion join his household. In the diary of Richard Blechynden, a civil engineer and building contractor, and an official assistant to Calcutta's surveyor of roads, there is the reference as to how he acquired one of his *bibis*. He got his bibi in the 1790s in a typical manner. Luteeb came, Blechynden wrote,

> 'and told me that a very pretty Bebe was ... in great Distress so much so that she would actually sell herself to anyone that would pay her Debts.'[17]

Blechynden was prevailed upon to meet the lady, Nancy, who 'laid such a scene of distress open' to him that he landed up paying off all her debts, took her to be his *bibi* and asked her to live at his garden-house. The next day he sent a palanquin for her, and she came in that to live with him.

The will of Samuel Mageough of Behrampore mentions Nancy, one of two of his kept women. He adds for the executors of his will,

> I hope the mother of the child, from her youth and good disposition may be provided for by getting a good master.[18]

It was also common for a *bibi* to have been kept by various European men during her lifetime, just as it was common for a British man to have many native women as his concubines at different times or even simultaneously. Wills did give out information on both the accounts. Charles Cordery of Calcutta in his will dated 1793, mentions his,

> Housekeeper and well-beloved friend Elizabeth Maclean, alias, Elizabeth Stagg, alias, Elizabeth Bruce, alias Elizabeth Cordery.[19]

He left every kind of his property to her, which she could enjoy at her free will. Now, here it seems that one woman was being kept by several British men and that she had adopted their surnames during each of her stays. It is for legal purposes that Mr Cordery mentions all her aliases in his will where he leaves all his real and personal property to her without any reference to anyone else from his family, etc. There are other wills too that often carry such details for the sake of legal clarity.

Even the above-mentioned Nancy, one of the *bibis* of Blechynden was living with a certain Mr Cooper before she came to live in with him. Blechynden's detailed narrative says Mr Cooper abandoned her on account of his marriage. It was not uncommon to have a *bibi* recommended, as in the case of William Hickey, an English barrister in Calcutta after the death of his English wife. He wrote in his memoirs, 'My friend, Bob Pott, now consigned to me from Moorshedabad a very pretty native girl, whom he recommended for my own private use. Her name was Kiraun.'[20]

Another way to get a *bibi* was of course to buy one on one's own. Though not in Bengal, Claude Martin in Awadh mentions having bought four women in his will.[21] We will come to his will in a while, but a copy of his will housed in High Court, Calcutta does describe having purchased the native Boulogne, nicknamed Lise, through a Frenchman, who had purchased her from 'cruel and inhuman' parents.

There is an interesting anecdote about an engineer sent to Gualier (Gwalior), published in Hicky's Bengal Gazette.' This engineer was ordered to go and 'clear the fort a number of little huts and rubbish.' There he observed 'a very pretty girl about 10 years of age carrying stones on her head, her figure struck one very forcibly.' He went on, 'tho' in rags and employed in so dirty an occupation she had the appearance of something superior to her present situation, her easy deportment, her playful disposition, with her comrades in employment, and of a most engaging sweetness of countenance all determined me to enquire and find out if possible, who she was.'[22]

He then found out the necessary information through his 'Hircarrah' and went to her house where she lived with her old and infirm mother. He then offered them work, which seems to have alarmed the mother,

> I could see her delicacy was alarmed ... and I solemnly declare that she raised an idea in my mind at the moment that. I never had a thought of before. I blushed at the question, but it was not a guilty blush.[23]

He went on to announce that he had intended to send them down the country to his family and thus gave her mother money beforehand. Her mother took the money then but came back an hour later furious and said, 'she had been talking to woman since she left me, who assured her that firngy (foreigner or white, in this case) men never gave any money to Girls but for base purposes.' She also proclaimed that 'she would rather kill her daughter with her own hands, than (let) her to be a Cujbie to any Firngy in the world.'

The anecdote brings out certain interesting points, firstly, the terms in which he described the girl. She is just about 10 years old, but he probably held what a lot of Europeans at that time believed, as discussed previously, the belief that girls in tropical climates physically matured earlier.

As discussed earlier, the will of Major Andrew Wilson Hearsey of the Bengal Establishment, ascribes the existence of his 'illegitimate' children, to the 'vigour of youth, under the influence of a hot climate,' as discussed in the previous chapter.[24] Others too added, as Alexander Dow, in 1770, declared that the 'languor occasioned by the hot climate of India' naturally inclined 'the native to indolence and ease.'[25] A medical manual in the section titled, 'The Passions,' blames

> the monotony of life and the apathy of mind, so conspicuous among Europeans residing in a hot climate, together with the obstacles to matrimony, often led to vicious and immoral natural connections with native females, which speedily sapped the foundation of principles imbibed in early youth.[26]

This view corroborates the perspectives in contemporary Europe. Hyam talks of the Cult of Romanticism, which led to the idealization of love and women; and lists the peculiarities of the British attitude to sexual practice around the 18th century. This view got imported to India gradually, especially around the end of the 18th century. It also helped to see the Indian and English women as completely different. Europe had a long tradition of identifying others through the monstrous physiognomy and sexual behaviour of women, a foil against which proper ordered, civilized whiteness could be measured.[27] It probably was suited to view things in striking contrast, especially which affirmed the British uprightness.

Another salient issue was the 'money' the British engineer offers the mother of the girl. The mother was convinced that '*firngy*' men give money to girls only for 'base' purposes. Despite describing the girl in 'physical' terms and offering her money, the British man claimed that he 'would not have violated the chastity of this little beauty.' But it was surely a fairly common practice to offer money for the girl child and later take her up as a *bibi*, as was in the case of General Claude Martin. His will carried an explanation with regard to his way of acquiring mistresses,

> the four women under mentioned ... I have acquired them not as term slaves tho paid a considerable for but the sum I paid was a present to the relations that I might have had a right on them as not to be claimed by anybody and those I acquired for to be the companion of my good and bad fortune and they were to be with me for life. I had them when in their childhood and I had them educated as virtuously as I could.[28]

According to him, they were bought, for he mentions having 'paid' money, but he differentiates it from slavery. There is also a clear reference to a conjugal relationship between him and his 'bought' women. He wrote about his women in a very conscientious way:

> they are innocent of any guilt I am culpable on the sin if they have owed compliance to my command as their duties having every reason to be well satisfied of their services for the reason my sincere wish is to give them their proper reward in this world.[29]

He certainly does that in his long will, where he mentions his 'amiable' Boulogne in loving terms, describes having her educated when she was just nine years old, and then goes on praising her for her humanity and generosity, leaving her well provided for.

We also notice the role of the native servants, like the hircarrah and even others staying in mixed-race social space. The next chapter discusses a certain Miss Kitty, who introduced a native girl to a French man, who rapes her, assuming her presence in a mixed-race locality as her sexual availability.[30] Richard Blechynden's native concubines including the mother of his children, were generally recruited through servants or arrived as supplicants.[31] Subedar Sita Ram writing in 1861, mentioned how most of his officers had native women living with the *sahibs*. 'The sepoys themselves were sometimes instrumental in persuading the officers to take their female relations into their service but such men were usually low caste, or else Mahommedans.'[32]

Paid for Their Service

Peter Robb, while talking of Blechynden's *bibis* holds them to be 'paid servants' and 'never a wife, though expected to be faithful.'[33] Many a time these *bibis* were paid in cash or kind. It is difficult to generalize about the nature of payment because there was no fixed criterion, nor was it always mentioned, given the various kinds of living arrangements. But what is certain is that there was payment involved, whereby these women got paid. In almost all the cases, the mistress was fully provided for by the man she cohabited with; and she ran her household independently.

The issue of money or the payments involved, as it turned out was often a contentious one between the cohabiting couples. There was always payment or emoluments involved in such connections, but it was not always a cordial connection. It came up in the court cases such as the one where Henry Pyne allegedly stole some pieces of jewellery from his ex-*bibi* Peerun's house.[34] The court case will come up in detail in the next chapter, but what is noteworthy here is that Peerun's sister, who was one of the witnesses testified that Peerun had also 'presented a petition against him … claiming her pay.'[35]

There are such references in court cases too where the payment became the bone of contention. James Macknicol, a coach-maker from Calcutta fleetingly mentions a servant named Rose, whom he gives sicca rupees 1,500, along with some household goods. But then, in the codicil to the will (1789), he writes,

> With respect to my housekeeper who has this day left me without any cause that no part of what is mentioned in my former be given her as I have settled all and every matter respecting what emoluments she has or shall receive from my estate to this day.[36]

This will has a clear reference to a certain kind of emolument since he writes that he has 'settled' every matter of that respect. But having said that, what also seems clear is that she would have no claims on his property if the relationship was ended. Moreover, this will use the words, housekeeper and servant interchangeably, which again blurs the line between the two words and roles.

Another such case is that of Peter Daniel of Patna in the year 1783, who talks about 'Maria D'Rozario who is my formerly Girl to whom I owe by consience [*sic*] the allowance of a few months.' We will discuss this case in detail in the next chapter, but Peter Daniel does mention that his previous concubine had taken a bond 'forcibly' from him. What is clear is that there was some sort of payment or allowance which he was referring to.[37] Though the wills generally do not talk about contention over emoluments or wages of these women directly, it was the court cases that have information on them. So, this will remains exceptional for it spells out the information other wills do not provide us with.

Along with loyalty, another aspect that is mentioned frequently regarding the women is the 'services' or the 'good services' or the care she provided the men with. At times, the wills 'compensated' the women for the above-mentioned. Lieutenant Colonel in the military service of the United Company of Merchants of England, trading to the East Indies and leaving

India, John Bateman of Calcutta, wrote in his will (1799) about the girl who 'is now living with me named Khannum Commonie whose care and attention during my illness merits my warmest acknowledgement.'[38] He leaves her sicca rupees 10,000, for her sole use. The will only mentions a friend after her to whom he leaves 2,000 sicca rupees. The will of John Diehle of Behrampore, written in the year 1799, mentions the term 'my maid servant,' who is remembered in his will for her good services. He writes,

> I leave and bequeath unto my maid servant Selvin by name, the sum of sicca rupees one hundred in token of her good services to me. This sum of money must be taken from the amount that will remain for my son Charles [does not establish if she is Charles's mother].[39]

In another will, John Bottomly of Bankipore, gave a surplus of what was left after all his accounts were settled to 'my good woman Naneey as a compensation for her good services to me.'[40] He also leaves her his 'premises at Dinapore with all the buildings or building materials' to be her sole property, as a further compensation for the attention shown to me.' Thomas Longcroft, who did not live in Bengal and died in Koli in 1811, was granted probate in Calcutta. His will mentions his native partner Mobarick Jehan, whom he left 8,000 rupees for 'her very attentive kindness during the long period she has lived with me.'[41] He specifically acknowledged her services while he was suffering from a grave illness. This was probably to emphasize to the executioners of his will, as he is leaving her a large sum of money, just for her use.

Lieutenant James Brown, in 1783, bequeathed a legacy of 1,000 current rupees to his 'female servant, commonly named Kale, the mother of my said children as a testament of my regards for her faithful services.'[42] Kenneth McKenzy, a Mariner from Calcutta, in 1774, towards the end of his will asked his trustees to pay the interest of most money and best security 'unto my girl Katherina monthly (as an acknowledgement for her care of me during my several indispositions) for and during her natural life.' After a year, he added 400 rupees over the said 1,000 rupees for her in a codicil to the will.[43]

The last few wills, and many more perhaps, lead us to some important questions: Did non-marital cohabitations in early colonial India, where local women could be exchanged for money, or were brought into a household with native servants, and paid to serve the colonial man, although without a legal contract, fall under the category of service? This is particularly important since a lot of bequests were left to them highlighting their service, or their role as mothers of the mixed-race children. Did the exchange of money make British men possess the women on the one hand, and on the other, make it equally possible for the relationships to be called off by either party?

Could this money-based effect be seen as part of the 'care economy' of the 18th-century early colonial world?

Companion – 'To Take Care'

The British Government had initially encouraged having a native concubine, especially for the army, as it was favourable to building the army. Concubinage with the local women also 'permitted permanent settlement and rapid growth by cheaper means than the importation of European women.'[44] This becomes clearer when one thinks of the large numbers of soldiers, who would have been difficult to control and were desperately needed by the Company. Thus, the Government adopted a different attitude towards the European soldiery,

> Who are allowed to marry native women; many of whom conduct themselves; when thus situated, in the most unexceptionable manner. Whether married, or not, each soldier is generally provided with a companion, who takes care of his linen, aids in cleaning his accoutrements, dresses his hair, and sometimes proves no bad hand at a bread.[45]

Williamson went on to mention the 'famous rows' they could cause once in a while, but on the whole, they 'may be considered highly serviceable; especially during illness, at which time their attendance is valuable.' A native officer in the Bengal Army, Sita Ram, narrated in his memoirs, 'Most of our officers had Hindustanee women living with them, and these had a great influence in the regiment; and they always pretended to have more than what they really had, in order they might be bribed to ask sahebs for indulgences for the sepoys.'[46]

Samuel Sneade Brown, a magistrate in the Indian Civil Service, as late as the 1830s, spoke of many soldiers attaching themselves to 'attractive' Indian women – which he held more moral than a destructive round of dissipation. He in fact found 'them' a great deal affectionate,

> I have observed that those who have lived with a native woman for any length of time never marry a European … so amusingly playful, so anxious to oblige and please, that a person after being accustomed to their society shrinks from the idea of encountering the whims or yielding to the fancies of an Englishwoman.[47]

Apart from concubinage in the cantonment, there was also rampant prostitution, which, despite being problematic, did serve the English Army stationed at Calcutta. There were 'British official attempts to revamp the profession, first to meet the needs of the "Tommies" and alter under various pressures of what constituted colonial ethos of Victorian society at that time.'[48] Around that time, public brothels had sprouted in the cities and towns of Bengal. And British soldiers had developed quite a reputation for their drunken brawls in Calcutta.

> They thronged the Lal Bazar area ... which was known as 'Flag Street' because of the strings of flags across the street leading to eating houses, grog shops and brothels. Soldiers and sailors drank and fought to their hearts' content in Flag Street.[49]

This is precisely what the authorities had feared – British soldiers wandering beyond the controlled environment of the cantonment into the unknown places where they could get infected or worse get tempted to 'Oriental' vices. Thus, the typical cantonment came to have 'regimental bazars as well as a central bazar, and the soldiers were expected to satisfy their needs there.'[50] Charles D'Oyly had his own views on it. Speaking of 'changing character of Indians,' he said,

> Whether from that circumstance, or the great influx of young officers ... that arrived from Europe, between the years 1778 and 1783, it is certain that the prime sets of dancing girls quitted the cities, and repaired to the several cantonments, where they met the most liberal encouragement.[51]

He went on to describe the charms of Kaunum and her influence on these European men:

> Those who did not witness the dominion she held over a numerous train of abject followers, would never credit, that a haughty, ugly, filthy, black woman, could, solely by grace of her motions, and the novelty of some Cashmerian airs, hold in complete subjection, and render absolutely tributary, many scores of fine young British officers! Nay, even the more discreet and experienced, many of whom could not, with propriety say, 'Time has not thinned my flowing hair, nor bent me with his iron hand,' were found among the most fervent of the proud Kaunum's admirers.[52]

These were more clandestine and may be temporary 'affairs,' but the relationships forged between the native women and the British men were certainly more complex than that. The set-up in this domain of domesticity was, mostly sans marriage, but it did have certain features common to most formal marital households. It was like a parallel universe for Britons abroad, where *bibis* were accorded a level of respect and status that would never have been allowed to a concubine on home turf.[53] Second, the household set-up with a native woman came within the purview of the legal space, since the rule of law did amount to settling the domestic discords rather than punishing their existence and there is even a debate on whether concubinage was a legal contract or not.[54]

Third, there are many wills that mention native women partners as servants, and a few that also refer to them as slaves. At times, the British men while bequeathing money or material objects did refer to these women for their 'care during illness,' etc., which makes it difficult to ascertain the relationships between the British master and his female servants/slaves. The use of terms like housekeeper, servant, my girl interchangeably does not let one define the status of these women clearly. These women were bought as slaves in a few cases and at times, the boundaries between a housekeeper and a servant girl were blurred. The wills usually mentioned slaves, as they were at times bequeathed or given their freedom.[55] Indrani Chatterjee, as discussed earlier, looked at them as slave-concubines. For her, the interchangeability of nomenclature indicated the interpenetration of the structures of the household and the market in the lives of these specific females.[56] Recently, Nitin Sinha in his work on domestic servants in colonial Calcutta, contends that the quintessential presence of a servant-like character, of a domestic-service/servitude-like relationship, and of the continuous potential to reconfigure that relationship through patronage and resistance is integral to servants' past in colonial India.[57] Although not specifically about native concubine, it talks about the domestic servants in mixed-race households, in various roles, as a perennial presence.

The will of Robert Maxwell of Calcutta (1792) is one such case. There is mention of a female servant whom he bequeathed everything, without any reference to anyone else in his will; he even provided for the unborn child she was pregnant with. He left all his money, even the amounts due to him to 'my female servant Diana … in consideration of her faithful services, as a support and maintenance for herself and the infant of which she is now enceinte should it survive.'[58] They clearly shared conjugal relations, and no one else comes close to being mentioned in his will, but she was referred to as his servant.

Captain Williamson tried to give a clear picture to his European readers of the households set up by the European men with native women and also of 'plurality.' Like most Europeans writing at that time, he too noticed the predominance of Muslim mistresses and wrote how a Muslim woman 'under the protection' of a European was held by her countrymen in no disrespect and was treated as though she were married to him. According to Muslim law, there were various degrees of marriages, from the 'most strict' form of conjugal attachment to a more 'loose' one too. Fanny Parkes too had expressed her surprise at it:

> It is difficult to say what sort of bridal contract is gone through between a Moslem beauty and a Christian Gentleman, but the ceremony is supposed to be binding; at least it is considered so in India, a native female not losing the respect of her associates by forming such a connexion.[59]

At the time when building a house for a mistress was considered a sure sign of prestige and honour among the elite Indians of Calcutta, the native mistress of the elite European men also got separate establishments. Blechynden had simultaneous *bibis*, one at his townhouse and another at his garden-house. In other instances, the '*Beebeeghar*' (house for *bibi*) was adjacent to the main bungalow, where the *bibi* resided with her retinue of female servants. At times, an entire property was devoted to maintaining a *bibi*, as suggested by this advertisement:

> To be sold by private sale, a garden-house and grounds situated at Taltolah bazar, which to any gentleman about to leave India, who may be solicitous to provide for an Hindostanee Female friend, will be found a most desirable purchase.[60]

Mixed-Race Social Space

It is true that *bibi*, despite being socially acceptable during the last quarter of the 18th century, did not accompany 'her man' to European social gatherings, though she certainly interacted with other European men. Blechynden mentioned in his diary that Colonel Erskine's *bibi* gave him a gold ring to wear 'for her sake.'[61] Thomas Jones, a conductor of the Ordnance in the Honourable Company's service mentions two of his mistresses at the station of Chunargur, in 1791. One was Lucy, his *bibi* and mother to his two children, to whom he left 300 Benaras sicca rupees along with clothes, gold, and silver ornaments. He then mentioned, Mary or Mannoo 'my woman or housekeeper,' who he left 100 Benaras sicca rupees along with clothes and precious jewellery. He added, 'the flat gold pump seal now at my watch belongs to her the said Mary, having been given to her by Mr Henry George, a house conductor of Ordnance and I desire that the seal be given to her.'[62] There seems to be a kind of affectionate friendship between Mary or Mannoo, and Thomas Jone's friend, and he wanted for her to have that gift that was in fact given to her. We do not get to hear much about such friendships, and it is interesting how one can pick such social details from these wills too, making it possible to imagine the socialization of mixed-race domesticities. Similarly, John Herbert of Dacca in his will from 1795 left a ring for his 'true and faithful servant Sameeda,' given to her as a keepsake by Mr Manington.[63]

Even William Hickey's friends treated his *bibi*, Jemadanee, very affectionately. A friend of his, Mr Mee, inquired after her in all his letters, and wrote in a letter dated January 14, 1793,

> I hope ... that the lively and good tempered Bibee Sauheb is in the perfect health. I lately met with some ornaments, fresh from Paris which from being so, I think she will admire and cry 'Wah! Wah!' at ... My best love to her and beg her to wear them for my sake.[64]

Lieutenant Philip Herbert clearly mentions a friendship between his *bibi* Kaunum and the *bibi* of Lieutenant F. William Blundele, namely Nouran in his will (1781). He left a sum of 1,000 sicca rupees to the son of Lieutenant F. William Blundele and Nouran on the account of the 'friendship subsisting' between Kaunum and Nouran; and 'the regard I have for the child.'[65] This does speak of a friendship between the two families, with similar domestic arrangements.

The native woman did not go to the social gatherings where large numbers of Europeans were present, but it does not mean that she did not have any social connection. While the reasons for this may not be apparent, it could be attributed to the fact that their socialization was more attuned to establishing acquaintances within domestic set-ups, which were similar in nature to their own. There was certainly no interaction with all-European households as a domestic unit, probably due to a sort of morality mostly over the white women, who were to be kept away from such setups.

Polygamy

It was common for a British man to have kept more than one mistress during his stay in India and at times in a polygamous set-up too. It should again be read keeping in mind the idea of class, as to which men kept or could keep more than one domestic partner at a time, almost modelled after the Mughals and Nawabs, whose opulent shoes they were stepping in. One of the features of the much-mocked figure of the Nabob, was a harem of multiple concubines. David Ochterlony, the Resident of Delhi (1803–1825), apparently had 13 mistresses among Indian women.[66]

A will by a Bengal merchant, William Driver, dated July 30, 1784, mentioned four 'dear beloved children' and mentioned Sophea as their mother. He also mentioned another woman by the name Rosear, whom he left one 1,000 rupees and claims her to be the mother of one of the children.[67] Both the women happened to be his concubines, either at the same time or with an interval. The will mentioned that both women bore him children. Similarly, Robert Harvey of Calcutta, in 1811, wrote in his detailed will,

> to pay unto my servant girl Constantia De Sauza better known by the name of Jenny, monthly, and every month during her natural life, the interest of the sum equivalent to six sixteenth of the net proceeds of my estate, and a legacy of 50 sicca rupees one month after my decease.
>
> Secondly, I give and bequeath to my servant girl Kitty the interest of the sum equivalent to four sixteenths of the net proceeds of my estate, which is to be paid to her monthly during her natural life, and a legacy of fifty sicca rupees one month after my decease.
>
> Thirdly, I give and bequeath unto the child of my late servant Girl Susannah names Cecelia Sureen, but better known by the name of mamney, the interest of the sum equivalent to six sixteenth of the net proceeds of my estate … and which interest is to be continued to her during her natural life, whether she be single or married.
>
> … it is to be understood that upon the death of one or both of the above mentioned two persons, that is to say Jenny and Kitty, her or their part on the interest of my estate bequeathed to them, is to revert to and to become the property of the afore mentioned child Cecila Sureen, and upon her death that the whole of my estate, Principal and interest, be divided between the children, if she have any, Lawfully begotten, if the above mentioned Cecilia Sureen, or in default one of her issue, to such charitable purposes, as my executors in their discretion shall deem proper.[68]

Both these wills clearly mention more than one mistress, although we are not told if they all lived with the British men at the same time. Another interesting aspect in second will is Robert Harvey's emphasis on his daughter begetting lawful children, if they were to claim his legacy. Such were the subtle ways of controlling the future life of his daughter, probably discouraging her from entering a non-marital connection, such as one she was born into.

Also, while these may or may not be a case of polygamous households where more than one mistress lived with the man simultaneously, in another case, Samuel Mageough of Behrampore (1791) mentioned earlier, there is a clear mention of both of his *bibis* Neuran and Nancy living with him at the same time.

> each of the girls who now live with me one named Neuran, the other Nancy, an annuity or more properly a monthly allowance of twenty-three Sicca Rupees.[69]

He also added that at his decease

> the girl who has lived with me the greatest part of the time I've been in the country, if living with me at the time of my death, is to

> be paid up and to receive immediately one hundred and fifty sicca rupees with liberty to proceed where she pleases.

He also expressed his wish for Nancy to remain with the child, in the immediate care of his executors, till the child reached the proper age to be sent to Europe for education.

> I hope the mother of the child, from her youth and good disposition may be provided for by getting a good master.[70]

John Erskine, probably the same Colonel John Eskine whose *bibi* gave Blechendyn 'a gold ring to wear for her sake,' mentioned four native women in his will.[71] He was a Major General in the service of Honourable United East India Company and wrote in his will from Chunar, in 1799, that he had left bequests to Noor Bebee (who was also the mother of his natural daughter Emma), Sheroo Khanum, Vizieran, and Banoo. He mentioned all of them to be residing with him in his bungalow, except Banoo, whom he mentioned 'having taken care of for many years.' Even the bequeaths were different for them. Noor Bebee got a monthly sum of 100 sicca rupees, Sheroo Khanum got a monthly sum of 60 sicca rupees, and Vizirean and Banoo both received monthly sums of 30 sicca rupees each for their natural lives.[72]

John Pearce, of Midnapore in the Soubah (Suba) of Orissa, 'under and subject to the Presidency of Fort William in Bengal,' in 1785 mentioned two women in his will.

> Likewise, to pay to each of my two girls, named Purbetty and Roojey now living with me as follows viz to the former one thousand sicca rupees, and to the latter two thousand sicca rupees. … This gift being over and above the sundry plots or parcels of lands or gardens with their several erections or tanks and thereon and there in. And over and above all money, gift or other things whatever I have occasionally given them during my life and for which they have or have not the proper papers or writings, and should any of these papers through inattention be found amongst my papers, I hereby desire they may be restored to both, or either in whose name such paper or writing may be made out in. I hereby likewise desire that they may be allowed without any let or hindrances or interrogatories being put to them to possess and enjoy whatever they are or may be in possession of at the day of my death, be it money, trinkets of gold, silver or cloths or any other thing whatever. And they may be allowed to remove themselves, and everything they have in, or chuse [*sic*] to take from the house in the jungal in which they sometimes live and opposite my dwelling house called Windsor and to go to either of their other abodes in the country.[73]

In another example, Christian Knudson in his will (1792), bequeathed 3,000 sicca rupees to Cadigee Canym along with the house at Danish settlement at Fredrick Nagoor, the same amount went to Biby Caryman and the Bunglow at Calcutta, as well as to Noor Nissa Bibee, 1,000 sicca rupees went to Himut Begum, and 500 sicca rupees to Techina. He also willed to divide his furniture, horse carriages, boats, etc. between 'Canym Sahib i.e., Kadigee Canym and Bibee Caryman.'[74]

Major John Fairfax of the Bengal Establishment, in 1782, mentioned his three children, all born of three different women – Rajeh, Manoo, and Esabania, all natives of Hindostan.[75] The women were mentioned just as mothers to his children. He wanted all the three children – Soldier (to be christened Harry), Maria, and Harriot – to be sent to England, to be educated 'in a manner suitable to their circumstances, and that their fortunes be remitted as soon as possible after my demise.' He divided his estate into three equal parts for his children, but the women did not get anything, other than a mention as mothers of his children.

Now, these cases clearly show one British man maintaining more than one mistress often at the same time. In the first will, the mother of the child, Nancy receives preferential treatment over the other one. He had good words to say about her, in fact, he also wrote to his executors to provide for her by getting her another good master, due to her 'youth and good disposition.' He did not mention any other family member and left everything to the child by Nancy and if she was to give birth to another one, it would be divided between the two offspring. He also clearly wrote that the women were free to go wherever they wished.

In the second will, the differentiated legacy could be due to seniority within the household or may be because Techina could have been a slave girl. Christian Knudson mentioned three children without establishing who had mothered whom. One similarity in the two wills is the lack of control over the women and absence of possible sexual jealousy. Many wills put conditions on the women for them to receive the legacies, at times, for as long as they lived but at times, also after the death of the man. Lieutenant Bartholomew William Healy (1793) left a monthly allowance and household furniture, etc., for his housekeeper Lucy's support, 'so long as she may live single and behaves herself to their (Executors') satisfaction.'[76] Here, the right to decide the 'right' kind of behaviour was left to the executors of his will. It could also be possible that in service of another white man, he was supposed to be providing for her.

Conditions Apply

Many a time the British men expressed that the legacies to be paid to their women on condition that they were still in their keeping at the time of their decease, staying with them or servicing them. Some of these relationships, and whether she may have had any bequest, depended upon her being or not being with him when he was writing the will. It could have also meant completion of her services to him, and hence, no responsibility towards her.

Robert Holme's will (1786), left the interest of 8,000 sicca rupees to his housekeeper, Bibby Connom, but also stated that in case of her marriage or going into the keeping of another man, the interest was to cease and the principal to go to his brother and sister instead.[77] Lieutenant Daniel Stewart, a Cornet in the Twenty-fourth Regiment of the Light–Dragons, in his will wrote about,

> my female friend Zorun Nissa Beghum the mother of my children sum of thirty rupees to be paid unto her on the last day of each month by my Executor or Executors hereafter mentioned.[78]

This monthly allowance was to be continued during her natural life provided she remained single and did not go into keeping with another but in which case it was to directly cease and the same would go towards the support and education of his children. Major Isaac Barraud, of Artillery in Bengal Establishment in 1788 turned all his property in a trust. He then mentioned that Susannah, the mother of two of his children, who was to get interest on a sum,

> during her natural life under the following limitation that she neither marries nor goes under the control of any other master to the detriment of our children, which I leave to the judgement of my trustees and executors, in which event I cut her off from every advantage she may inherit by this my last will, allowing her only in that event during her life one hundred current rupees per mensem, and to take with her, her cloaths [*sic*] and effects only and I also bequeath unto her the use or monthly rent during life of my two houses...under the foregoing limitation, and neither of them nor any part or portion of them to be left in her power to alienate or dispose of being to remain as part of my property.[79]

Major Barraud then bequeathed 10,000 current rupees to each of his three children, as well as the right to use the house in Dhee, Calcutta, of six cottahs, which was not to be disposed of during the natural life of their mother or till the youngest child reached 21 years of age. Here, money to his *bibi* was conditioned on her remaining single, and he did not shy away from emphasizing it.

John Andrews, in his will written in the year 1807, bequeathed to his woman the interest of 15,000 sicca rupees (which he has bequeathed to his two natural children from her). He also wrote that in case of the death of the two children, the interest of either or both halves were to go to her, along with 3,000 sicca rupees was to be put in Company's paper for her support. Then he put the condition,

> but if she marries or goes in keeping with any one else I shall only give her sicca rupees Two thousand and she will not be allowed or permitted to have any command over her children's money.[80]

He says she can only share the interest from the money if she kept herself 'chaste and behaves with that propriety as she has done for these three years past.' Thomas Nisbet, Serjeant Major of the 32nd Battalion of Native Infantry of Honourable United East India Company, residing upon his own estate at Howrah, near the Orphan School, Calcutta. He bequeathed to 'Nancy, Native woman living with me/But with and under the provisions specified.'[81] He wanted the rent from the part of his estate leased to Neter Robistoon to go to her during her natural life, along with the movable effects of every kind. However, on her decease, it was to be sold, and the money remitted to his children. However, he wanted to make it very clear that 'Nancy is only to receive the house and estate after my death and only while she continues to live single.'[82]

Along with the weight of morality, there is a clear separation of the mistress from her children. Though there are cases where men have left money, etc. for the women they had previously kept or even if someone had 'gone into the keeping of another man.' There are also documents that showed men being comfortable mentioning the previous keepers or even the present keepers of their ex-mistresses. Evident in the passages above, is that men did try and control the sexuality of their women or it was certainly a concern and they made it clear through the legacies they left to them in their wills with conditions being put on their 'proper behaviour.' Richard Blechynden's detailed diaries can be called upon to address this. This was a widespread agreement that it was demeaning to abandon a *bibi*, and hence there are multiple cases, where Blechynden took care, by making payments towards some of his friends' *bibis*.[83] One reason for the sense of responsibility for the *bibis* was that none was regarded as a prostitute, though there was a gradation of status, as Blechynden himself had temporary *bibis* from time to time.[84] The sense of responsibility was considered to have been passed on to another man, if she went in another man's 'keeping,' and so did any monetary responsibility. As mentioned earlier, not all men left bequeaths for their mistresses, current or previous, as there are some wills where only children are mentioned.

Some wills found it difficult to even come up with proper adjectives for the relationship. The reason is difficult to fathom, because it does not, in any way, hinder the legal implications of the will, even when these places are left blank. For example, Lieutenant Christopher Kelly left a bequest to a girl named Mary in 1788.

> To a girl named Mary, now living with me, who has been my faithful ______ these four years the sum of twelve hundred sicca rupees, to be ______ in the best security ... that she may regularly draw ... at the rate of ten or twelve ... in monthly payment without ______ whatsoever during her life.[85]

There were also very concise wills, that neither express nor share much, and often do not mention the names of the mistresses, her mention is simply alluded to her service and role. But then, those are mostly the wills that belong to men from the lower social classes, where the bequeaths were smaller sums. This practice of mistresses not being mentioned, overlooked, or even written about at length, separate or their relation to the man, was not uncommon among elite men too. Similarly, there were wills that do not concern themselves with what the native concubine would do once the British man had passed away, moved back, or even when their relationship had been terminated by either party. As already noted, the will of Charles Cordery mentions his 'Housekeeper and well-beloved friend Elizabeth Maclean, alias, Elizabeth Stagg, alias, Elizabeth Bruce, alias Elizabeth Cordery' clearly the case of the woman having lived with various keepers. The will appears 'loving' in its overall language and leaves everything at her disposal and for her sole use.[86]

Similarly, there are wills that show a deep concern for the native mistress to be well provided for. There are many such wills in the section on familial intimacy, where such concerns are aplenty. Lieutenant Henery Himing in the Bengal Establishment, in a will dated July 18, 1784, bequeathed

> unto the girl formerly kept by me and who was under the charge of Mr James Wordsworth one thousand sicca rupees to purchase an annuity for life and this to be purchased by my Executors on her account taking care to have good security and the money deposited in such a manner that the income may be regularly and monthly paid, or of should be inconvenient quarterly.[87]

The last will did not name the woman, though she is left provided for, and that too at par with the woman who was cohabiting with him. In fact, this is also a will that hints at a discord or a change of heart vis-à-vis the present concubine. Henery Himing left a bequest of 1,000 sicca rupees for the girl, 'now in the keeping by me.' An addition was made to the will on the same day that it was filed/drafted (July 18, 1784), changing the amount to only 200 sicca rupees. Another change was made on July 21, 1784, by H. Himing, who left nothing to the current mistress.

Lieutenant Francis Forde in the Royal Navy of Chittagong mentions his 'faithful servant Balinda' whom he left an interest of 4,000 arcot [*sic*] rupees. He wanted it to be at the rate of 20 rupees per month, and remainder for the repair for her bungalow where she was staying, but only for as long as she lived.[88] Another of such numerous wills, was by John Evers of Calcutta (June 17, 1799),

> First, I leave devise and bequeath unto my faithful Girl Lucia the sum of one thousand and five hundred sicca rupees / S. Rs. 1500 lawfull money of Bengal. Also, all my plates, chairs, tables, cot with all its furniture and one of my best chests – and also all her own clothes and chests.[89]

Though we will take up the right to property due to these women only for their natural life, and the bequest of solely the interest on a primary sum in the next chapter, it requires a brief mention here too. While it is true that most of these women did not have complete rights over the property of their men, certain features of a marital connect were expected and maintained. For instance, the native mistress was expected to be 'faithful,' this word makes frequent occurrence in the wills. Now faithfulness was mentioned as an important aspect of their relationship, non-marital but it extended to most aspects of the conjugal boundaries.

'My Faithful Servant'

Being 'faithful' or a 'good woman,' having provided good services or having given him attention and care, etc. were cited in the wills as reasons for leaving her a share of the wealth he had acquired during his lifetime. If not a reason, this was the service and role in the confines of the household, in the life of the British man, and in the early colonial scheme of things. Blechynden's diaries show his expectations from his *bibi* as a part-time companion, housekeeper, and sometimes childminder, all in one.[90] Diaries may have reflected a lot of engagement with thoughts and ideas, but the will is usually not the appropriate document for such expressions. However, the frequency with which the faithfulness of the native mistress is mentioned, along with terms like 'trusty' which are often used for long-term companionships, and at others, what these women represented in a British man's life away from 'home.' The frequent use of these terms implies the kind of onus that was put on the concubine's being faithful, as a part of the relationship, or how she was being rewarded in the wills for being faithful.

Henry Bourke of Calcutta, at Fort William, writing in 1787 in his will, gave 'his trusty housekeeper Reetah' a sum of 2,500 sicca rupees, along with some household objects, wearing apparel, etc.[91] Likewise, John Vickers, ensign in the services of the Honourable Company of Merchants in England trading to the East Indies, Bengal Establishment in 1797, mentioned his 'worthy woman and companion Johannah Rozarah Seeveenah in consideration of her long good and faithful services.'[92] He left her his

> large and elegant puckah built house with all godowns and other appurtenances ... enclosed by a wall situated lying and being to the southward of the cantonment of Behrampore in Bengal for and during the term of her natural life

He also left her 500 sicca rupees, along with her clothes and jewellery. He did mention children but established no clear relationship between the chil dren and his *bibi*. John Gilbert, in 1794, desired that four gold *mohurs* be paid to 'my girl Flora' in consideration of her attention to him.[93] He also left household objects and his utensils to her. A merchant of Patna, Henry Righton, in 1790, bequeathed 'unto Ann Mountain for her long and faithfull [*sic*] services all my household furniture, cloaths [*sic*], plate and stock of every sort and kind and inquest.'[94]

Thomas Ballias, a private soldier in the 76th Regiment of Fort and Captain Watsons Company, left to

> Mary (a native woman of the country) as the only and least token I can leave her of my approbation of her good conduct and affection towards me during the seven years that she cohabited with me, the whole of my arrears of pay ... clothing, prize money together with all and every other debt or debts due to me.[95]

Lieutenant Michael Constance Davoren mentioned his housekeeper Mrs Elizabeth Ramsey, 'my present housekeeper, who has born me three children.' He then went on to mention the bequeath to her 'as a reward for her faithful and affectionate attachment during the many years she has lived with me.' He did not mention marriage but used the same name for her. However, he highlights her role and attachment to her in the will.[96]

Richard Burton also wrote about the *bubu* (another word for native mistress) for her indispensability in terms of the role she played in everyday life during the 'tenure of her office.' He says,

> The bubu is all but indispensable to the student, and she teaches him not only Hindostani grammar, but the syntaxes of native life. She keeps house for him, never allowing him to save money, or, if possible, to waste it. She keeps the servants in order. She has an infallible recipe to prevent maternity, especially if her tenure of office depends on such compact. She looks after him in sickness, and is one of the best of nurses, and as it is not good for a man to live alone, she makes him a manner of home.[97]

Another interesting feature that one notices is that some British men adding their surname to that of a native woman in the wills. It is there in many wills, probably as a sense of identification, affinity, patriarchal assumption, or as a conjugal rite. Though it could have been just used for legal documentation, considering it was being mentioned in a will. It might have made claiming the bequeath easier. Richard Seager of Calcutta, in 1799, bequeaths to his

> much esteemed old Housekeeper by name of Hannah Carter (lately known by the name of Hannah Carter but since living with me known by the name of Hannah Seager) the rest residue and remainder of the whole such property.[98]

He also appoints her the executrix of his will. We keep coming to the exceptional case of Charles Cordery, where the woman was known by various surnames, which may have been those of her keepers. Though this was not a rule but still common, another parallel one could draw to marital relationships. Thomas Lowry of Artillery Corps filed his will at Chunar in July 1808. Where he mentions a native woman, his well-beloved companion Mary Lowry. He always mentions her name with such loving care throughout the will, and with his surname. He leaves her all his ready money and all his just debts due to him for her. He adds later that in event of death of his son, Edward Lowry, any property he has bequeathed to him, shall go to Edward's mother, the said Mary Lowry.[99]

Mariner Robert Hammond's will (1792) is one such case among others. His native live-in partner is referred to by her name Mary Dil Jonny (*Dil Jaani*), who is commonly known by his surname.

> I give and bequeath unto my old companion Mary Dill Jonny, commonly called Mary Hammond, in consideration of her long and faithful services all my garden houses and grounds at Havera, to hold for her natural life. … All the residue of my estate after my funeral expenses are paid I leave to the aforementioned Mary Dill Jonny commonly called Mary Hammond.[100]

John Ogilvy, a former Mariner leaves 1,000 current rupees to 'the girle [*sic*] named Nannie … for her good services in taking care and nursing a child of mine.'[101] It was to be laid out to her best advantage, in a secure manner, he writes. While establishing her to be the mother of his natural son, he does refer to her as 'his mother Nannie Ogilvy' and puts a condition on the son to let the mother and his sisters stay in the house he has bequeathed to him. Though the will does not establish any relation between the Nannie and his daughters, he does use his surname for her to relate the mother and son. Although he also left Nannie

> all my wearing apparel and housald [*sic*] furniture such as tables, chairs, chests and coots and bedding and with cooking utensils and two silver spoons large and two small with my name upon them for her to remember me when she looks upon them.

There are many more such wills, spelling out the words, like faithful, loyal, good companion, trusty, etc. These are loaded words, especially because they were being used not for their 'lawfully wedded companions,' but for their 'kept' native women. But how these gendered expectations remained a virtue to be spoken of well and even at times to leave a compensation for, is interesting. So, for most of the British men 'living' with the native women, being faithful was important as long as the relationship existed, but for some also after the relationship had ended.

Seeing the details of these wills, it would be unfair to sum all these wills under a blanket category, as one witnesses layers of everyday details, and degrees of intimacies. The conjugal and sexual aspect was certainly common to them, but they also make such interesting micro-histories, especially concerning the women who do not appear in any other source material.

There are wills where the intimacies or lack of them, came upon different terms. The terms had to be derived by reading the terms of the wills carefully. Faithful servants, trusty housekeepers, contentious episodes, and so on have been mentioned. There is yet another aspect of intimacy that was spelt out in the wills. There were wills that read like letters, or even better as testimonies to the emotions involved. It would be beyond the scope of this work to take up those myriad emotions, and interpersonal connections. However, the expression of intimacies does provide another dimension to this endeavour of researching the wills.

Families – Here and There

Before discussing the familial intimacies that were experienced in these relationships, as suggested by some wills, there is a need to look at the references to the families back in Europe. A lot of these men who were writing these wills mention their parents, siblings, nephews, nieces, friends, even wives and legitimate children, apart from the Indian mixed-race relationships and children born out of these relationships. These two families, the one in India and the one in Europe, are often juxtaposed in the wills.

John Vickers of the Bengal Establishment, in his will written in 1797, mentioned his four legitimate children, whom he left 1,000 sicca rupees each. Thereafter, he also mentioned the youngest daughter, presumably by his mistress. He also gave a reference of a long-term domestic arrangement with a native woman in his will and left his house to his native mistress.

> My large and elegant puckah built house with all the godowns and other appurtenances ... to my worthy woman and companion Johannah Rozarah Seeveenah in consideration of her long good and faithful services to me.[102]

William Collier of Calcutta mentioned his father in his will and then gave out certain details about his relationship with Nancy. This too appears to be a case of a household of a British man and a native woman that had been established for long. He writes about 'my girl Nancy who has lived with me upwards of three years and who has always been known and called by the name of Nancy.'[103]

Christopher Webb Turner of Calcutta talked about his housekeeper in an otherwise concise will.[104] He said his housekeeper Nancy De Rozario had lived with him for the past five years, from 1795 onwards. He left her with 1,500 sicca rupees. These are a few of such examples of wills which are household establishments that have been in operation for a long time, consisting of the British man and the 'native' woman. There are other wills in which the only point at which the British men talk about their 'family' is at the mention of their native woman and their natural children. Only a few wills have details about these relationships where the men mention how they viewed these domestic arrangements.

Some wills establish the existence of an English wife as well as a native woman partner, along with children from either or both relationships. Charles Roberts, formerly in the service of the Late James Miller, Esquire, who subsequently served Doctor John Shoolbred, both of Calcutta, wrote his will in 1811. There, he mentioned his wife Elizabeth Roberts of Gloucestershire as well as their two children. Thereafter, in his extremely elaborate will, which is produced in another chapter, he mentioned his two natural children. He also mentioned two mistresses, as being the mothers of the above-mentioned two natural children and the mother of his natural daughter Fanny Roberts to be his 'trusty housekeeper Mrs Anna Coridaja, otherwise called Billo's mother.' He left 500 sicca rupees to her as well as to the other woman he had mentioned, 'Sophy De Rozario, the mother of my natural son James Roberts.' It is difficult to clearly gauge the kind of domestic set-up they had for both the native women may have been living with him, and that too simultaneously.

William Price Wattell of Dinapore, Behar, in 1820, wrote in his will that his dwelling house at Dinapore, if not disposed of till his demise, be disposed of in a lottery.[105] He then proceeded with bequests, where his 'beloved wife Sarah Wattell' should receive all her personal jewels, house, silver plate, and house furniture she was permitted to select for her personal use, and a sum of 8,000 rupees exclusive of an allowance for education and clothing for their infant children. He also said that 'the sum of two thousand four hundred rupees in deposit with Messers P. Stewart and Robertson the interest is a provision for Beebee Nancy during her natural life.' After her decease, it was to become a property of Samuel, George, and Adelaide Wattell, his children, in equal shares of 8,00 rupees, together with 1,000 rupees each to these two sons and a daughter payable by his executors at 12 months after his death. He did not say whether the children were natural and mentioned only his wife Sarah as the mother of his children, so we can presume all three were her children. But both, his wife as well as *bibi* were mentioned and taken care of. However, one cannot help but notice a monetary hierarchy, where the wife got a larger share, complete control over the money for her own use, while his *bibi* had to make do with a lesser grant with stipulated conditions related to it. He also chose to reserve a more affectionate term like 'beloved' for his wife.

A merchant of Patna, William Anthony Camedys, in 1793, mentioned his married wife Mrs Hannah Camedys to whom he left 'one shilling of lawful money of Great Britain.' He also referred to a Rose Elizabeth, whom he called 'my beloved friend and a good companion,' who was the executrix of his will. He left her 'the residue and remainder of his property, estate, lands, tenements, hereditaments with my goods, plates, jewels, bonds, arrears of rent with all other property whatsoever.'[106]

William Lowrie of Chittagong in the province of Bengal, in 1784, wrote his will, what he bequeathed to his three natural children – William, Thomas, and Margaret. He made a provision for leaving both sons 6,000 sicca rupees each and his daughter 8,000 sicca rupees with interest, as and when they turned 21. He mentioned Francisca Pierrah, a Portuguese woman, inhabitant of Chittagong, to be their mother, to whom he did not leave anything, nor did she get a mention in his will other than the fact that she was the mother of his three children. He left the residue and remainder of his real and personal estate to his 'loving wife Jean Lowrie and to her heirs.'[107]

This interracial cohabitation and its attachments, be it permanent or temporary, co-existed with the natal family and/or the family by marriage back in Europe. The reference to both in a will was a common phenomenon, again keeping in mind the nature of wills, as a source. One also needs to look at wills that went on to talk about a sense of family within the mixed-race domestic space.

Familial Intimacy

There are wills in which the only point at which the British men talk about their 'family' is with reference to their native partners, and at times the children borne by her. It is true that the wills were not a detailed account, but there were some men like William Hickey or Richard Blechynden, who wrote about their *bibis* at great length in their memoirs and diaries. There are also some wills that go on to give out various details about these relationships. There are certain wills that mention British wives as well as native concubines. It is interesting to read how some of these men viewed this native 'connection' as the only relation to be mentioned in probably their last documents, i.e., the will.

Pilot William Watts of Calcutta bequeathed unto 'my girl or companion the sum of ten thousand sicca rupees together with half my furniture and rest of my estate.'[108] Another Pilot, Joseph Friend mentioned 'my girl' Mattalena Desaw, whom he made the sole executrix of his will and left her,

> all my ready money, debt, dues and demands that may become due unto me at the time of my decease after all my just debts are paid. Furthermore, I give into the said girl all my wearing apparel, goods… chattels, tenements that I may be possessed of at the time of my decease.[109]

Cornelius Seavander mentioned the 'love and friendship connection which has long subsisted' and that he still bore it for Rozie D. Rozario. He left her half the amount of his outstanding balances, household furniture, jewellery, half of his garden to her, with the other half for the executor of his will.[110] There are wills like that of William Higgins, a corporal in the 5th Battalion of Infantry, who in 1791, bequeathed 'unto my native woman Hannah' all the worldly effects, together with his pay arrears, clothing, and any other money due to him.[111] Hannah was the only person mentioned in his will. Even in brief wills, only the native woman gets a mention, though occasionally. John Reily, a Private in His Majesty's 16th Regiment of Foot, in his will in 1799 talked about his 'beloved girl Mangama' who is the only one mentioned in the will.

> First, I will & bequeath unto my trusty & well-beloved girl Mangama, all my pay and arrears of pay. Ready money, wearing apparel, & beding [*sic*] together with any sum or sums of money which may become due to me at my decease or may become payable after.[112]

There are many such wills, where the only person to be mentioned is the native mistress. This by no means suggests that such men did not have families in Europe. Some of them might be returning home once they decided so, some coming to completion of their commission in the army, and so on. However, because most of these interracial unions were not bound by formal marriage, the British men were not under any obligation to make a provision for these women in their wills. Captain Peter Cullen, stationed at Futty Ghur in 1793, mentioned a native woman who was living with him at that time. He only described her as 'a native woman' but left her an 'ample and due provision.' He directed the executors of his will to make such provisions for her during her life. After the payment of debts, etc. he insisted that they ensured she got assistance and subsistence, etc.[113] Similarly, Edward Dawson, of Fort of Chunar, in 1785 wrote about, 'my girl Ritta Penny, commonly called by me Nancy,' in his will to whom he left all the cash found in his house, debts due to him in India, goods, chattels, clothes, furniture, valuables, pay, arrears, and 'in short everything I can call mine of whatever kind, substance, and sort.'[114] He then urged his executors for a favour, i.e., their protection and assistance in settling her affairs before they helped her find a boat for Calcutta, as well as a suitable accommodation. He expected them to 'give her every aid and advice in their power.'[115]

Lieutenant Natheniel Leonard of Artillery mentioned his three children, without referring to them as either 'natural' or illegitimate, 'born of the body of a Native woman of Hindostan' who he called Winifred. This will reads like a letter addressed to all his relatives, whom he left nothing in his will. There is a sense of duty towards his 'family' in India. In an attempt to be fair, he wrote,

> the mother of my children would be destitute of support and my own mother be in embarrced [*sic*] circumstances in the decline of life should I omit to appropriate what property I am now possessed of towards their support – It is therefore my will that whatever I am possessed of to the amount of three thousand sicca rupees and no more, be put at interest to the best advantage.[116]

He then wanted the interest of the sum to be paid to his *bibi* as well as his mother, equally. He seemed aware that, 'Probably my relations will blame me for putting my mother and female companion on a footing,' because he had left nothing to them. But he went on in that same tone about his children too and deeply regretful that they would have to be sent to an orphanage. Now, this is interesting because he seemed aware of the fact that he was leaving almost all his property to his children from a 'native woman of Hindostan' and that it would not be received well by his relatives. At the same time what is established with certainty is a sense of domesticity, the native connection seemed more like a 'family' for him for he spoke very warmly about them.

Thomas Deane Pearse mentioned two native women whom he had cohabited with. He took great pain to establish Punna Purree, 'a native of Hindostan' as his wedded wife. He chose his will in order to carry forward the information so that all the claims to his property by the native woman, his wife Punna Purree and her son were not refuted by anyone. He wrote,

> First I do declare and call God to witness that I am married to Punna Purree a native of Hindostan who since the said marriage is become Punna Purree Pearse and I do firmly believe that our marriage tho' for many years kept a secret was in every respect lawfull and if were not so I most assuredly would have gone through every possible form to have made it so.[117]

He also mentions his fear that some of his relations in an attempt to benefit from his fortunes might raise doubts regarding his marriage. He, in any case, bequeathed 9,000 sicca rupees with interest from April 1, 1780, to be given to Punna Purree Pearse, the sum which he had borrowed from her to build his house. He then divided his property into ten parts.

> I bequeath to my wife Punna Purree Pearse or if my marriage with her should be defective, I bequeath to Punna Purree, a native of Hindostan the mother of Thomas Deane Mahomet Pearse three tenth parts of the neat produce of my estate together with all her jewels and household furniture and also whole produce arising from the sale of a piece or pieces of ground in Chowrunghee near Calcutta.[118]

He also mentioned his 'female friend Moortee … who has lived with me many years in my zenana and bore me two female children, long since dead.' He left her money which he claimed to have been borrowed from her, 3,000 with interest from April 1, 1780. He also gave her a certain share from the sale of his property in the codicil to the will and then further added provisions for any child who was to be borne by both the women, his wife as well as by 'beebee Moortee.'

Another will that needs a mention here is the case of William Palmer, who talked of

> Beeby Fyze Bukch Saheeba Begum who has been my affectionate friend and companion during a period of more than thirty-five years. The house which I now inhibit near the cantonment of Behrampore and which I purchased … to her own use and benefit and to her own free disposal forever.[119]

These documents are interesting because they bring out this unique aspect of domesticity to the forefront. The sexual and conjugal relations become very clear and so does the affection that the partners shared, but in some of the wills, bequeaths were made only to the Indian or native family that the British men had started during their stay in India.

All the relationships discussed in this chapter had the conjugal element common to them; the native women who were taken on as concubines in various ways were a part of the households of the British men here. So, in sharing the confined space of the house in terms of co-residence, the concubinage in its entirety was conjugal as well as domestic. But there is a need to look at domesticity as a more fluid space, which developed over a certain duration and in terms of the constant sharing of space which was not 'unchanging.' The numerous relationships mentioned, do develop quite differently from each other, but within the framework of conjugality.

At another level, it is important to realize how such relationships were more acceptable for the large numbers of soldiers and not so much for the civil officers at the turn of the first quarter of the 19th century. Therefore, the number of wills available for that period declines. It was not possible for such an 'arrangement' to end abruptly, but the number of British men coming out in open with these relationships may have gone down. It would be doubtful to assume that the changing official attitudes would have led to the abandonment of a practice that suited their needs, both at the physical and economic as well as the personal level; but certainly, the number of wills mentioning the native woman does decline.

The terms of the relationship, including the issue of payment, were often dealt with on an interpersonal level and did not require any official policy. What and how much the women were paid, often depended on the man and his earnings too. Even then, there was no protection or policy towards ensuring the same. A reading of the wills reveals the variety of such domestic configurations, and it makes clear that such relationships were not merely sexual, but also had various other dimensions to them. These everyday, intimate interactions between the early British colonialists and the 'natives' were multifaceted. Certain households were set up more closely on the concepts of 'domesticity,' because in certain wills, the only familial connection mentioned at all or in detail were the native ones. It was a sense of responsibility towards the 'family,' not in terms of their rights (because they were not legal marital relationships) that one gets to read in some of them. In certain other cases, some were comfortable by not having any provision for the woman who they cohabited with in their wills and thereby limiting it to a conjugal relation, because there was no provision for the woman to appeal for a share in his property as being rightfully hers. It is here, in trying to view these legal documents to create the interpersonal 'connections' between the native women and the British men, one is faced with questions regarding their legal aspects. The wills also record instances of discords and disputes within these everyday intimacies and interactions between the British man and the native woman in early colonial Bengal. Some wills also highlight some of these problems; the next chapter will discuss in greater detail when the legal aspect of these relationships comes into play.

Notes

1 'Appendix to the Report from the Select Committee of the House of Commons on the Affairs of the East India Company, 16th Aug. 1832 and Minute of Evidence' (London: Select Committee on the House of Lords, 1833), 311.
2 A.L. Stoler, 'Matters of Intimacy as Matters of State: A Response,' *The Journal of American History* 88, no. 3 (2001): 894.

3 J. Thirsk, *The Rural Economy of England: Collected Essays* (London: The Hambledon Press, 1984), 28–29.
4 A.L. Stoler, *Carnal Knowledge and Imperial Power: Race and the Intimate in Colonial Rule* (Berkeley: University of California Press, 2002), 2.
5 U. Narayan, 'Colonialism and Its Others: Considerations on Rights and Care Discourses,' *Hypatia* 10, no. 2 (1995): 135.
6 M. Kowaleski and P.J.P. Goldberg, eds., *Medieval Domesticity: Home, Housing, and Household in Medieval England* (Cambridge: Cambridge University Press, 2009), 2.
7 F. Riddy, '"Burgeis" Domesticity in Late Medieval England,' in *Medieval Domesticity: Home, Housing and Household in Medieval England*, ed. Maryanne Kowaleski and P.J.P. Goldberg (Cambridge: Cambridge University Press, 2009).
8 A. Blunt, 'Imperial Geographies of Home: British Domesticity in India, 1886–1925,' *Transactions of the Institute of British Geographers* 24 (1999): 24.
9 'High Court Calcutta – Original Side: Bengal Wills,' 5318.
10 'Oriental and India Office Collection: Bengal Wills,' L/AG/34/29/8.
11 Ibid., L/AG/34/29/5.
12 Ibid., L/AG/34/29/12.
13 Ibid., L/AG/34/29/14.
14 Ibid., L/AG/34/29/13.
15 Ibid.
16 D. Ghosh, 'Decoding the Nameless: Gender, Subjectivity, and Historical Methodologies in Reading the Archives of Colonial India,' in *A New Imperial History: Culture, Identity and Modernity in Britain and the Empire*, ed. Kathleen Wilson (Cambridge: Cambridge University Press, 2004), 303.
17 P. Robb, *Sex and Sensibility: Richard Blechynden's Calcutta Diaries, 1791–1822* (New Delhi: Oxford University Press, 2011), 52.
18 'Oriental and India Office Collection: Bengal Wills,' L/AG/34/29/7.
19 Ibid., L/AG/34/29/8.
20 A. Spencer, ed., *Memoirs of William Hickey (1749–1792)*, 4 vols. (London: Hurst & Blackett, Ltd., 1923), Vol. 3, 276.
21 'Oriental and India Office Collection: Bengal Wills,' L/AG/34/29/12.
22 'Hicky's Bengal Gazette,' (Calcutta), 1781: 28 July to 4 August.
23 Ibid.
24 'High Court Calcutta – Original Side: Bengal Wills,' 5246.
25 A. Dow, *The History of Hindostan; Translated from the Persian, to Which Are Prefixed Two Dissertations; the First Concerning the Hindoos and the Second on the Origin and Nature of Despotism in India*, 3 vols. (London: Printed for J. Walker, 1812), Vol. 1, lxvii.
26 J. Johnson, *Influence of Tropical Climates on European Constitutions: Being a Treatise on the Principal Diseases Incidental to Europeans in the East and West Indies, Mediterranean, and Coast of Africa* (New York: W.E. Dean, Printer, No. 3 Wall Street, 1826), 421.
27 J. Morgan, '"Some Could Suckle over Their Shoulder": Male Travelers, Female Bodies, and the Gendering of Racial Ideology, 1500–1770,' *William and Mary Quarterly* 54, no. 1 (1997).
28 'Oriental and India Office Collection: Bengal Wills,' L/AG/34/29/12.
29 Ibid., L/AG/34/39/12.
30 'The Hyde Papers and Hyde Reports' (Calcutta: National Library Calcutta), Reel 5: December 12, 1793.
31 Robb, *Sex and Sensibility: Richard Blechynden's Calcutta Diaries, 1791–1822*, 35.

32 Sitaram, *From Sepoy to Subadar: Being the Life and Adventures of a Native Officer of the Bengal Army Written and Related by Himself*, trans. Lieut. Col. Norgate, ed. D.C. Philott, (Baptist Mission,Calcutta, 1911), 15.
33 P. Robb, 'Clash of Cultures? An Englishman in Calcutta in the 1790s. An Inaugural Lecture Given on 12 March 1998' (London: School of Oriental and African Studies, University of London, 1998), 41.
34 'The Hyde Papers and Hyde Reports,' 1789, Reel 11.
35 Ibid.
36 'Oriental and India Office Collection: Bengal Wills,' L/AG/34/29/8.
37 Ibid., L/AG/34/29/6.
38 'High Court Calcutta – Original Side: Bengal Wills,' 5309.
39 'Oriental and India Office Collection: Bengal Wills,' L/AG/34/29/11.
40 'High Court Calcutta – Original Side: Bengal Wills,' 5312.
41 Ibid., 7202.
42 'Oriental and India Office Collection: Bengal Wills,' L/AG/34/29/6.
43 'Bengal Proceedings,' in *India Office Records* (London: British Library), IOR/P/154/56.
44 Stoler, *Carnal Knowledge and Imperial Power: Race and the Intimate in Colonial Rule*, 48.
45 Capt. T. Williamson, *The East India Vade-Mecum; or Complete Guide to Gentlemen Intended for the Civil, Military or Naval Service of the East India Company*, 2 vols. (London: Printed for Black, Parry, and Kingsbury, 1810), Vol. 1, 457–458.
46 Sitaram, *From Sepoy to Subadar: Being the Life and Adventures of a Native Officer of the Bengal Army Written and Related by Himself*, trans. Lieut. Col. Norgate, ed. D.C. Philott, (Calcutta, Baptist Mission, 1911), 15.
47 R. Hyam, *Empire and Sexuality: The British Experience* (Manchester: Manchester University Press, 2017), 117.
48 S. Banerjee, *Dangerous Outcast: The Prostitute in Nineteenth Century Bengal* (Calcutta: Seagull Books, 1998), 2.
49 Ibid., 52.
50 K. Ballhatchet, *Race, Sex and Class under the Raj: Imperial Attitudes and Policies and Their Critics 1793–1905* (London: Weidenfeld and Nicolson, 1980), 3.
51 Capt. T. Williamson and F.W. Blagdon, *The Europeans in India; from a Collection of Drawings by Charles Doyley Esq … Accompanied by a Brief History of Ancient and Modern India from the Earliest Periods of Antiquity to the Termination of the Late Maharatta War* (London: Edward Orme, Bond Street, 1813), Plate XV.
52 Ibid.
53 Violet Fenn, *Sex and Sexuality in Victorian Britain* (Philadelphia: Pen and Sword Books, 2020), 36.
54 'The Hyde Papers and Hyde Reports,' Reel 17.
55 M. Finn, 'Slaves out of Context: Domestic Slavery and the Anglo-Indian Family, C. 1780–1830,' *Transactions of the Royal Historical Society, Sixth Series* 19 (2009).
56 I. Chatterjee, 'Colouring Subalternity: Slaves, Concubines and Social Orphans in Early Colonial India,' in *Subaltern Studies*, ed. G. Bhadra, G. Prakash, and S. Tharu (Delhi: Oxford University Press, 1999).
57 N. Sinha, 'Who Is (Not) a Servant, Anyway? Domestic Servants and Service in Early Colonial India,' *Modern Asian Studies* 54, no. 3 (2020).
58 'Oriental and India Office Collection: Bengal Wills,' L/AG/34/29/8.
59 F. Parkes, *Wanderings of a Pilgrim in Search of the Picturesque, During Four and Twenty Years in the East with Revelations of Life in the Zenana,*

Illustrated with Sketches from Nature (London: Pelham Richardson, 23, Cornhill, 1850), 412.
60 T. Wilkinson, *Two Monsoons* (London: Duckworth, 1976), 118.
61 Robb, 'Clash of Cultures? An Englishman in Calcutta in the 1790s. An Inaugural Lecture Given on 12 March 1998,' 44.
62 'Oriental and India Office Collection: Bengal Wills,' L/AG/34/29/7.
63 Ibid., L/AG/34/29/11.
64 Spencer, *Memoirs of William Hickey (1749–1792)*, Vol. 4, 89.
65 'Oriental and India Office Collection: Bengal Wills,' L/AG/34/29/5.
66 Hyam, *Empire and Sexuality: The British Experience*, 115.
67 'Oriental and India Office Collection: Bengal Wills,' L/AG/34/29/5.
68 'High Court Calcutta – Original Side: Bengal Wills,' 7185.
69 'Oriental and India Office Collection: Bengal Wills,' L/AG/34/29/7.
70 Ibid.
71 Robb, 'Clash of Cultures? An Englishman in Calcutta in the 1790s. An Inaugural Lecture Given on 12 March 1998,' 44.
72 Oriental and India Office Collection: Bengal Wills, L/AG/34/29/11.
73 Ibid., L/AG/34/29/6.
74 Ibid., L/AG/34/29/8.
75 Ibid., L/AG/34/29/5.
76 Ibid., L/AG/34/29/8.
77 Ibid.
78 'High Court Calcutta – Original Side: Bengal Wills,' 7255.
79 'Oriental and India Office Collection: Bengal Wills,' L/AG/34/29/7.
80 'High Court Calcutta – Original Side: Bengal Wills,' 7121.
81 Ibid., 5368.
82 Ibid.
83 Robb, *Sex and Sensibility: Richard Blechynden's Calcutta Diaries, 1791–1822*.
84 Ibid., 37.
85 'Oriental and India Office Collection: Bengal Wills,' L/AG/34/29/8.
86 Ibid.
87 Ibid., L/AG/34/29/5.
88 Ibid., L/AG/34/29/6.
89 'High Court Calcutta – Original Side: Bengal Wills,' 5334.
90 Robb, *Sex and Sensibility: Richard Blechynden's Calcutta Diaries, 1791–1822*, 125.
91 'Oriental and India Office Collection: Bengal Wills,' L/AG/34/29/6.
92 Ibid., L/AG/34/29/11.
93 Ibid., L/AG/34/29/8.
94 Ibid., L/AG/34/29/7.
95 Ibid., L/AG/34/29/11.
96 Ibid., L/AG/34/29/12.
97 I. Burton, *The Life of Captain Sir Richard Burton, with Numerous Portraits, Illustrations and Maps*, 2 vols., vol. 1 (London: Chapman & Hall, Ltd., 1893), 135.
98 'Oriental and India Office Collection: Bengal Wills,' L/AG/34/29/13.
99 'High Court Calcutta – Original Side: Bengal Wills,' 7200.
100 'Oriental and India Office Collection: Bengal Wills,' L/AG/34/29/7.
101 Ibid.
102 Ibid., L/AG/34/29/11.
103 Ibid.
104 Ibid., L/AG/34/29/14.

105 'High Court Calcutta – Original Side: Bengal Wills,' 9121.
106 'Oriental and India Office Collection: Bengal Wills,' L/AG/34/29/8.
107 Ibid., L/AG/34/29/5.
108 Ibid.
109 Ibid.
110 Ibid.
111 Ibid., L/AG/34/29/7.
112 'High Court Calcutta – Original Side: Bengal Wills,' 5303.
113 'Oriental and India Office Collection: Bengal Wills,' L/AG/34/29/8.
114 Ibid.
115 Ibid.
116 Ibid.
117 Ibid., L/AG/34/29/6.
118 Ibid.
119 'High Court Calcutta – Original Side: Bengal Wills,' 8052.

4

LEGALITY

Property, Violence, and Discord

> All persons living or domesticated in the family of a British subject and within his walls, receiving wages from him, and deriving authority or power from that situation was intended to be subjected to jurisdiction when they are charged with the commission of crime.[1]

William Orby Hunter's attorney, Mr Carrington made this statement during the case where Hunter was being prosecuted along with his bibi named Baugwan Konwar, for seriously wounding and ill-treating their female servants. This was a disputed domesticity case, where the voices of different stakeholders can be heard. The native women spoke about themselves and their lives, and gave out the details of the mixed-race relationship of William Orby Hunter and Baugwan Konwar. Although the case mentions that Hunter had 'carnal' relations with all the women in his service, it, however, did not talk about that; instead, it established Hunter as a British subject in order to investigate his interracial domesticity. During this case, both the attorneys argued against each other on the nature of Baugwan Konwar's relationship with him with legal precedents as to whether concubinage was a contract or a service under English law. Baugwan Konwar's relationship with him with legal precedents as to whether concubinage was a contract or a service under English law.

The legal archives of early colonial Bengal are filled with information if one were to go looking for the histories of these women. In the proceedings of the court cases, it is also possible to hear the voices of the women once they are summoned as witnesses and through their testimonies. If the wills and probates provide us with bequests and various ways in which the mixed-race connection could exist, the court cases present the more disagreeable aspects of it. Issues such as conflict over money, cases of stealing, violence, the rape of native women, and so on bring out the emerging issues of race, money, social hierarchy, and tensions within

 DOI: 10.4324/9781003315186-4

the mixed-race space. The way a case was presented, argued, and the role of testimonies – together could impact the outcome of the case, bringing the racial tension to the forefront. The early colonial sense of the 'other' starts becoming visible in the everyday legal spaces too. Despite a rhetorical stance of legal equality, and a promise to treat all subjects equally, at the end of the day, the law's paramount purpose was to maintain Britain's hold in India.[2] The paternalistic attitude of the chastisement of a female relative, servant, and a slave was expected to just stop short of grave physical harm including murder, but at the same time, the judicial credibility given to male narratives of 'shame and disgrace,' 'sudden anger' and 'great provocation' as a mitigatory factor, readmitted patriarchal prerogative under the aegis of the role of law.[3] These court cases, particularly the one cited above, become interspersed with notions with racial, gendered, and classist undertones.

Legal primary sources provide us with detailed, fine-grained accounts of the everyday lives of non-elites, and of their legal consciousness.[4] The court cases, especially their language through testimonies help us look at these households in a different way that wills are often unable to do. As witnesses, one hears the native women speak, come face to face with the rule of law, and speak about themselves and their lived experiences in the testimonies. Given that women entering these intimate relationships often come from marginalized groups, their presence can be felt in legal records more than in any other archive. Despite that women remained at the peripheries of official documentation, even during high colonialism, because most of the colonial concerns at that time, like property-owning, education, professional qualifications, military, and official service were male domains. It was in the legal construction of the family, particularly the definition of the conjugal bond and the relationship between parents and children, that the state sought to locate the female as an object of governance.[5]

Jenny Kermode and Garthine Walker argue that despite the circumscribed lives of the women in early modern England, the ways in which these women used the courts to bring their own concerns into an officially sanctioned arena is telling.[6] Their work rejects the notion that women in the world of legality were mere bystanders, which is why the binary of the public and the private space needs to be crossed, since women are moving in and out of these quite easily. Even in the case of Bengal, wills and court cases, and the issues they delineate, present domesticity as a contested and fluid space. These domestic setups were not bound by any legal contract and hence could be dissolved by either party. Issues such as discord, disagreement, or even theft, show that native women were certainly not mere victims, but often active participants in the everydayness of the relationship, at times with a certain leverage.

Bequeath – Until Her Natural Life

The bequeaths to native companions by their British 'keepers' have been discussed previously including what they reflect. That said, the legal details of these bequeaths too are pertinent, especially in the context of the legal proprietorship of these women over these. While many well-to-do British Company servants or even those that were not Company officials, often left the interest on a sum to their concubines. Except for a few of these women, most of them just got the right to use the property 'during their natural lives' or the interest from the money that the men left them. We have relatively fewer examples of the native mistress or servant girl getting complete rights over the piece of land or even the money left to them. She, generally, did not have the right to use the property as her own or to even dispose of it at her free will. In most cases, the man left specific instructions as to what was to be done with the 'woman's' share after her death in his last will. The property or the principal sum usually reverted to his natural or legitimate children, at times to natal family members in case the native woman was not granted complete rights to it.

Despite a concern in many wills to start the payment to the native woman right after the demise of the will maker, the complete right to property, or the principal sum was not hers to have. Robert Doughlas of Artillery in India, in his will from 1797 wanted 2,500 sicca rupees to be used to purchase the Company's bonds out of all the cash in his possession and the amount acquired from selling his effects. He wanted the interest on that amount to be given to 'Bibbee Pole a native woman who has lived with me many years and behaved well.'[7] He further clarified what that meant, 'she, Bibbee Pole, to receive such interest for the course of her life, and by no means to sell or take any sum of money in lieu of it.' The bonds were to ultimately go to his sister Mrs Hannah Shellern, or her children, in case of her demise.

Dirck Smith, in 1783, mentioned his 'one and only son, William Soverine Smith' without establishing any link between him and his native woman partner, Soffiah [*sic*] De Rozario. He could have been his natural son because he gave the responsibility for his son 'to be properly instructed and educated' to his executors.[8] To Soffiah, he left 'one thousand Arcott rupees, but specifies that she is entitled to only the interest, and not the principal.' He also leaves her household furniture, her gold and silver jewels, clothes, etc.

Two concisely written wills from year 1801, of Major Samuel Jones, Commanding Ram Ghur Battalion, and Captain William Dunn in Artillery, Bengal Establishment, refer only to their *bibis*, who were both left with an interest on a large sum, but only for their natural lives. Major Samuel Jones left an interest on 4,000 sicca rupees to Maadah Bux Bebee, for her life.[9]

Similarly, Captain William Dunn mentioned a 'native woman Ameerbux' who was living with him at that time. He left her an interest on 6,000 sicca rupees for her natural life.[10]

Furthermore, as some of the court cases indicate, what was given to women could also turn into a matter of dispute in some cases. There are some wills where disputes over money and matters like stealing are mentioned, like in the case of Peter Daniel whose ex-mistress Mary D'Rozario stole a bond from his home.[11] However, they are mostly exceptions.

Looking at contemporary women in marital relationships in Britain, one gets a dismal picture as far as women enjoying property rights were concerned. Barbara Kreps's work shows how under common law, married women of all classes were united under the extensive property disabilities of coverture, the legal status of married women: husband and wife were legally as well as spiritually considered one flesh and one body, but the coverture reserved to the husband alone the role as that body's head.[12] As far as their rights were concerned, married women lost not just their legal capacity for any independent action, as far as their property, real estate, or even clothes were concerned, they were also disadvantaged in disputes over custody and access to their children.[13] Here too, despite the regular presence of native women as intimate partners in British subjects' households in the Bengal Presidency, there is an absence of any law pertaining to her role, or ensuring any special rights to women, who may not have been married, but who were serving the early colonial households in large numbers, in these intimate relationships.

Looking at the Law of Coverture, one figures how the native mistress in the will of her 'keeper,' was not bequeathed the entire property most of the time. There were some elite British men, who left their living grounds to their concubine(s); in most cases, the concubine got her apparels, jewellery, goods, objects, and even the rate of interest over a sum, that ultimately the principal reverted to their children or the British man's natal family. Very few women got complete ownership of the property, or interest as well as the primary sum. It certainly reflected a hierarchy, differentiation, and difference in fortune among the white men present in India at that time.

James Connor, a Pilot in the service, writing in 1792 mentioned Anna De Rozario, to whom he left all his goods, household furniture, chattels, money due to him as well as a piece of ground with a bungalow and out-houses consisting of six *cottahs* situated north of Bow Bazaar. It could be for her sole use only if she remitted 500 sicca rupees to his mother in 12 months' time from his death, that she could have complete right to sell, mortgage, or dispose of any part of the property he left to her.[14] Robert McFarlane of Calcutta, in 1797, mentioned 'my housekeeper Mary Warrick (commonly called Mary Macky).'[15] He left her his household objects, silver crockery, etc., all his money, and alcohol too.

Much before Indian laws were opened to debate, reform, and revival, the limited rights of women to property were discussed there too. Tirthankar Roy and Anand V. Swamy mention several suits in the 1780s and 1790s, where the rights of an Indian widow were accepted as an annuity of a share of the property and absolute power of disposal, only while she lives.[16] Their work shows an actual increase in joint family suits closer to the mid-19th century, even there, precedence was preferred in judgement than consultation.

When She Bequeaths

As we engage with legal sources, it becomes imperative to ask, if they can be summed just as 'colonial' archives? How does one study the native presence, their words, and their versions in it? Do the native voices qualify as a valid component of the colonial archive, or as something more organic, where a mixed-race society came into play? Despite translation, one hears natives and sees their version of their historical place. For a historian, that engagement can be the beginning of a re-search, where the archive is not just content for analysis, but it became a way to socially locate those, otherwise written off by their silence. Does the colonial archive make up for the fact that the native presence remains, representative and beyond their own language? No, it does not. But then again, it provides the native players with a leverage to be 'heard.' Even if their language is lost, often what they say is not.

Writing about women's voices in Tudor (late 15th to early 17th century) wills, Susan E. James considers certain information available only in women writing their wills. She analyzes the diverse ways in which these women employ the legal and emotional tools provided by the will-making process to distribute their possessions, comment on their lives, and exercise their authority over events that will take place only after their demise.[17] Although a little before the early colonial times, the act of writing wills often makes up for women's writing, and subsequently, their voice.

In the case of South Asia, John Dawson Mayne, Advocate-General of the Madras Presidency (1868–1872), pointed out the perplexity of the English lawyers over the origin and growth of testamentary power among the Hindus.[18] For him, no synonym for the wills in the native language was an indicator of it being an English influence in the Presidency towns. Inheritance laws are culture-specific; however, it was only at a later stage that the Hindus occasionally did make wills, like Indian Muslims did.[19] With that in mind, when one comes across a few wills written by native women in the early colonial times, it certainly reflects the socio-cultural impact of the European presence in India. The fact is that these native women, most of whom were part of the Indo-European cultural space, had found the writing of will probably as a way to ensure the division of property as they would have wished.

The few wills by these women certainly give us a glimpse into their lives, more importantly, through their words. It was also one of the ways in which they came face to face with the British judiciary in early colonial Bengal. The wills legally provided many of them with a certain share in the property of the men they cohabited with. But the share was not lawfully theirs since it always depended on the will of the British man, their husband or 'keeper.'

Most of the time these women only received the right on the share or interest on a sum for use during their natural life, though there were some instances where they got complete rights over property, or even money. What about the jewellery, and other material possessions women got in these wills? How these *bibis* disposed of the clothes, jewellery, and other material objects they either bought or that were bequeathed to them remains unknown.

There are certainly only a few of these, which the wills by the British men suggest, only a few women got complete rights over the property left to them by their keepers. Durba Ghosh in her book suggests that native women leaving wills in the colonial period shows a shift in their cultural context and that they often accommodated several modes of self-representation at the same time.[20] It would not be wrong to say that some of these women extended the role of British law into their lives by leaving wills with bequests for their family, friends, etc. These wills are one of the ways to know the domestic life of the native women, in their words. It also goes on to show that some of these women did have certain property in their hands and could bequeath it. There are wills where they leave bequests for their family and mention the material goods, thus relating their daily lives. They mention friends, other relationships, godchildren, servants, slaves, and so on.

I would like to begin with a will of Elizabeth, in year 1800. In the will, she called herself a native woman, formerly a companion to the Late Conductor Ferrier, and mentioned that she was now living with Sergeant T. Fitzpatrick. She bequeathed '1500 sicca rupees, her house and land in division no 2 Emombaug Lane, street no 19, house no. 21' to her daughter Isabella Ferrier.[21] She also mentioned a son, William Hume, to whom she left 500 sicca rupees. To another son, John Butter Fitzpatrick, she left the residue of her property, jewellery, etc.

Elizabeth Rodrigues in her will dated 1799 wrote,[22]

> I Elizabeth Rodrigues otherwise called Beebee Betty of Calcutta at Fort William in Bengal. … I desire to be privately buried in a decent manner. … It is my desire and request that after my death my executor will see either at publick or private sale as he may think most advantages to my estate my large lower roomed Brick House at

> Ronney Modee Golly in Calcutta and from the produce thereof apply to be following purpose that is to say –
>
> I give and bequeath unto my beloved son named James Rodrigues my house and ground situated in Bow bazaar and all my gold ... I give and bequeath unto my lawfull husband George Rodrigues Five cottahs of ground with a house annex to my Large brick house, my silver things and furniture.

Elizabeth mentioned her son and 'lawful' husband to whom she bequeathed the property. She, however, referred to herself as Beebee Betty, the name she was popularly known by. She mentioned her alias for the sake of legal clarity. She may have been a native woman, more popularly called Betty, a common name given to the native women who entered conjugal relations with the British men and the term *bibi* or *beebee* often used for the native (including mixed race, as discussed earlier) women in a mixed-race conjugality. It should be noted that the property seemed to belong solely to her, as she went on to bequeath it as its sole owner and later mentioned that she had lent Mr Bready

> a sum of sicca rupees one thousand and eight and all the rest and the residue of my estate and effects my executor is to lay out the same at interest on good, sufficient, security and the interest arising therefore to be applied yearly for...the benefit of my soul.[23]

Clearly establishing her control over both – her property as well as the money that had been given on loan and from which interest was being earned. Though there is no reference to her religion, all she had to say was that she wanted to be buried privately and that she wanted her money to be spent on her after-death rituals, etc. which she did not spell out. She nominated her 'lawful' husband as the executor of her last will. She might have converted to Christianity as well; it is not mentioned in her will.

Another such will by Bebee Zenut of the town of Calcutta, was written in the year 1824. The will records her speaking in the 'Hindostanee language' and was written by the deponent of William David of Calcutta. She bequeathed the property that belonged to her as follows,[24]

> First, I leave and bequeath to my son George Ricketts and my granddaughter Amelia Ricketts share and share alike, the whole of the ground and house erected thereon situated at Collingah. Secondly, the remainder of my effects of whatever description I leave and bequeath to my granddaughter Amelia Ricketts above mentioned.

In the inventory of effects belonging to Bebee Zenut of Collengah, the house she bequeathed was described as a 'brick wall built tenement or dwelling house containing Five cottahs more or less of ground situated in … Bagaun Collingah.'[25] Now, Bibi Zenut was Lieutenant John Henry Ricketts' partner, whose son John William Ricketts was sent to Upper Military Orphanage, Calcutta. He had fathered an illegitimate daughter Amelia, who Zenut mentioned in her will.[26] She had property in the form of the house and the ground, of which she was the sole proprietor.

Another will by Bibee Sukeena (1822) directed the executors to 'sell and dispose of my lower roomed house with three cottahs of ground there unto belonging situated at Khyroomatters Lane in Calcutta.' Then she left one of the two equal parts of that to a nephew Hossain Ally, who was at Dacca, but only when he turned 17 years of age. She left the interest as well as the second share to 'Bibee Chaund alias Bibee Phutoon, brought up by me from her infancy and now the age of eleven years or thereabouts and residing with me.'[27] Now this will did not have any other bequeaths nor did Bibee Sukeena mention any other family member.

Mary D'Rozara wrote her will in December 1807, 'in bodily health and of sound disposing memory.' She willed,[28]

> that all my just debts and funeral charges be paid and discharged by my executors … I give and bequeath, to my Godson Charles Burrow, the sum of twenty sicca rupees of lawfull Bengal money. I give and bequeath to my good friend Bibby Cartonah [spelling unclear] one paticoat (sic), one Bodjoe, one chulee and also one gold ring.
>
> I give and bequeath to my Godaughter (sic) Fanny one string of pearls and also six sicca rupees lawful Bengall money.
>
> I give and bequeath to my Godaughter (sic) Rozaldo Hooper one string of pearls and one locket.
>
> It is my particular desire … to be buried in the Roman Catholic Church burying ground … the remainders after my property shall have been sold to be the best advantage shall before the use of my former servant George Williams. That is the remaining sum from my property shall be put to interest in secure hands and the said interest to be given to the above-mentioned George Williams should he at any time be in distress or want and should the said George William marry, and by his marriage have children he is then to be put in full possession of the full principal of the sum left by me for his use.

The next four wills, again written by native women, are compiled by Pradip Sinha in his book *On Calcutta's Urban History*, where an entire appendix titled 'Eurasians as an Ethnic Group in Calcutta – Some Judicial Documents' is an anthology of wills.[29] He produced parts of wills by Elizabeth Rebeira, alias Bebee Diana, Bebee Lucy, Bebee Nancy, and Bebee Bivan. These women, mentioned property, such as houses, jewellery, clothes, and sums of money which they bequeathed to family, friends, other bibis, servants (Consamah, *Khansamah* or cook in case of Bebee Nancy), tenants, and so on. It shows some of these women living through their social circle and the connections they came to form over time. None of these four wills have any reference to their partners or husbands, but some of them mention children, even adopted ones, and grandchildren.

In the will, Elizabeth Rebeira also gives her alias as Bebee Diana, an inhabitant of Calcutta, in 1821. She started by giving out to Bebee Susana her 'one pair of gold joomkah-ornament for the ears' and her old shawl together with all her wearing apparel (Sinha 1978: 199).[30] Next she said,

> I will that my houses and premises situated in Moonshee Tank near Chandney Choke remain in the hands of my Executors hereinafter named and the rent and income thereof collected and held in trust by them till such time the debt to which the said houses and premises are subject, be liquidated when I desire the said houses and premises be disposed of ... and the proceeds thereof, equally divided between my adopted daughters Johanna Almeida alias _ lane Thomas and Helen Lewis her daughter respectively.

She added that 'a piece or parcel or ground measuring about seven cottahs, be the same more or less, with godowns thereon in the front situate in Chandney Choke.'

Bebee Lucy's will from 1822 mentioned herself as,

> Bebee Lucy of Taultullah Bazaar in the town of Calcutta. I give and ... all that my messuage tenement, brick built dwelling house situated lying and being at Tadtullah Bazaar in the said town of Calcutta unto Charles Phillips his heirs and assignees for ever and I give and bequeath unto the said Charles Phillips his executors administrators or assignees all my other property of whatsoever nature kind or condition the same may be. I appoint Meer Mooksood Ally of the said town of Calcutta executor of this will. I hereby revoke all former wills by me made. In witness whereof I have hereunto put my hand and seal this fifteenth day of August in the year of Christ One thousand eight hundred and twenty-two. [31]

Bebbee Nancy in her will filed on 5 May 1830 gave to her daughter Mrs. Amelia Eaglestone, the wife of Mr. Eaglestone, the sum of Sicca Rupees 2000/-. Then went on to give,

> to my grandson, George Alexander Eaglestone, the sum of Sicca Rupees 2000/-, to my Consamah Burkootoollah now living in my service Sicca Rs. 1000/- and I give to my tenant Alla Box Broadman ... to Shaik Budderuddy of Durramtollah Street in the town of Calcutta coach-maker ... my two adjoining lower roomed houses in Dingabhungah and a piece or parcel of ground thereunto belonging measuring ten cottahs ... upon trust not to sell or dispose of the same...and to pay and expend the rents ... towards keeping 11p annually my funeral rites and giving charity...to indigent people of my caste.[32]

Shaik Budderuddy was made sole Executor of the will.

Bebee Bivan, an inhabitant of Calcutta, in her will dated September 15, 1815 gave to her only son, Robert James (Durie), the sum of sicca rupees 3,600 and 'a certain piece or parcel of ground situated in Bolee Congee [Ballygunge] consisting of twenty-live cottahs of ground more or less.' She directed that 'after my decease the household furniture, jewels, and other property [were] to be sold and after paying [for] my funeral rites, and ceremonies according to the Mahomedan religion.'[33]

John Herbert of Dacca, whose will was mentioned in the previous chapter, claimed that

> the house, and outhouses, ground and appurtenances thereunto belonging at Tisgong in which the before mentioned Sameeda now lives and resides, is her own property, she having purchased and paid me the value for the same; and I do further hereby declare that all the furniture of every kind, plate and everything else in the said house, is her (Sameeda's) own property.[34]

Though this is not a will written by Sameeda but stated that she had purchased multiple immovable properties from John Herbert, by paying him money. He specified that in his will. He also added that Sameeda held two patta of land at Tizagong,[35] which, he said, was planted with cotton and other trees. So, he clarified her ownership of the land, among other properties she owned.

So, what is certain is that some among these women, who were independent in a certain sense and encountered the mixed-race social sphere, were probably even born out of such mixed-race conjugal relationships. They preferred distributing their acquired, bequeathed, or even purchased property by willing it, rather than in a more informal distribution. Considering the Hindus did not have the concept of writing of will, and despite the Muslims having such a concept, these native women chose to file their wills in the Calcutta Supreme Court in the late 18th and early 19th centuries, shows the social circle of many native concubines. They were not just a part of the mixed-race domesticities and residences, but they also chose to go to British law in matters pertaining to property distribution. Also, may be their social acceptability was much more attuned to the British judicial system since they had been part of British households or in mixed-race locations.

Under the Purview of Court – Disputed Domesticities

The most obvious way in which these mixed-race relationships were brought to the legal purview was by the hearing of the court cases that were filed and fought at the Calcutta Supreme Court. Europeans did not want to be judged by or litigate in indigenous courts – nor, in some cases, did the indigenous social actors who were tied by interest, culture, or blood to the colonizers.[36]

The British man who was also a British subject, or even a European man working for the English East India Company, could not have been tried by the 'native' laws. Therefore, any allegation against him came down to the 'rule of law' that the British tried to establish. The cases reveal the various ways in which the native women encountered the British men, the individuals with whom they were in a relationship as well as the law, to which she could now appeal.

As the preceding chapter discussed; the working of these conjugal connections took place in various ways. The native woman in such a domestic connection could be a well-kept *bibi*, but she could also be a housekeeper expected to provide services beyond that of a sexual partner. This chapter discusses instances of violence against underage girls, perceived as potential sexual partners. There was an ex-mistress petitioning for her 'allowance,' or just a native woman seeking legal recourse for facing violence at the hands of a British man. After all, the interface between the two categories, the British men in the Company's service and the native woman, was not and should not be limited to concubinage. The social spaces they occupied, were brought closer as the individual intimacies were established. The mixed-race intersections went beyond individuals, as can be seen in the court cases.

Contradicting the imperial promise of law and order, the enduring problem of white violence vividly revealed the disorder and terror brought about by colonial contact.[37] There are several court cases which talk about crimes which involve the native woman and the British man, at times on the same side and at others against one another. The cases are different from one another, but they do involve British men and native women, who were in some ways a part of the mixed-race localities and lives in Bengal. The cases speak at length about not only how the law viewed the degrees of intimacy/relationship between the two but even became the ground for debates, questioning, stereotyping as well as for the 'legality' of this intimacy.

The intervention of the early colonial structure became a site for these intimacies to be played out in the public space. It also let the 'rule of law' enter these mixed-race households established by the British men with women native to India. On the one hand, it is the British law treating its own subjects of Great Britain, but then it has also to an extent established its authority and jurisdiction over the 'women,' native to India but living in the 'house' of as well as being a part of the 'domestic' setup of the British male. I would like to argue that law even in the nascent colonial period ensured the services of these women by acknowledging their existence, making sure these relationships existed without hindrance. The early modern law did include these women in these legal spaces as a part of British men's household structures, but over time, created a distance from the children born out of these relationships due to their Indian side. Mixed-race progeny will be looked at in the next chapter, but no legal rights were designed for such commonplace relationships, despite the large number of mixed-race children. As the actual numbers of mixed-race children being sent to Europe went down considerably, it was the Indianness of both the *bibi* and her children that came to be frowned upon.

As the chapter stated in the beginning, the legal authority of the Supreme Court of Calcutta extended over the colonized women subjects in British households in the Presidency. They came under the purview of the Supreme Court by virtue of being within 'the walls of,' servicing and being 'paid wages' by a British subject. This book argues that she was servicing the British man, his household, and by extension, the emerging colonial structure.

The Company's early legal system relied upon a sharp line of distinction between the Company servants and the native Indians and had no means to deal with non-Company Europeans in India.[38] The early colonial state was trying to imbibe the local versions of law gradually. It moved beyond the earlier charters, like that of 1668, which had very narrowly brought down the establishment of the courts in the English factories in India to be modelled on the English ones. In the early years of the East India Company rule in India, Hastings set up an administrative structure which included a dual court system: the Presidency courts, with the English judges and lawyers, offset by the *mofussil* courts (including the *sadr* [chief] court) which were presided over by the judge/collector who entertained Indian pleaders.[39] The Crown Courts were tribunals of English law with jurisdiction over everyone within the limits of the Presidency and in all cases involving the British anywhere on the subcontinent.[40] In an attempt to rule with a combination of mutual political agreements, Article 23 of the Regulation II (1772), attempted to 'save' the rights of the Hindus and the Muslims to be governed by their respective religious laws in matters pertaining to their inheritance, marriage, caste, and religious institutions.[41] These regulations applied to the lower or mofussil courts, but it was the Act of Settlement, 1781, which extended the principles underlying Hasting's plan to the Supreme Court of Bengal.[42]

As mentioned earlier, the native concubines were tried in the courts meant to try the British subjects in India, due to their residence within the domestic space of a British subject and/or by receiving wages from them. It would also make the definition of household broad, for it covered servants or anyone getting their wages from that household. This included the native women who were the mistresses or *bibis* of the house as well as the women who were servants/slaves (who could be the conjugal partners of the man as well). Such cases put to trial the native women sometimes, who at times also appealed to the Supreme Court against the British men. The matters involved were varied, as mentioned above, but provide an abundance of historical evidence regarding the legal viewpoint, biases, and attitudes towards the native women, who met the British men as well as towards their interpersonal relationships. We even get to hear other native witnesses to the alleged crimes and thereby their impressions on how they viewed this connection. These cases have information about the domestic setup, certain details that corroborate information found in wills.

This chapter opens with details about a brutally violent case. Mussamaut Ajanassi, a servant girl in the household of Baugwan Konwar and William Orby Hunter, of the province Bihar, accused Konwar and Orby of wounding and ill-treating her and two other slave girls and fettering their feet with iron chains. It was the most appallingly brutal and revolting instance of gender violence in the entire record of 'European Misconduct in India, 1766–1824.'[43] The testimonies of both Hunter and Konwar were contradictory. Each blamed the other and even the witnesses were divided while relating their versions of the events. According to Mussamaut Ajanassi,

> the tip of my nose and a part of each ear has been cut off by Taje Bibi by the order of Mr William Hunter. He gave that order with regard to me several times before it was done and on different days.[44]

She went on to describe the details of the relationship that Baugwan Konwar and William Hunter shared. Baugwan Konwar received rupees 250 a month from Hunter as wages, which Ajanassi claimed to have seen. She used to work for her. As far as Baugwan Konwar was concerned, in Ajnassi's words,

> I never saw BK take care of W. Hunter's cloathes, nor give him his hookah, nor give a cup of tea or bread or butter but I have seen him bring tea, bread and butter to her.

She indicated that Baugwan Konwar functioned as the mistress of the house. As the case proceeded, it came to light that Hunter had carnal relations with all other women too, but Konwar was his concubine while others were clearly servants and even slaves. This was probably why the acts of corporeal violence were particularly gruesome and conveyed a sense of ownership evident from the feet in iron fetters. On being questioned as to why this was done to her, she said that William Hunter had locked every passage of the *zenana* because he feared that the servants may steal his things and run off. Hence the iron fetters. Baugwan Konwar, too, came across as an extremely violent mistress towards her slave girls in other testimonies.

Baugwan Konwar was clearly the *bibi* of Hunter, but the other female servants established that he had physical relations with them as well, even after this brutal incident. Punnah in her testimony mentioned that she received wages from Baugwan Konwar but that it was Hunter's money. There appeared to be no contestation over the fact that he established sexual relations with Baugwan Konwar's servants who were living in his household. Out of these women, Ajanassi was a slave, a fact Punnah established along with the fact that she herself was not one. Another female servant Taje Bibi, added that Ajanassi belonged to Baugwan Konwar's mother and when Baugwan Konwar came to live with Hunter, Ajanassi came along.[45]

Taje Bibi, a slave from Delhi, admitted to having inflicted the violence but added that it was done at her master's behest. According to her, he claimed that he would get it done by taking the girls out and getting their ears and nose cut by a barber. So, she said, that the mistress, Baugwan Konwar instead asked her to make a mark herself. In her testimony, Taje Bibi admitted that the master had sexual relations with both – Punnah and Mussamaut Ajanassi, both before and after the incident. She remained quiet when asked about her own relations with him.

> I know that Ajanassi had carnal relations with William Hunter and that Punnah had like wise.[46]

Hunter's personal servants, like his bearer and *abdar*, Bussunt, testified in his favour. The bearer even said that servants were not subjected to any cruelty during the time of Mr Hunter's earlier *bibis*. Hunter failed to uphold his responsibilities towards his concubines and therefore he was given a sentence. The verdict also stated that Hunter was sentenced because the crimes took place in his household unit and that he lacked the authority to put a check on the occurrence of such crimes.

Though both Hunter and his *bibi* were declared guilty, it was Baugwan Konwar who was pronounced guilty for having ordered Taje Bibi to cut off parts of Ajanassi's nose and ears, putting fetters and imprisoning Ajanassi and the two other servants. Konwar was awarded a six-month jail sentence.[47]

This case was important for various reasons, for here the natives talk about their own relationships, the wages they were paid by the British man, the relationship they shared, the nature of work that Baugwan Konwar did at home, indicating the clear difference between the status of *bibi* and the servant girls. But most importantly, the issue of concubinage was openly discussed in the court. Mr Lewison, Baugwan Konwar's attorney argued that she could not come under the court's jurisdiction because she is only Hunter's concubine and not under his services for any work, etc. He 'objects to the subjection of Bagwan Konwer[48] to the jurisdiction.' Lewison argued that in the case of Konwar, 'no service was performed by her to William Hunter, but that of a concubine.' He went on, 'by the evidence it appears that she was employed in no household service. Unless she is subject to the jurisdiction by serving him as a concubine, she is not in his service at all.' He continued arguing that concubinage was not a service since it was not a 'legal contract.' As far as employment was concerned, he added, 'employment must mean a lawful employment. To make his case, he referred to Sarah Walker vs William Perkins, where 'an agreement to live together in a state of fornication, any bond given in support of such agreement is illegal and void.'[49]

In response to these objections, Hunter's attorney, Mr Carrington made the statement with which we started this chapter. For him, any person

> living or domesticated in the family of a British subject and within his walls, receiving wages from him, and deriving authority or power from that situation was intended to be subjected to jurisdiction when they are charged with the commission of crime.

Regarding concubinage, he said it was 'known to the law of England as a species of employment' and that there is an essential difference between concubinage and prostitution. He also gave precedents to argue that 'In whatever shape bonds, gifts or annuities to concubines have come before court of justice, they have been maintained, except where there has been fraud.' So, for Mr Carrington, Baugwan Konwar lived for several years in Hunter's house, was one of his domestics, a member of his family, living in his family and receiving monthly wages.' He argued, that 'it remains therefore only to be considered whether there is such a relation as Pater familias acknowledged by law of England.' He concluded by placing concubinage as a service, by arguing:[50]

> that concubinage is no relation known to the law may be inferred right on the opposite side because it is no legal addition; but the same might be said of servant. That there is such a character as Master of a family known to the law and imposing a responsibility upon such master for everyone that resides in his home … this

> woman having resided several years In WH's house, having eaten his bread and received his wages, was she, or was she not a domestick for whose conduct he was responsible
>
> Did not the legislature mean to subject all persons so domesticated in an English family to the jurisdiction of the court.
>
> These employments are not legal employments. These instances are sufficient to show that the word employed is used by the legislature as descriptive of illegal acts, and that it is to be considered *Secundum Subjectam Materiam*.[51]
>
> I contend that a person unlawfully employed for 7 years by Mr Hunter has still been employed by him, within the meaning of the charter which was to rescue the British name from disgrace by subjecting to trial (by a jury in this court) every British subject and every person living in the house of a British subject however employed by him, receiving wages from him.
>
> The prevention of oppression which it was intended to prevent, could only be prevented by bringing to justice here not only Englishmen themselves, but everyone accused that lives in the house of an Englishman.
>
> The object of this charter was to meet crimes committed by persons unlawfully employed as well as by those whose employment under a British subject was lawful.

The other statement by Hunter's lawyer, advocating different punishments for them both, carries stereotypes, and propagates white superiority. Thus, choosing to lay all the blame on her,

> In considering who is most likely to have committed those acts, let it be remembered that William Hunter was born in a country of humanity, and educated in the habits of an English Gentleman; that Baugwan Konawar has been bred up in vice and habituated to it.

Another case of burglary and larceny involved Henry Pyne, a Company merchant of Chittagong, who allegedly broke into the house of Peerun, his *bibi* previously. Peerun's brother testified that Pyne broke into their dwelling,

> As soon as he began to kick the door open I began to cry out. … He did not inquire after Peerun Bibi. … I did not know for what he was looking … he took a small box … which was in the chest … he then broke open (the box). … Many people had come around hearing my clamour … he took out little bundle of rupees. There were 200 Arcot rupees.[52]

Along with the above-mentioned money, Pyne allegedly took 200 pieces of silver worth 20 Pounds, one gold ornament for the waist valued at 5 Pounds and some gold beads worth 5 pounds. Various natives including Peerun's brother and sister, their neighbours as well as Pyne's servants testified in the case. The neighbours testified to the above-mentioned version, and that the straw-hut dwelling house was not built by Mr Pyne.

The other version described the scene as Peerun having invited Pyne over to her house, which he visited again at night at her request. According to Pyne's native servant,

> I do not know that Peerun has any property. My master spent twenty-six rupees and built her a house. My master did not turn Peerun out of the house.[53]

One of the issues that was taken up by the defendants was that Peerun was a 'bad' woman. The above-mentioned servant also quoted his master refusing her invite to visit her house at first claiming that she was a bad woman. A British witness John Strong, who knew the defendant also gave a statement from 'general report in Chittagong' pronouncing Peerun to be, 'a most infamous woman and not worth a farthing.' According to him, he had known Pyne for eight months and claimed that 'he bore the character of an honest, industrious and hardworking man.' Another servant of Pyne's added that how the woman (Peerun) 'was not worth two *cowries*.'[54] It is interesting how Peerun's being a bad woman was highlighted by both of Pyne's witnesses in almost a similar way in two different languages, but no mention of Pyne's ruthlessness or personality was made. In fact, the last witness, James Dunkin, said he knew Pyne for 20 years and added that Pyne was 'connected with a respectable family in the south of Ireland, and I have always understood him to be a man who behaved properly and well.' The verdict was declared in Pyne's favour without more witnesses being called upon, as 'not guilty.'

One pertinent issue that came up in the testimony was that of money and jewellery, and whether they belonged to Peerun. Her sister while giving out the account of how Peerun acquired all that money and jewellery mentioned that Peerun was first kept by Mr Jeffery and then by Mr Creighton. Peerun's sister testified regarding the contentious jewellery and money that was being questioned to have been Peerun's in the first place. It was emphasized that the money and jewellery were given to Peerun by her former 'keepers' and that she did not receive any money from Pyne for the time she had lived with him. What they were highlighting is that the money and ornaments did, in fact, belong to Peerun. Peerun's sister had testified how Pyne had taken away all that Peerun had, though Peerun was not present there to testify all this. Her sister testified,

> She had both these ornaments before she went to live with the prisoner, with whom she lived almost six months. The 200 rupees she did not get from the prisoner. She never received a cowry from him. She went with him to Dinapore ... and other places and whenever she asked for monthly pay, he used to say that he would pay ... at their return to Chittagong she demanded money, thereupon he turned her off.[55]

She also added that two months after that he asked Peerun to come back to live with him, which she refused and that she had also 'presented a petition against him ... claiming her pay.' What was certainly clear in the case was that Peerun and Pyne had had a conjugal relationship which did come to an end in six months, and not very amicably. Her claiming her pay meant it was denied to her and must have been one of the reasons to call off their domestic arrangements.

This case also showed that Peerun was receiving pay from Pyne. Also, her brother and sister presented her as the sole bread-earner for their family and described her living with previous 'keepers' as well. But the verdict, without hearing all the evidence, was given as 'not guilty.' Again, keeping a mistress or a *bibi* was not a legal contract; therefore, there was no way of ascertaining the wages that could/would have been rightfully hers. Perhaps, the testimonies of the natives against an 'English Gentleman,' as in the previous case, did not hold much ground, and the case was dismissed. But the matter certainly had a valid contention and basis because after a few months of this case, Pyne's licence to remain in India was revoked and he was asked to go back to England. Ironically, the officials noted that Henry Pyne was well-known in Chittagong as an oppressive landlord and employer to the local natives and they wrote, 'we have thought from his general bad character and mode of behaviour ... that he should not be indulged with permission to remain in this country.'[56]

These cases deal directly with the mistress or the *bibi* living in the domestic setup of and with the British men along with other servants. The female servants though clearly waiting on the 'Bibi' also had conjugal relations with their British master. Apart from blurring the boundaries between the *bibi* and the servant girl, cases like Hunter–Baugwan Kunwar, provide clear evidence that both groups of women, were serving the same British man.

In the preceding chapter too, references to the mistress were accompanied by the services she provided. Like Lieutenant Richard Fennell mentioned in his will,

> I give to Bhowdry, a little girl what has been with me from an infant and been particularly useful and diligent in all my sickness 300 Sonnat rupees, to Cozella my eldest girl and took into my house

> at the famine 300 Sonnat rupees, to Bundee 200 Sonnat rupees provided they are with me at my decease.[57]

Here, Bhowdry gets a mention for her useful and diligent services in sickness, he does not name her in any other way, nor is she mentioned like Cozella, 'my eldest girl'. Reading it along with many other similar wills tells us that Bhowdry must have been his partner, but it was her 'usefulness' in his sickness, for which she was mentioned. This was how the *bibi* and the servant woman, both serving in the same household, could not be told apart in most cases. Nor should we try to. The aspects of service and serviceability, in a mixed-race household, did carry possibilities of the sexual and the intimate. As the previous chapter showed, *bibi*, especially in other than a few elite households, was mentioned for her multitudinous roles – sexual partner, mother, housekeeper, servant, caretaker, and so on.

The native Indian women in other economic roles such as ayah or the governess also existed in contemporary sources, and so did the female servant, which was mentioned in multiple ways, for it involved numerous roles. Terms such as 'my servant girl' and 'my housekeeper' need to be taken literally, for most of these women provided labour beyond sexual labour to these men. This was also why just the term 'concubine' would simply fall short to effectively convey what all these *bibis* did in these mixed-race households. Usage of terms like servant needs to be taken beyond just its literal meaning, to mean imbibe a sexual partner as well as a domestic servant, especially where the will insinuates. These women, in various ways, provided the British men in Bengal, and elsewhere, with comforts within the confines of the domestic structure. Concubinage could be banned by the colonial administration, but the quotidian comforts of colonial life created by the constant presence of native nursemaids and housekeepers, washerwomen and watchmen, cooks, and gardeners – who serviced and nurtured these European selves – could not.[58]

In the next section, we will consider cases involving assault and rape. In those cases, the native women being considered potential sexual partners is highlighted by the European men, and both resulted in their acquittal. At no point did the law condemn or question the legality of such households. Peerun and Baugwan Konwar were clearly mistresses, and are not mentioned as servants or housekeepers, it probably did not come in the description of their roles, or what their partners expected of them too. Peerun's receiving pay was mentioned in the testimony and Baugwan Konwar's role as the mistress over a household with servants and slaves was established too. However, throughout the trial, their racial identity was made the point to be focussed upon – Peerun's in the testimonies from Pyne's witnesses and Baugwan Konwar's in the ruling itself.

Violence and Assault

A case of the assault and rape of a native girl Mary Serraun, by a Frenchman Pierre or Peter (the case mentions both spellings of his name) Bouton, a merchant in the East India Company's service, the victim, aged 'ten years or ten years and five months' was bought by John Drake, a watch-maker by profession. John Drake said,

> I christened her about five years and five months ago. I bought her from a Portuguese man called Antony for 20 Rs and a Cape bottle of Gin about seven years ago. I considered her a slave until I christened her.[59]

He described in his testimony that the girl was brought to him by Mr Blaquiere, along with the prisoner. He testified that the girl was 'bleeding and in a very bad condition.' On being asked if the girl was a maid when she had left his home, which was a day or two ago, he said that the girl surely was when she left his house. But then he also added that seeing her condition and the profuse bleeding made him believe that she was not a maid at the time when Mr Blaquiere had brought her back or that at least some attempt had been made. He described,

> She asked me that day for leave to go and see a sight of festival. … I gave her leave and two lesser girls who are my only servants, to go one at a time. I saw Mary go out at 8 'o'clock in the morning, I did not see her come back. The next time I saw her was before Mr Blaquiere.[60]

Justice Hyde asked the Frenchman, named Peter Bouton if he was not ashamed to lie about such a young girl, to which the man replied that the girl (Mary) had already been debauched and that she was not a 'maid' when he first saw her. That is when Kitty de Rozario, a native Catholic, who knew the prisoner testified that she was

> about sixteen years old. I do not know whether I am eighteen. I know that girl. I knew that prisoner about four months ago. He came to dine at a French man's house, I do not know the French man's name.

She lived near his house, neither though did she say that she was kept by any European man nor had she received any money from the men, who lived in her neighbourhood. In her version,

> the Frenchman and I live in the same compound. … In the evening that Frenchman and the prisoner sat out drinking tea at the Frenchman's door … at that time it was that the girl came and asked me for water, and I gave it … as she was going the prisoner called this girl and she went to him … the prisoner did not come to

> my house to her. The Prisoner asked the girl if she would stay, or live with him, the girl said yes. Then he asked her if she was a maid. She said, no. Then he drank his tea and took her by the hand and went away. The next time I saw her was the next day after she came and drank water at my house. ... When I saw her the next day she was sick. She was deflowered by this man. ... Chokedars and others told me the Prisoner had acknowledged it.[61]

Along with this statement, she said that probably the girl did not understand his intentions when he asked her to come to live with him and that she was too young to have answered whether she was a maid.

Thereafter, the 'Hindoo' midwife, Sidoo *dhye* (*dhai*) testified,

> I attend at the police office when I am sent for. I am a mid-wife. I know this girl. I knew her when her mistress was alive. The girl is not above ten years old. ... She has not had her monthly discharges of woman neither before nor after that time. When I was ordered at the police office, and examined her she had a discharge of blood which seemed to have occasioned by her having been deflowered. The bleeding continued ten days and it was a month and a half before the sores were cured. She appeared when re-examined her as much a child as the private parts as she appeared five years ago.[62]

Before we talk about Sidoo dhye's statement, it is imperative to consider what the prisoner had to say. The prisoner accepted to have carried her from the house of 'Bibi Kitty,' thinking her to be of 12 years of age. He defended himself on the grounds that Bibi Kitty had told him that the girl was not a virgin. That he did not take her by force or against her will. He accepts having a 'connection' with her, not by force but because 'she was willing.' He said that she made no noise and was willing. He, in fact, quoted the girl saying that she had already been 'deflowered' by a boy. After this, the case resulted in his acquittal.

The case centred on Mary's being a virgin or not, and the only person whose testimony seems to have sealed the case was Pierre Bouton himself. Similarly, on the question of Mary's age too, what he thought clinched the case for him, and not Mary's actual age. His having thought she was 12, that he was informed she wasn't a virgin, and that she was willing. This also brings one to Sidoo *dhye*, who in her own words stated that she worked with the police regularly. Despite Sidoo *dhye*'s detailed physical examination proving the girl to be of ten years of age, having the private parts of a child in that she had not menstruated, the case acquitted Pierre Bouton, claiming the sex to be 'consensual' or that the European man having been kept in dark about the girl's age and virginity.

The girl's being physically present in an area where the Europeans resided probably was taken as a point towards her being a potential sexual or conjugal partner since Bouton had offered to take her as his conjugal partner. The reference to Bibi Kitty as being the native woman who helped organize the 'arrangement' by offering Mary to him and telling him that she was 12 years of age worked in Bouton's favour. Therefore, the 'misinformation' (if it was taken like that) came from a native woman, who could have herself been a sex worker living in the same compound as the Frenchman.

The Sidoo *dhye*, on the other hand, worked for the police in cases like these and others. As was the practice in early modern Europe too, midwives were called on in primary investigations and then later as witnesses or even as medical practitioners in various circumstances.[63] In fact, rape was one such crime where the midwife's evidence could secure a conviction.[64] In this case too, her statements established that there was a discharge of blood and the girl had also been inflicted with severe sores due to physical assault. But in the final judgement, the midwife's testimony was not considered.

In fact, one needs to ask, what happened to the native women's voices that were retrieved from the legal sources. Were they heard at that time? It seemed the statements of the native women, both Bibi Kitty and Sidoo *dhye* were neither collated nor considered. The mention of injuries on Mary's body, profuse bleeding, and even testimonies by the practitioner John Drake and his witnesses were not taken into consideration while delivering the verdict. Supposing they were considered, Pierre Bouton's statement claiming that he was misinformed about Mary's age and the fact that he thought she was not a virgin, held sway. He was questioned and shamed for it by Justice Hyde, but that had no bearing on the final verdict. In this instance, Sidoo *dhye*, despite working for the police was viewed as a native, whose account was considered less pertinent than that of a medical examiner, who must have examined Mary when the rape was reported.

Sidoo *dhye* had also mentioned having examined Mary about five years prior to this incident; coinciding with the time when John Drake had christened her, which could mean that Mary might have been examined (for being a virgin) at the time when John Drake decided to tear her slave papers and let her enter his household. John Drake had also testified that he was sure that Mary was a 'maid' when she left his house and before she was 'deflowered.' He refused to take her back into his household after she was deflowered when asked by Judge Hyde. Therefore, the girl being a maid when Pierre Bouton raped her could not be ascertained, nor could the fact about the Frenchman's ignorance about her correct age, resulting in his acquittal.

Another case also involves rape of a Hindu girl called Clara in 1796, who was a servant of Noonoo Benson, a native woman and widow of Sergeant Benson. The defendant was also a sergeant; a friend of Sergeant Benson named William Tripp. The girl professed to be a Hindu and said,

> I suppose I am fifteen years old – I am not twenty. About a month ago the one evening, the prisoner came to my mistress's house and told her that some mulmull clothes were offered for sale at the artillery Barrack, my mistress said she wanted to buy some. ... He replied send your girl with me and I'll give her two pieces to bring to you. Accordingly, she sent me with him, and I went ... I observed that I was not going towards the artillery barracks but another way ... he took me into a narrow unfrequented passage.[65]

Clara then gave a very graphic and detailed description of the physical assault and rape by Sergeant William Tripp. She also claimed to be a virgin at the time of the incident, a fact ascertained by Noonoo Benson, who also testified that Clara had not yet started menstruating. Clara then named several British witnesses in the cantonment area who she ran into when the defendant had left her after he committed the act with her 'forcibly.' She gave a list of witnesses at the barracks who had seen her with a blood-stained petticoat, namely Sergeant William Marshall, Sergeant Lyon, Sergeant Major Fitzgerald, and Sergeant Dick.

Sergeant William Marshall gave his witness statement in which he said that he saw bloodstains on the trousers of the defendant when he met him after the incident and that he was slightly agitated. He also mentioned having seen the girl in the above-mentioned condition. But the last testimony was given by Surgeon Thomas Lyon, who had examined the girl,

> That was said to be ravished, and to see if there were marks of violence. I examined her private parts. I saw not a particle of blood, nor any laceration, no wound, nor any the smallest appearance of recent violence. It appeared to me that she has not recently lost her virginity. Nor been lain with by violence. I saw no marks of violence at all.[66]

This testimony was taken to be the final verdict and Sergeant William Tripp was acquitted. The statement of the surgeon had established that the girl was sexually mature, by having lost her virginity 'not recently.' In the light of the medical examination, it could be assumed that the rape became a lesser crime (contingent on the girl having lost her virginity prior to this incident) or that it was taken at face value wherein the surgeon was steadfast in his belief that the girl had no marks of bodily violence, despite the claim of other witnesses, including other men of the British army, to the contrary.

This case is different from the previous one where it was the medical testimony of the native lady or Sidoo *dhye* that was not considered at all, thereby either questioning her knowledge of medicine or that she was a native, the common denominator being that in both cases, the girls were not believed to be virgins that became the ground on which both men were acquitted. The other fact being, of course, that both the native girls were living in British or mixed-race localities which made them potential conjugal partners. Them not being virgins or at least the alleged victim's having been allured on those grounds made the cases weaker for the native girls. There seems to be a certain mistrust over the testimonies given by the natives, and the fear that the natives could bend and use 'law' against the British.

There is another case, in 1836, involving the rape of a nine-year-old girl named Peerun by John Chilton Lambton Carter in the Barracks at Fort William.[67] Several persons from the victim's family, including the victim herself, her mother, aunts, and servants, gave testimonies spelling out details about the family's attachment to the regiment and that two of the women of the family, who were widowed were living with the British men at the Military Cantonment in Calcutta. The girl had gone to the barracks with a servant, who used to go to give food to her aunt, Motee Khunum *Bibi* of Captain Amsworth at Fort William.

The defendant's witnesses, his servants as well as friends, testified Peerun to be a prostitute claiming that her aunt had arranged the rendezvous between the two. Carter defended himself by saying,

> 'I believed her (Peerun) to be a prostitute and did not in any way use the least violence towards her, I consider the whole of this got up by the relatives of this girl with a view to extort money from me.'[68]

Despite the testimony by two medical personnel, confirming the wounds on Peerun's body and profuse bleeding, the case did not even go to the jury because the clerk did not find 'sufficient evidence' to send to them.

In another case of violence, recorded in the Hyde papers, in November 1777, where the plaintiff Deepoo Bhy (Bai), alleged that,

> In the month of August about twelve at night Meenah came into my house, she and an European and a Sepoy with a Sword in his hand came into my house they broke the two outward doors. I was asleep she came into the room, she pull'd my cloaths, she desired the European to strike me. I was ill, I could hardly get up, I cried out for Justice on Lord Saheb.[69]

She claimed the prisoner, Meenah wanted the European to murder her. She said,

> I cried out for Justice, I said you are robbing my house, she said I have robbed, and I will rob though it cost me a thousand Rupees. The European talked moors, he said Chub-ro [keep quiet], likewise said why do you not make a noise. There was an Hircarrah, a Sepoy, and a musaulchy. The musaulchy brought a musaul alight.

> The European said did I ever come to your house; this Woman brought me. She first threaten'd, if you make a noise, I will kill you. The three strings of beads were gone, and the paunjeb, two brass pots, and one peticoat. She left her chest in the House of a Bearer. This peticoat was found there.

The next testimony was given by Melu/Uclu (her name is spelt as Uclu in rest of the document), a slave of Depoo Bhy.

> I sleep in the same room as my mistress. About four months ago I heard a knocking at the door. They broke the doors and came in. They were not Mat Doors. There were four persons came up stairs. Four bearers were on the Stairs. She came for my Mistress's daughter.

Afterwards during her evidence, she said,

> the Prisoner and the others came to search for a Girl, who she call'd the daughter of Deepoo Bhy the Prosecutrix, who had before, as Ucloo had said been taken by fraud from Deepoo Bhy togather with Uclu herself, and who Uclu expected to find there. She also said while the prisoner was looking about the house for this girl, Uclu saw the Sepoy steal the gold beads.

The jury was asked to go through the evidence if they had any doubts, but they all acknowledged that there was no felony,

> Though the breaking the house was a trespass, and not coming there for the purpose of committing a felony, even if it were true as this witness said, that a felony had been committed by the sepoy that would not charge the prisoner, no more than the European, or other persons there, with the guilty of the felony committed by the sepoy. The Jury expressed themselves convinced that no felony was committed; and without going through all the Evidence brought in their Verdict Not Guilty.[70]

Since the prisoner did not commit the theft, and it was a case of felony, she was declared not guilty. No cognizance of the claim by either Depoo or Uclu, for theft by the sepoy was taken into consideration. Also, the case did not go into giving out the details of the connection between the European man and Meenah. However, despite trespassing and stealing, they were let off because technically it was not the prisoner who had stolen.

If we look at the cases dealing with the rape of native women by the European men in early colonial Bengal, they cannot be simply explained as being cases of women physically 'available' in the vicinity of 'white' or mixed-race residences. Though what is true is that staying in a mixed-race space did bring them in closer proximity to the British, making the native colonized women more vulnerable to mixed-race violence. In racial and gender hierarchies, she remained most vulnerable. Also, in these rape cases, the defendants presented the victims as older and sexually mature despite the two of them claiming to be ten and nine years of age and as not having protested to the physical relations. So, there was no denial of a physical relation with the girls. The argument about sexual 'ripening' of women from East, as a travel literature and orientalist trope, has been discussed previously. However, it was not just that. As these cases show, European men considering them sexually mature could itself be taken as consent by them.

In fact, while looking through the cases, there was an interesting statement made by Justice Impey, during a case of burglary that he tried.[71] This case was against Gungaram, who was found guilty of burglary at Gunsam's home. Now, Gunsam swore he found the prisoner in his house at night and that on his seizing the prisoner, he drew a little knife from the cloth he wore around him and attempted to stab him. He said he found the string that tied the door of his house had been cut. Gungaram, in his defence, stated that he had, in fact, gone into Gunsam's house to sleep with his wife, and not to steal. Even the knife that he carried was only to cut the string tied to the door.

> Impey asked Gunsam the age of his wife. He said thirty-Five. That not being reckoned a young woman in his Country makes the Story improbable. Impey asked the Prisoner what the name of the woman was? he said he did not know. That is another Circumstance which makes that story improbable. He said he had been with her only twice before.

They go on to discuss whether petty larceny would be considered a felony or not, but this statement about Gunsam's wife's age becomes an interesting way in which legal spaces also reflect a lot of what the travel writings had been publishing about the native women and their bodies. The debate around the age of consent started much later, in the second half of the 19th century; until then it was not of great concern, except for Pierre Bouton being shamed for being with 'a girl so young'. However, he was also ultimately acquitted.

Also, if the rape victim was seen as consenting and presented so by the defendants during the trials, the case went in their favour. The most important figure in 18th-century English legal thought on rape was Sir Matthew Hale, who defined rape as vaginal penetration by a man (or men) of a female above the age of ten years and against her will.[72] But he was also wary of false charges, for he considered it to be an accusation easily made, and harder to be defended by the accused party. Even in cases of intraracial (Indian-on-Indian) rape around the same time, he considered the woman's prior sexual history, fresh complaint (an immediate police report), and marks of physical violence, all as crucial pieces of evidence to make sure the woman had not consented earlier.[73] The girls' age in rape cases discussed does not become the central point in the first case.

In the above-mentioned interracial rape cases, the medical examination by Sidoo *dhye* and Surgeon Thomas Lyon had an entirely different impact on the outcome of their respective cases. Unlike Surgeon Thomas Lyon's examination, Sidoo dhye's statement was not viewed as the expression of her medical know-how. In fact, all the cases resulting in acquittal did have these factors in common and as the victim in the last case sums it up, the cases were seen as an attempt by the girls' families to make money out of the European men. The involvement of other native women, living with the British men being known to the girls, was also probably seen as a sign of the victims being 'potential' cohabiting partners of the white men, and hence being sexually 'available.'

Disputed Domesticities

All disputes within such households were not so grave as to be taken to the court, but nonetheless show that domesticities were a complex matter. Although one would not expect wills to carry such details, some wills talked about the problems and disputes. James Macknicol, who was a coachmaker in Calcutta, in his will from 1789 fleetingly mentioned his servant, Rose. He left her 1,500 rupees, some household furniture, and the rent of a small house as long as she lived and kept the same in repair. However, in a codicil added on May 26, 1792, he revoked his bequest to her.

> with respect to my housekeeper who has this day left me without any cause that no part of what is mentioned in my former will be given her as I have settled all and every matter respecting what emoluments (sic) she has or shall receive from my estate to this day.[74]

In his will dated December 10, 1798, James Thomas mentions,

> a native woman the mother of my four children which she has borne to me the sum of 20 Calcutta Sicca Rupees to be paid her monthly, and every month during her natural life by my executors ... (All the rest of the estate) I give and bequeath unto my children by the said

> Maria, by name James, John, Margret and Hannah, if one of them die underage or unmarried, the share of him or her is to go to unto amongst the survivor of them.[75]

Then in a codicil added to the will next year, i.e., in 1799, he revoked the last will. He wrote, 'It is necessary to revoke my will in favour of the woman who I consider the mother of my children and to leave everything to the children after paying my lawful debts.'[76] In both these wills, some kind of discord between the couple, which resulted in such codicils. Both the codicils carried out instructions of refusal to give her any part of his property, leaving it to only the children. It certainly adds an interesting aspect to our understanding of domesticity as a contested space and shows mixed-race domesticities too in quite a different perspective.

Henry Himing, in his will dated July 18, 1784, left 'unto the girl by kept and now in keeping by me – the like sum of one thousand sicca rupees, with the same intention to be applied by my executors in the like.'[77] He had already mentioned an ex-mistress to whom he had left the same amount with an intention of an annuity to be bought in her name. He altered the will on the same day after having put his signature on it, and then wrote, 'I do after my intention with respect to the girl latterly kept by me – I leave her only two hundred rupees.'[78] Three days later, he changed it again whereby he left her with nothing, without giving any reasons. He did not mention the names of either of his women in the will, though provided the name of the previous 'keeper' of his ex-mistress.

Similarly, John Roop of Calcutta city, mentioned having married Maria Roop in a Portuguese church, but then got a divorce from her 'by a Portugese Padre.'[79] He mentioned her 'bad behaviour' as the reason for divorcing her. Nonetheless, he left her the interest of 5,000 sicca rupees, during her natural life from his property in his last will.

Another kind of dispute is projected in a will by Peter Daniel, son of Jacob Daniel of Patna (1783),

> Mary D'Rozario who is my formerly Girl to who I owe by conscious the allowance of a few months as for a bond she will produce in my name she has given me a fake account and took a bond from me by force and she … signed in the said bond is taken her part and made me sign the bond by force this demand is originally false and my house with its compound and sundry furniture are in her possession, the bill of sale of the said house is in her possession too.[80]

This kind of document was an exception and not the rule. The native mistress taking the bond and appropriating the British man's signature forcefully seems like an act of defiance on the part of the woman, because the man also confessed not having paid her allowance of a few months. He also mentioned another woman, who lived with him, Maria De Costa and he wrote that he was not left with anything to leave for her.

As discussed earlier, the issue of faithfulness was also a potential cause for disputes, as it was a highly valued aspect of the domestic setup the British man established with the native woman. William Hickey's diary mentioned such a case regarding a native girl Kiraun,

> After cohabiting with her a twelve month she produced me a young gentleman whom I certainly imagined to be of my own begetting, though somewhat surprised at the darkness of my son and heir's complexion; still, that surprise did not amount to any suspicion of the fidelity of my companion. Young Mahogany was therefore received and acknowledged as my offspring, until returning from the country one day quite unexpectedly, and entering Madam Kiraun's apartments by a private door of which I had a key, I found her closely locked in the arms of a handsome lad, one of my kitmuddars with the infant by her side, all three being in a deep sleep from which I awakened the two elders.[81]

After this, he confronted her and got to know that she was involved with him since the beginning of her stay with Hickey. Therefore, it was concluded that the child was fathered by the *kitmuddar*, so he immediately asked her to leave, though due to her distressed condition later he continued to give her a monthly pension. This too was a sort of discord that did not come up in the legal arena. But many a time men did expect women to remain single even after they had left or died, making it a condition for bequeathment.

Ichebad Keirk, who was a Master in the Marine at Calcutta, in his will dated 1792, left his housekeeper Hannah 500 sicca rupees, to be paid immediately after his death.[82] He added the interest of 1,000 sicca rupees to be paid quarterly by his executors as long she continued to be single or lived with a European, but not otherwise. Here what Blechynden often expressed in his diary, there prevailed the fear of the women joining the 'disreputable' rank of being a prostitute.

Carl Christian Warmann, in his will signed and sealed at Patna in 1788, asked his executors to make provisions for the maintenance of the mother of his children from whom he had 'reasons to be dissatisfied.' Without going into its details, he asked them to

> recover for me any outstanding debts due to me as well as to dispose of all my effects for the care, convenience and benefit of my children being a girl and a boy. But as I have reason to be dissatisfied with the mother it is my wish a provision should be made to prevent her from coming to the extremities of indigence and want.[83]

Even the two court cases where Hunter–Konwar's and Pyne–Peerun's domesticities were discussed certainly present the disputed aspect of the interracial households. The interesting aspects like an entire debate on the nature of concubinage vis-à vis the domestic service were something that did not go beyond that court case. Nor did they change the larger system of mixed-race concubinage.

However, both the disputes brought forth the social and interpersonal aspects of the legal archive, particularly through the testimonies of witnesses, and statements made by attorneys. They were a clear reflection of the thinking of the time, the everydayness even within the disputed claims, and in the case of Hunter–Konwar, a conversation around the violence that the bodies of the lower-class women would have faced.

Though both cases involved disputes of different kinds, they both also presented relationships gone sour and being fought in the court. In the case of Peerun Bibi, despite having travelled to Chittagong with Pyne, she not only had to petition for her pay but also ended up getting her jewellery and money stolen. It was also the case where despite the official proof of Pyne's ruthlessness, it was Peerun who had to face personal defamation at the hand of Pyne's witness, who used similar, rhetorical comments in two different languages.

The language towards Baugwan Konwar and her brutality was coloured by a certain preconceived image of the 'natives' and their propensity to such 'vices' than Hunter in Carrington's summation. Despite being written in the space as legally 'morally superior' as the High Court, it carried similar stereotypes that the European travel literature had fed the people in Europe since early modern times. It was certainly accompanied by a paternalistic attitude with which the law penetrated the lives of the Indians by the last quarter of the 18th century, living in the British households. The Hunter–Konwar case is a good example of how her attorney appealed to the superior moral British sense, in extending the 'rule of law' to Baugwan Konwar as an extension of William Hunter's household. Such courtesy, however, was never extended to women cohabiting with British men, not getting any share in the British man's property as rightfully theirs.

In the 17th century, the English East India Company (not to forget the Portuguese and Dutch East India Company before them as well) had encouraged the mixed community. In 1687, the Court of Directors wrote to their officials at Madras about the 'marriage of our soldiers to the native women,'

> A matter of such consequence to posterity that we shall be content to encourage it with some expense and have been thinking for the future to appoint a Pagoda to be paid to the Mother of any child

> that shall hereafter be born, of any such marriage, upon the day the child be christened if you think this small encouragement will increase the number of such marriages.[84]

That was in the 17th century, when the clandestine affairs between the British men and 'native' women were not only accepted but even encouraged. The British tried to step into the Portuguese and Dutch shoes in this matter. By the late 18th century, the cases concerning these households were being presided over by the Supreme Court at Calcutta. But despite that, the law did not offer any protection to any rights of these women, because there was no 'contract' of a legal kind. Disputes that came to court from such households saw an intervention by the presence of British law, which stepped into these households, but just that. However, in the Madras military, in 1797, some provision was made to provide Rs 5 per month to European wives, but no such sanction was given to Indian wives or mistresses.[85] Then, by 1825 the provision was extended to 'Half Cast' wives, and by 1829 even Indian widows were expected to get similar rights as the European and Anglo-Indian widows, if they could show a written confirmation of their marriage from the Church of England's chaplain.[86]

So, we can see, that the early colonial and of course, colonial state intervened in interracial domesticities, but mostly to keep the racial, gender, class, and other hierarchies in place. The continuation of native partners and their acceptance in the army, and their condemnation in civil spaces, is one of the most contradictory aspects of emerging colonial structures. However, this emerging colonial and racial consciousness was nowhere more visible than towards the mixed-race children. The children of mixed race were prohibited from entering the covenanted services in 1791 by the Company Directors – thereby, frowning upon such households and conjugal relations, that had existed in large numbers and had served the Company officials, merchants, and others, as a part of their early colonial enterprise in Bengal and elsewhere in India.

Notes

1 'The Hyde Papers and Hyde Reports' (Calcutta: National Library Calcutta), Reel 17, December 23, 1796.

2 E. Kolsky, *Colonial Justice in British India: White Violence and the Rule of Law* (Cambridge: Cambridge University Press, 2010).

3 R. Singha, *A Despotism of Law: Crime and Justice in Early Colonial India.* (Delhi:Oxford University Press,1998 122–123.

4 Mitra Sharafi, 'South Asian Legal History,' *Annual Review of Law and Social Science* 11, no. 1 (2015): 319.
5 R. Singha, 'Colonial Law and Infrastructural Power: Reconstructing Community, Locating the Female Subject,' *Studies in History* 19, no. 1 (2003): 90.
6 J. Kermode and G. Walker, eds., *Women, Crime and the Courts in Early Modern England* (London: University College London Press, 1994; reprint, Taylor & Francis e-Library, 2005), 7.
7 'High Court Calcutta – Original Side: Bengal Wills,' 5326.
8 'Oriental and India Office Collection: Bengal Wills,' L/AG/34/29/7.
9 Ibid., L/AG/34/29/13.
10 Ibid.
11 Ibid., L/AG/34/29/6.
12 B.I. Kreps, 'The Paradox of Women: The Legal Position of Early Modern Wives and Thomas Dekker's the Honest Whore,' *ELH* 69, no. 1 (2002): 86.
13 Kermode and Walker, *Women, Crime and the Courts in Early Modern England*, 6.
14 'Oriental and India Office Collection: Bengal Wills,' L/AG/34/29/7.
15 Ibid., L/AG/34/29/13.
16 T. Roy and A.V. Swamy, *Law and Economy in Colonial India* (Chicago: University of Chicago Press, 2016), 90.
17 S.E. James, *Women's Voices in Tudor Wills, 1485–1603: Authority, Influence and Material Culture* (Surrey: Ashgate, 2015), 4.
18 J.D. Mayne, *A Treatise on Hindu Law and Usage* (London: Stevens and Haynes, 1878), 322.
19 P. Olivelle and D.R. Davis Jr., eds., *The Oxford History of Hinduism: Hindu Law – a New History of Dharmaśāstra* (Oxford: Oxford University Press, 2010), 164.
20 D. Ghosh, *Sex and Family in Colonial India: The Making of Empire* (Cambridge: Cambridge University Press, 2008), 136.
21 'Oriental and India Office Collection: Bengal Wills,' L/AG/34/29/14.
22 'High Court Calcutta – Original Side: Bengal Wills,' 5302.
23 Ibid.
24 Ibid., 9901.
25 Ibid.
26 C.J. Hawes, *Poor Relations: The Making of a Eurasian Community in British India, 1773–1833* (Surrey: Curzon Press, 1996), 167–168.
27 'High Court Calcutta – Original Side: Bengal Wills,' 9412.
28 Ibid., 7153.
29 P. Sinha, *Calcutta in Urban History* (Calcutta: Firma KLM Pvt. Ltd., 1978).
30 Ibid., 199.
31 Ibid.
32 Ibid., 200.
33 Ibid.
34 'Oriental and India Office Collection: Bengal Wills,' L/AG/34/29/11.
35 The name of the place is spelt in two different ways in this will.
36 L. Benton, *Law and Colonial Cultures: Legal Regimes in World History, 1400–1900* (Cambridge: Cambridge University Press, 2001), 127.
37 Kolsky, *Colonial Justice in British India: White Violence and the Rule of Law*, 8.
38 Ibid., 31.
39 J. Nair, *Women and Law in Colonial India: A Social History* (Bangalore: Kali for Women, 1996), 23.
40 Kolsky, *Colonial Justice in British India: White Violence and the Rule of Law*, 31.

41 Livia Holden, ed., *Legal Pluralism and Governance in South Asia and Diasporas* (London: Routledge, 2015), 7.
42 U. Baxi, 'People's Law in India, the Hindu Society,' in *Asian Indigenous Law in Interaction with Received Law*, ed. Masaji Chiba (London: Kegan Paul International, 1986), 224.
43 Kolsky, *Colonial Justice in British India: White Violence and the Rule of Law*.
44 'The Hyde Papers and Hyde Reports,' reel 17, December 23, 1796–January 12, 1797.
45 Ibid.
46 Ibid.
47 Ibid.
48 Different spellings of Baugwan Konwar's name are used throughout the case. This work will use all the different spellings.
49 W. Cruise, *A Digest of the Laws of England Respecting Real Property* (London: Printed for J. Butterworth & Sons, 1818), 507.
50 'The Hyde Papers and Hyde Reports,' reel 17, December 23, 1796–January 12, 1797.
51 In Latin, meaning according to the subject matter.
52 'The Hyde Papers and Hyde Reports,' reel 11, December 15, 1789.
53 Ibid.
54 Ibid.
55 Ibid.
56 Ghosh, *Sex and Family in Colonial India: The Making of Empire*, 194.
57 'Bengal Proceedings,' in *India Office Records* (London: British Library), IOR/P/154/56.
58 A.L. Stoler, *Carnal Knowledge and Imperial Power: Race and the Intimate in Colonial Rule* (Berkeley: University of California Press, 2002), 6.
59 'The Hyde Papers and Hyde Reports,' reel 5, December 12, 1793.
60 Ibid.
61 Ibid.
62 Ibid.
63 D. Harley, 'Provincial Midwives in England: Lancashire and Chechire, 1660–1760,' in *The Art of Midwifery: Early Modern Midwives in Europe*, ed. H. Marland (London: Routledge, 1993), 36.
64 Ibid., 37.
65 'The Hyde Papers and Hyde Reports,' reel 17, December 10, 1796.
66 Ibid.
67 Ghosh, *Sex and Family in Colonial India: The Making of Empire*, 200–203.
68 Ibid
69 'Hyde Books, ' https://hydebooks.njit.edu/browse.php?id=70
70 Ibid. https://hydebooks.njit.edu/browse.php?id=70
71 Ibid. https://hydebooks.njit.edu/browse.php?id=79
72 E. Kolsky, 'The Rule of Colonial Indifference: Rape on Trial in Early Colonial India, 1805–57,' *The Journal of Asian Studies* 69, no. 4 (2010): 1096.
73 Ibid., 1097.
74 'Oriental and India Office Collection: Bengal Wills,' L/AG/34/29/8.
75 'High Court Calcutta – Original Side: Bengal Wills,' 5305.
76 Ibid.
77 'Oriental and India Office Collection: Bengal Wills,' L/AG/34/29/5.
78 Ibid.
79 Ibid., L/AG/34/29/11.
80 Ibid., L/AG/34/29/6.

81 A. Spencer, ed., *Memoirs of William Hickey (1749–1792)*, 4 vols. (London: Hurst & Blackett, Ltd., 1923), Vol. 3, 276.
82 'Oriental and India Office Collection: Bengal Wills,' L/AG/34/29/7.
83 Ibid., L/AG/34/29/6.
84 K. Ballhatchet, *Race, Sex and Class under the Raj: Imperial Attitudes and Policies and Their Critics 1793-1905* (London: Weidenfeld and Nicolson, 1980), 96–97.
85 E. Wald, 'From Begums and Bibis to Abandoned Females and Idle Women: Sexual Relationships, Venereal Disease and the Redefinition of Prostitution in Early Nineteenth-Century India,' *Indian Economic and Social History Review* 46, no. 1 (2009): 10.
86 Ibid., 10–11.

5

INTERRACIAL PROGENY

> I bequeath to my natural daughter whom I have called Elizabeth and who goes home to Europe in the same ship with myself the sum of three-thousand-pound sterling to be paid to her on attaining the age of 21 years or the day of marriage whichever shall first happen.[1]

> I recommend to my children to conduct themselves prudently, pay proper respect and attention to their mother in all things proper and do nothing of importance without previously consulting two or three honest, prudent respectable people respecting the propriety of the measure. I like wise recommend them not to associate with or form a family connection with black or dark brown native Portigees or any other low description of people – but with honest industrious Europeans of respectable character education and connexion or their children being moderately white and, in a situation, to maintain them comfortably.[2]

The first will by Major Thomas Adderley in the service of the Honourable United Company of Merchants of England, trading for East Indies, written in 1783, stated that he was aboard a ship to Europe. He mentioned his natural daughter going home with him. Although he did not mention the mother of his natural daughter, this will did not lay any conditions on his daughter, including her marrying or staying in Europe. He entrusted his executors to take care of her even if she chose to return to India.

The second will, written as late as 1819, is Charles Nicholson Senior's, who is chastising his 'British' children for their imprudent behaviour. He left his large garden house at Sealdah to his son Charles and his two daughters, Sarah and Jane Nicholson, granting them the liberty to dispose it of to the best of their advantage, if they wanted. However, his feelings towards forming a 'family connection with black or dark brown native Portigees or any other low description of people,' pointed to the widening social distance

DOI: 10.4324/9781003315186-5

between the Europeans and Indians, even the 'mixed-race' children. The children born of such mixed-race connections were subject to different policies at the behest of the East India Company and the British Government at different times. With the changes that the heyday of the colonial state brought in, its symptoms had started to become visible in the intimate spaces first. The inclusion of the Eurasians in 'respectable' European society, both in India and in Europe, came to be questioned on moral and scientific grounds, as will be discussed in the chapter. Most of the Eurasians born in the late 18th- and early 19th-century India, were born out of wedlock; however, as this work shows, such relationships were extremely common. Such cohabitation was not just accepted in society as commonplace, they were the interpersonal aspect of an emerging colonial state, where the existence of mixed-race households was as symptomatic of the early colonial as it could get. As discussed in previous chapters, one of the ways in which the native mistress found mentioned in the will was for her reproductive role, as the mother of the British man's children. There was no denying that at the micro-level, these women were crucial to the workings of the English East India Company and its early colonial phase in South Asia. However, in the confines of a mixed-race household, the children who were born in these conjugal relations were mentioned more often and in much more detail than the native women. The wills became a testimony as to how important the emerging colonial state and the British men considered the role of these women as mothers; despite the fact that these children were rarely left with the mothers.

The change came with the evolving political role of the British in the Indian subcontinent. As the British role in India came to be politically consolidated, racial prejudices began to become visible. As the century progressed, 'scientific' ideas of race intensified the fear of degeneration, particularly the mixing of racial blood. An article in *The Calcutta Review*, as late as 1881, gave the usual perspective of how the mixed-blood children were viewed at that time,

> Portuguese, Dutch, French, and English adventurers and settlers left behind them a race of men, which, because of the less desirable qualities inherited from their mothers, their intercourse with natives, low class natives in many cases, as servants during that period of life when the future character is formed and crystallized. ... The lax morality in which many were cradled, the enervating effects of the climate of the country on races of European extraction, and other causes, such as the tendency, which has manifested itself more or less markedly wherever a mixed race has been produced, for the pure race of the fathers to repudiate the equality of the mixed one, in many instances to treat its members with dignity or scant courtesy – all these causes, and such as these, tended still

> further to burden Eurasians, and hedge them round with a mass of retarding conditions in their life's progress, which in the case of many individuals, required an effort little short of heroic to overcome, and which in the case of many more will require a force little short of the marvellous to triumph over.[3]

Careful reading of these wills also brings out a testimony of kinship patterns that were established by individuals within a larger colonial super-structure. They uncover how these mixed-race children were being mentioned and provided for by their European fathers, and at the same time, also reflect the policy shift noticeable in government records and official attitudes. Along with these questions, the changes in the way the Anglo-Indians or the Eurasians came to be viewed in these wills must be addressed. Once again, these wills went beyond pure provision clauses and additionally provided an account of the personal space prevalent at that time, as a source or testament of it, but with time, even they began to reflect the shift in these mixed-race households, much before they made a full-fledged presence in the political sphere. In fact, the early curiosity about the east and all that it represented, could very easily be turned the other way into the process of 'othering.'

The change in the official attitude, evident in various government records, could be witnessed in the wills too. The mention of the native mistress declined significantly by the second decade of the 19th century, but even before that, it was the mixed-race children who were no more being sent back home to Europe. They were being identified with 'native-ness' now more than ever. It would perhaps be unreasonable to assume that it was happening because there was a decline in the number of men having 'liaisons' with native women. I would like to argue that it was not the native concubine but rather a reference to her that became less acceptable to the emerging colonial social and political standards.

The change in the British political role and attitude around the last decade of the 18th century as discussed in Chapter 1, consequently affected the relationships between the Indians and the British. The transition began once the Company servants became more than merchants and took up the roles of diplomats, administrators, judges, etc. Cornwallis hastened this transformation in his capacity as Governor-General from 1786 to 1793. This was the period when the rift between the Indians and the British began to widen. At the social level, the changes were manifested to maintain a 'British' way of life. The 'natural companion' of the Nabob or the native mistress no longer suited the needs of the new type of civilian. The 'respectable' English women have been often held responsible for widening the social and racial rift between the Indians and the British, and subsequently for the 'demise' of the native mistress. *The Calcutta Review* declared categorically how the inability of the 19th-century administrators, soldiers, and policymakers to understand or effectively communicate with Indians was due, at least in part, to the arrival of larger number of English women after 1815, and thus to the establishment of traditional patterns of English family life, values, and social institutions.[4]

The Coming of Memsahib

It was often conveyed in the 19th century- and even later writings that how one of the reasons the native mistress ceased to exist in European spaces was because the number of white women travelling to India, went up. Hence, the Englishwoman and her arrival in India were used as a trope not only to define the social distancing from the natives but also to express the resultant 'uselessness' of the native mistress. Memsahibs were presented as carriers of Anglican morality without situating them within the colonial framework and the policy of racial exclusiveness. Many scholars have taken a slightly moderate view regarding the role of the English woman.[5] Others, however, viewed the Englishwoman as being a costly companion as a double-faced coin that had both its pros and cons. If it made them a status symbol for an Englishman, it also worked against them by making them face competition from their Indian counterparts.[6] Nupur Chaudhuri elaborates upon the little attention paid to the inner dynamics of the Memsahib's private sphere in the colonial environment by colonial scholars.[7] Without any legal voice, economic power, or political say, the Memsahibs' gendered portrayal not only pitted white women versus the native women, it also reduced the Memsahibs to these stereotypes of being overbearing and self-centred individuals. Maintaining a native mistress was considered cheaper because in most cases, she worked as a housekeeper as well. Marrying a British woman meant a household with several servants as well as maintaining a very different lifestyle in India, which came to be a big expense. East India Company was perhaps wary of letting the number of European women exceed beyond a point, 'fearful that any such change might pose a threat to the stability of their relationships with Indian rulers.'[8] Therefore, all travellers would obtain prior permission to travel, and in the case of a Miss Campbell, who arrived without permission, she was ordered to be returned to England in 1755.

However, once the sea-lanes were cleared following the Waterloo (1815), it meant that more English women could travel safely to join their husbands or other male relatives in India. However, it would be wrong to see the Memsahibs in isolation from the rest of the developments. The widening gulf between the Indians and the British, emphasis on a racialized British 'character,' and the coming of 'Memsahibs' in large numbers cannot be a mere coincidence. They are mere representations of a shift in the character of the British empire. Memsahibs did get positioned as bearers of Anglican morality, but they should also be seen as a part of the whole policy of racial exclusiveness. Thus, the Memsahib behaved the way she was supposed to, 'her limitations were largely imposed upon her.'[9] Janaki Nair brings forth another aspect of the literary productions of Englishwomen in India, which she says was far from random or scattered observations of the exotica, as it 'fulfilled a number of ideological functions as a part of colonial discourse.'[10]

We arguably cannot see the white women independently, and away from the larger political shifts and the move to a colonial state. In fact, the European woman was expected to shoulder the burden of her gender as well as race, especially while in the colony. One of the principal architects of the French colonial education policy, George Hardy, commented as late as 1929 that 'a man remains a man as long as he stays under the gaze of a woman of his race',[11] both gendering and racializing their presence. The expectation was that by virtue of their own domesticity, Victorian women could neutralize the threat of the 'other,' and thus, the white women were attributed with the potential to repair and reform not only their husbands but also the nation.[12] Thus, this attitude was exclusive to their treatment of race relations but reflected even in the ways their own selves were to be constructed. Miscegenation was something to be avoided, on physical, moral, and political grounds as one moved towards the 19th century. This almost went hand in hand with the governmental policies and the resultant treatment vis-à-vis the children of mixed race in India.

Once the British began to disapprove of the mixed races, it led to the Victorian intellectuals becoming obsessed with the question of whether the 'lower races' could even be counted among the same species as their colonizers, the answer to which, notably was thought to rest on the fertility and vigour of the offspring of these interracial unions.[13] These shifts and changes from the previous century were reflected in various interactions of the early 19th century. The encouragement given by all European trading companies to mixed races in the earlier centuries in India began to change by the time the 18th century came to a close. Similar shifts can be noted in the wills that were left by the British fathers. The 18th century held numerous examples of these children born from native women being sent to Europe to their respective families by most elite men or were left well-provided for, along with a provision for their future and education in India.

This is especially true of the older wills. Another point, quite common to many wills is how many native mistresses were mentioned only as the 'mother of the child' of the European man and many of them had no reference to the mother but only referred to the child born out of their relationship.

Bequest for Children in the Wills

Most of the discussion on mixed-race children centres around the official policy and the hardened racial attitudes of the 19th century. How does one look at these children as a part of these intimacies and everyday life of the interracial household? Of course, the colonial boundaries became most visible in relation to the native mistress and mixed-race children. Nonetheless, one can study what was being left for these children in the wills and how they were mentioned. We construct these are personal histories that are taking place, in bits and pieces, in these wills.

William Collier of Calcutta, in 1793, bequeathed an annual interest of 1,000 sicca rupees to Nancy, whom he refers to as 'his girl.'[14] He mentioned she had been living with him for more than three years and had a child, 'born in his house and whom I believe to be my child.' He gave out the details of his son, who he named Joseph William Collier, and that he was baptized in the New Church in Calcutta on April 17, 1791. He left Joseph a sum of 8,000 sicca rupees that was to be paid to him when he turned 18. He then directed the executors of his will to use the interest of the said sum on his education in Calcutta, and any residue to him was to also go to his son John William Collier. Other than his *bibi* and son, the only other person to be mentioned in the will was his father.

The reference to children could be done in an extremely matter-of-fact tone, for wills are solemn documents. However, at times additional terms of endearment and not-so-necessary details give away a more affectionate bond or an expressive British man. It is especially true of the children, who are left better provided for, than their native mothers. They do carry the hereditary line, and property is passed on to them, with a little more comfort. In a crisply written will, John Henchman in 1799, left the interest of two-fourths of his property to a faithful woman by the name Johnny 'by whom I have two dear boys.' He divided two-fourths of his property between the mother and his boys, mentioned affectionately by him.[15] In a will written in the year 1775 by Pickering Robinson of *Bauleah* in Bengal, he mentioned his family including a daughter in England. He left Ann Reynold Robinson, his daughter in England, the estate held by his father and a sum of 20,000 current rupees or 2,000 Pound Sterling. He then mentioned his two infants, Sally and John, born of a native woman called Sarah.

> I bequeath the sum of twenty thousand current rupees to each which as it is my intention the infants should be educated and brought up in England.[16]

He also left the sum of 4,000 current rupees to their mother, but in case she married against the wishes of the trustees or died single, that sum was to revert to his two children. The earlier chapters showed that such control over the bodies and services of native women continued even after her master had died or left for Europe. Her having gone into someone else's 'keeping' would often result in the forfeiture of any responsibility the British man may have felt for her. This will too, established the British man as the head of the household, settling the matters even after his death, through such detailed instructions. In this case, Robinson sent the two children to his family back home, while the native mistress stayed on in India. In a lot of earlier wills, the mixed-race children were sent back to the family of their fathers. As will be discussed in the next section, this practice was quite commonplace till about the last decade of the 18th century.

For instance, Captain Thomas Smith (1772) bequeathed his entire estate to his wife in England, namely Elizabeth Smith. He then mentioned,

> To my Bastard son named after myself Thomas Smith and now with Mrs Smith, I give and leave thirty pounds sterling per annum for his education in England, and his passage to be paid out of my estate, and when he arrives at the age of twenty-five years, he is to be paid one-hundred-pound sterling.[17]

Here too, there is a reference to his family in England, wherein the family was expected to treat the 'illegitimate' child like any other member of the family; in fact, he said, the child was already with 'Mrs Smith.' The term 'bastard' used here is slightly uncommon here and is not used in most of the wills.

John Abernethie wrote about his son from a native woman named Flora. His son was to be sent to Scotland to his brother Alexander Abernethie, which he said was to be done, 'as soon as his tender years will permit his undertaking so long a voyage.'[18]

Many of the wills had very precise bequeaths to the 'natural' children, focusing only on the legal details. Some of them did, however, mention certain other details like that of Harry Palmer, who was in the service of the East India Company in Bengal. He duly mentioned the birth date of the child as November 5, 1772 and appointed his friend Walter Ewer Jr as the executor of his will. He then left 2,500 hundred pounds for his 'dearly beloved son Charles Palmer,' which was to remain on interest till he was sent to England and used to have him educated in the best manner possible.[19]

John Watson, a surgeon in the Bengal Establishment penning down his last will in the year 1786, made no reference to the mother of his child. He left,

> two thousand Pound Sterling in Trust for my natural daughter Margret Sophia Watson to be paid to her on the day of her marriage ... I hereby direct that she shall be sent to my relations in Scotland.[20]

There was no mention of his mistress, not even in relation to the child. He also added that the daughter would have to marry with the consent of her guardians or the members of her Trust, clearly signalling a control on the family and relations whom she was being sent to. In quite a similar way, Major Thomas Adderley (1783), wrote his last will 'being aboard to embark on board a ship for Europe.' He had detailed provisions for the daughter, giving her the freedom to come back to India if she chose to.

> I bequeath to my natural daughter whom I have called Elizabeth and who goes home to Europe in the same ship with myself, the sum of three thousand Pound sterling to be paid to her on attaining the age of 21 years or the day of marriage whichever shall first happen.[21]

In this will, the British father referred to Europe as his natural daughter's home, clearly indicating that this was where she belonged. He entrusted his executors to take care of his daughter if she chose to return to India but nowhere does her mother appear in the document, not even as a reference, or as the parent of his daughter.

Captain Samuel Hunt in the 'Military service of the Hon. United Co. of Merchants trading to the East Indies on Bengal Establishment' left a detailed will (1787) for the benefit of his 'natural' son, without mentioning the mother. His son had already been sent to England the will tells us,

> I give and bequeath unto my Natural son John Hunt now about the age of ten or eleven years and residing in the Kingdom of Great Britain on his arriving at the age of twenty one years the sum of two thousand pounds sterling to be laid out in the best manner at the discretion of my executors in England, and the interest and produce thereof to be applied towards the maintenance and education of my said son James Hunt until he attains the age of twenty one years, and if more than sufficient for that purpose, the same to accumulate and be added to the principal for the benefit of the said James Hunt.[22]

Lieutenant Henry Frederick Bird left some of his property to his father and his friend Innis Delamain, among others. He wrote, 'In default of my honoured father's not being alive the whole of my property real or personal to devolve to and be equally divided between my two sons Horatio Bird and Ulysses Bird naturally born to me.'[23] There is no reference to their mother in the will. Lieutenant James Goldbourne too in 1791 mentioned his natural son Robert Goldbourne to whom he left all his property.[24] But there is no mention, not even a remembrance of the mother. Lieutenant James Pennington in 1796 mentioned his natural son Thomas, leaving him part of his property, but there is again no reference to the mistress or Thomas's mother.[25]

Charles Purling in his will, written in 1789 mentioned his English wife who got a large share of his property in the form of money and jewels. He also mentioned his three children – Louisa, Emilia, and John Charles. Then he talked about a natural daughter, Sarah Hope, whom he left 2,000 Pound Sterling.[26] The interest of that money was to be spent on her education and maintenance and the principal was to be handed to her when she turned 21 years of age. Now here, not only was the mother absent, but the child did not carry the second name of the father, nor did he provide for her to be sent to his family. Though he begged his friends and her guardians that they would 'out of friendship to me accept the trust' and offer her their protection, as well educate, and advise her.[27]

Thomas Chalcraft, a surgeon at Patna, mentioned Bebee Burkey as the mother of his five illegitimate children, all of whom carry his second name in the document. In his will, he bequeathed his mistress 2,000 sicca rupees and about his children he wrote,

> I give and bequeath unto my five illegitimate children viz the above-named Edward, George, James, Harry and Sally the sum of sicca rupees two thousand (*sa rs* 2000) to be lodged in the hands of the managers of the Orphan Fund in Calcutta to be put out by them at interest and to be equally divided among the above named five illegitimate children.[28]

Clearly, the children were to be sent to the Orphanage in Calcutta though he referred to his legitimate son John Chalcraft, who was in England. He left his son 600 Pound Sterling, a gold watch, a gold chain, and seals. His wife, Sally who was from Surrey, got the interest in whatever else he was left with.

The Orphan Society was established for children of such fathers who had either died or moved back to Europe. But then, what is clear is that the mother being Indian or native, belonging to a socially inferior class in most cases, had no right over her children. Also, the attempt to train and educate the child in the 'genteel' manner was left to the British side of the family. It also meant distancing the child away from the native mother and her influences. At times, friends as guardians of these children were duly mentioned in their wills. Robert Hammond's will has already been discussed in Chapter 3 (*Forging Intimacies*), who after leaving his garden house and grounds at Havera (Howrah) to his companion Mary Dil Jonny or Mary Hammond, mentions Mary Chapman. Mary was the natural daughter of the Late Chapman of Calcutta, who was to get those houses after Hammond's mistress's demise.[29] Samuel Mageough of Behrampore whose polygamous domestic setup has been discussed earlier, instructed that one of his *bibis*, Nancy who was probably the mother of the child stay with the child till he was of the proper age to be sent to Europe. But, he also gave instructions that Nancy and the child be immediately separated from the other women of his domestic set-up after his death.[30]

Even in cases when the mother did belong to an affluent family like in the case of Khair un-Nissah, the children were sent back to the family of James Achilles Kirkpatrick,

> Guardians of my said natural children Saheb Allum and Saheb Begum whom it is my wish, intention and most positive and urgent injunction, to have christened as soon as possible after their arrival in England, in order that they may become members of our holy Religion, and partakers of all its benefits, both temporal and eternal.[31]

Not all British men in India who took up native women made their last wills and out of all those who did, not all mentioned their native connections. There are also several wills that only mention the children borne out of the cohabitation with the native women as seen in detail in Chapter 3 (*Forging Intimacies*). So, the actual numbers of mixed-race children, would still be an under-estimation by studying these wills.

The whole idea of leaving the half-British children in India emerge in case the British father either did not want to acknowledge the familial relations with his 'illegitimate' children or when he could not afford to send them to Europe. In most cases, till the last decade of the 18th century, if the British man could afford and wanted to bring up the progeny of the 'native connection' in Europe, it was invariably arranged with the help of family or friends. However, the children who were left in India by their British or European fathers were taken care of by various societies for orphans established especially for such children. Special schools were set up for children of mixed race, 'half-castes,' or Anglo-Indian children. It started as an attempt to educate them and cultivate them in the European way, though these attitudes were to change later.

Natural vs Legitimate

From humid weather to being without a 'suitable' partner, various reasons were held accountable for the birth of 'natural' children. In legal parlance, 'natural' was a prefix for a child born outside the wedlock and carried the weight of morality with it. Hence, despite a social acceptance of the conjugal relationship between a British man and a native woman, a child born to them remained 'natural' throughout the wills. It was used as an antonym to the term 'legal' or 'lawful,' which denoted children born to married parents. An interesting footnote in the 'Selected document of the early nineteenth century Bengal' while referring to the term 'natural born' Chattopadhyay sarcastically writes, 'We hope that this term will not be supposed to imply anything but the opposite of alien.'[32].

As discussed earlier, Nathaniel Leonard's will is an extremely emotional expression towards his mixed-race family. He also tried to explain what the term 'natural' meant. He held the laws of 'nature' to be the strongest, thus justified having his children outside of wedlock. In fact, the term 'natural' for a child was a clear marker of a mixed-race intimacy, without a formal marriage. It certainly was a sort of umbrella term used for all the children who were born in a household where sexual relations existed between a British man and a native woman, but which had no 'legal' marriage. Captain Thomas Smith's will, who used the term 'bastard' extremely formally for his son born outside of wedlock, was an exception.

A former captain of the Infantry in the French Service and then a Major commanding a brigade in the service of Row Dowlut, Row Scindiah (Rao Daulat Rao Scindia), heir to the Late Madaje Schindiah (Mahadji Scindia), wrote,

> to my natural son, and to the natural child whether it be male or female who may come to the world from the body of my girl Mary, who is now again pregnant, the whole and every part of my estate.[33]

To his *bibi*, he bequeathed all her material belongings such as apparel, jewellery, and 2000 Bindrabund (probably Mominabad Bindraban mint) sicca rupees, provided she was still 'attached to him at the time of his death.' Although he gave her the liberty to use the money as she pleased, which meant not just the interest but the entire amount.

There are numerous instances that mention both the natural and the legitimate children in the same will. These distinctions were made, and emphasized in the will, for legal purposes; everything needed to be laid bare. John Monthreau described himself as a British subject residing in the province of Bengal and was a pensioner in the list of the Hon'ble East India Company in the Presidency of Fort William in Bengal. In his long will from 1811, he mentioned two mistresses, three natural children, one lawful daughter and one granddaughter.[34] He also mentioned another woman, whose status was not clarified, nor did he call her son Migual, his natural child. He also made a provision, that in the case of the death of all his natural children, everything he owned should go to the children of Mrs Roza Pool and Mr Thomas Collin, his grandchild. His will presents many aspects we have discussed all through this book – division of property, multiple native partners, names of children with no mention of their mother as well as those who have their mother's name mentioned, native partner getting property only during natural life, lawful as well as natural children being mentioned, and so on. His detailed will is as follows,[35]

First ... I will & direct that immediately after my death my executors [not clear] to be sold some part of my landed property. Messuage Tenement, together with my household furniture, apparel, plates, jewels as herein specified, that is to say, 1 biggah and ten cottahs of ground together with a brick built tower roomed house standing upon it in Dhee Intally, a garden at Dhee, a Birzee in Calcutta measuring one biggah and eleven cottahs and also eight cottahs of ground in Chadernagore, from the amount of residue of the above sale my executors are to pay my just debts and legacies & the remainder amount to be disposed off in the manner and form as follows.

I give and bequeath one-twelfth part of the amount residue for the sole use and benefit of my natural son John Monthreau & one biggah of ground in Dhee Intally by his acquiring the age of twenty-one years. This property to remain in the hands of my executors and they will lay it out to his advantage, and that the emoluments arising from interests and rents, should be paid towards defraying the expenses of his maintenance, clothing and education.

I give and bequeath from the amount residue one sixteenth part to my natural daughter Anneth & one Biggah of ground in Dhee Intally.

I give and bequeath from the amount residue one sixteenth part to my natural daughter Augatha [not clear] & one biggah of ground in Dhee Intally – these properties are to remain into the hands of my executors, & they will lay it out to their advantage & from the emoluments arising from interests and rents should be paid towards the expenses of their maintenance, clothing and education.

I give and bequeath three cottahs of ground in Dhee Intally to Anna D'Rozario for her good services to me, to live upon it during her natural life, & after her demise the ground to be sold in the best manner my executors will think proper & after paying her funeral charges which are not to exceed more than one hundred rupees, the remainder to be equally divided amongst my natural children John Monthreau, Anneth, and Augatha.

I give & bequeath unto my beloved and lawful daughter Roza Pool, the widow of Charles Pool & her children the sum of three hundred rupees.

I give and bequeath to my grand daughter Caroline Collin the sum of one hundred rupees.

I give and bequeath to Elizabeth D'Rozario the mother of my natural daughter Anneth the sum of fifty rupees.

I give and bequeath to Anna D'Rozario for her good services to me the sum of one hundred and fifty.

I give and bequeath to Jonnah D'Rozario, her son Migual the sum of eighty rupees.

Charles Roberts of Calcutta, who was discussed earlier, also wrote a detailed will in 1811, with various provisions for his family through marriage as well with his native mistress, in India.[36] He leaves the sum of sicca rupees six hundred and sixty-six, ten annas, eight pice (bronze coin during colonial times) to both his wife Elizabeth Roberts of Gloucestershire. He leaves the same amount to the eldest daughter Mary Anne Roberts and the youngest daughter Sarah Roberts. After this, his will mentions mostly his natural children and their mother,

> I leave and bequeath to my natural son James Roberts, horizontal gold watch, capped and jewelled, N222, John Ellicott, maker, London ... Item I leave & bequeath my natural son James Roberts, aforesaid, the sum of sicca rupees five hundred. Item I leave & bequeath my natural son James Roberts, aforesaid, all my plates, consisting of twelve silver teaspoons, one soup ladle, one tea pot and stand, & twelve tablespoons, the whole weighing one hundred and seventy two sicca weight & fourteen annas. Item I leave & bequeath my natural son James Roberts, aforesaid, my lower-roomed house& ground, formerly N. 88, now N. 95, Durrumtollah, possession, whereof, together, with the three above mentioned legacies, bequeathed to my natural son James Roberts, aforesaid, to be of the age of twenty-one years. In the event of the decease of my natural son James Roberts, during his minority or of his decease with or without issue, after he comes to the profession, in the former event, the above mentioned four legacies bequeathed to my natural son James Roberts, aforesaid, to devolve to my natural daughters Fanny Roberts. In the first case of the latter that is of his decease after he comes to the profession, having and leaving issue, then the above mentioned lower-roomed house & premises to descend to such his issue and to continue hereditary. And in the second case of the latter event, that is of his decease after he comes to the profession, without any issue, then the Lower-roomed house & premises only, before mentioned to devolve to my natural daughter Fanny Roberts, aforesaid, before she come to the age of seventeen years, or of her decease without an issue, after she come to the profession, in either of the above cases, the aforementioned house and premises to devolve to my family in England & to be equally divided among them, so that they share and share alike. But in the event of the decease of my natural daughter Fanny Roberts, aforesaid, after she come to the profession, & of her having and leaving an issue, & to continue hereditary. The lower-roomed house& premises aforementioned is/immediately from after my decease to his attaining the age of maturity to be rented in order to support him & his sister Fanny Roberts, aforesaid, to be left in the charge and management

> of my trusty Housekeeper, Mrs. Anna Coridaja, otherwise called Billoo's mother. Provided that all fixtures and furniture being in the aforesaid, lower-roomed house, at the time of my decease, to be equally divided between my natural son James Roberts, aforesaid, and my natural daughter Fanny Roberts, aforesaid & except my large cot, which I now use, is to be given to my natural daughter, Fanny Roberts, aforesaid. The sum of sicca rupees five hundred to be given to her at the age of seventeen years, but in the event of her decease before she come to that age the said legacy of five hundred sicca rupees to devolve to her mother, my trusty housekeeper, Mrs, Anna Coridaja, otherwise called Billoo's mother, aforesaid. Item I leave & bequeath to my natural daughter Fanny Roberts, aforesaid, my silver watch, N. 133, maker's name Thomas Walker, to be given to her at the age of seventeen years. Item I leave and bequeath to Sophy D'Rozario, the mother of my natural son James Roberts, aforesaid, the sum of sicca rupees five hundred, to be paid to her immediately after my decease, but in the event of her decease during my lifetime, the said legacy of five hundred sicca rupees to devolve to my natural son James Roberts, aforesaid. Item I leave and bequeath to my trusty housekeeper, Mrs. Anna Coridaja, otherwise called Billoo's mother, aforesaid, the sum of sicca rupees five hundred to be paid to her immediately after my decease.

Major General John Erskine, whose will we have discussed in the section on polygamous households, where he left differentiated bequeaths to his various native mistresses.[37] The woman 'Noor Bebee, mother of my daughter commonly called by the name Emamee,' got paid a higher monthly pension than other women. He divided his estate into three equal shares for,

> my dear daughter Mrs. Margaret Mackae, wife of Mr. John Mackae surgeon at Chittagong, one other third part to my son John Erskine, now residing in Chunar ... and remaining third part to my daughter commonly called or known by the name of Emamee.

To Send Them Home

Until a certain time, it was common for these wills to have laid down instructions for the mixed-race children be sent back home. The appointment of siblings, friends, and even a married wife to carry out these instructions was common. Of course, it depended upon the class of an individual, as to who could afford to send the child back to his own natal or married family, but it was considered the normal course. That the Indian mother would not have any right to the child was also an established norm. The children were usually baptized by the British father, and over time, by the end of the

18th and the start of the 19th century, the children were usually not sent back to Europe. The number of orphanages and educational institutions for 'half-castes' was all proof of an arrangement for a mixed-race progeny to be distinct from natives, and yet more distinct from the 'whites.'

Like many early wills, Joseph Shepherd of Fort William Calcutta, wrote in his will for his natural children in 1787 to be sent to England.[38]

> This is my particular wish that the boy and girl may be sent to England for their education and the boy to remain at school until his guardian or guardians shall think it proper time to put him in apprentice not exceeding the age of 15 or 16 years and to be bound for seven years to an ... stone seal engraver in the city of London, has there is a sufficiency in my estate allotted to him as his dividend it is my request that one or two hundred pounds may be given as a premium if necessary to put him to the first master of that branch of business.

Here too, the British father went as far as deciding a career in Europe for his natural son. Robert Gumly in his will mentioned his three natural children, from two different women.

> I will and bequeath unto my three natural children two of which (William and Elizabeth) are in Ireland and the other living with myself, the whole of my effects, goods and money to share and share alike except the undermentioned viz to Golab the mother of William and Elizabeth one thousand sicca rupees and to Jerrau the mother of the other child one thousand sicca rupees.[39]

James Hunter's will from 1785, which has been discussed in a previous chapter. He did not mention his *bibi* beyond being the mother of his child and left his natural daughter Sarah Hunter, by a Bengal woman, the sum of four thousand pounds sterling. The amount was to remain with his executors, whom he also appoints as Sarah's guardians, till she attains the age of twenty-one years, and then the money was to be at her disposal. In the event of her death, the amount was to get divided between his sisters. He also adds,

> if the said Sarah Hunter should marry with the consent of majority of her guardians, in that case the said sum of four thousand Pound sterling becomes her own property though she may not at that time of her marriage would have attained the age of 21 years.[40]

Lieutenant Francis Forde's will, also mentioned earlier where he referred to his two illegitimate children named Sarah and Francis, and their mother, his 'faithful servant,' Balinda.[41] He arranged for the interest of his estate to be put in such a way that when his natural children were of age, the interest would go to their maintenance and education. He mentioned that his children are already in England under the care of John Barnes, the executor of his will and their guardian. He added that he hoped, 'he will take the trouble to have them educated in the manner he may judge best for their advancement in life.' He wanted his son Francis to remember the tender care shown to him by Forde's friend Major and Mrs Ellerker to him during his early years. This was probably a reference to Francis travelling with them or having stayed with them earlier. This also brings another dimension that of the social network and ties of the British travelling to South Asia, and the role it played in shaping the lives of these mixed-race children. They were taken away from their parents, especially mothers, who did not have a right on these children. The fathers, if and when they wanted to send the children away, used their natal family and friends to help them out in trying to socialize these children into European life.

John Fairfax, Major in the Bengal Establishment mentioned three children, from three different native women. He mentioned the names of all three of his *bibis* – Rajeh, Maunoo, and Esanabia. He called all of them 'natives of Hindostan.' He mentioned each woman with each child – a boy 'commonly called Soldier' and who was to be called Harry when christened, Maria, and Harriot. He then divided his entire personal fortune into three parts, either in money or goods to be distributed equally among his three children. He then instructed his executors,

> till the above children Soldier or Harry, Maria and Harriot are of age or able to manage themselves – It is my desire that the above-named children be sent to England and educated in a manner that their fortunes be remitted there as soon as possible after my demise.[42]

He did not leave anything for the three native women.

Captain Nathaniel Alexander, in 1792, mentions that the interest on the money that he remitted to England plus the interest on all that he possessed was to go to his 'loving natural daughter commonly called Nancy Alexander and now or late at Mr Hodges school at Calcutta – and to be perfectly clear my said loving natural child is the daughter of a Black girl I kept for many years.'[43] He appointed his brother among others as executors of his will, and as her guardians. He wished for her to be sent to her guardians and requested that the interest of 500 Pound Sterling be paid as an annuity for life, 'to prevent a possibility of her ever-wanting subsistence.' The will emphasizes her being a daughter of a 'black girl,' and is always referred to with a lot of affection throughout the will.

Captain John Rolland in the 7th Native Regiment of Bengal Infantry, in 1801, mentioned a natural daughter Janet Preston Rolland commonly known as Jesse Rolland.[44] He mentioned how she was at school with Miss Lowis (sic) at Exeter and left all his property to her. He mentioned a woman named Khaunum, 'who has resided in my house upwards of 10 years,' leaving her 2000 rupees, but did not establish any connect between the two.

James Miller of Calcutta, whose wills described him as 'a senior merchant in the Civil Service of the United Company of Merchants of England trading to the East Indies,' mentioned that he had sent both his natural 'adopted' daughters to England. He also mentioned his 'dear' daughter, who the will informs was married, but there is no reference to his wife.[45] The will has detailed instructions about the upkeep of the house, which is left to his beeby during her natural life, and he ensures a pension for her too. He also ensures that major upkeep of the house is taken care from his money while she lives there. One of those wills sends the children to England, and has detailed instructions for the pension and house for the native mistress, who is their mother.

> Where as I granted & gave some years ago unto the mother of my natural adopted daughters Justica Margaret Miller & Harriet Miller both now in England by name Rupa Beeby & now residing at Mullunga in Calcutta my certain bond conditioned for the payment of Sicca rupees fifty of lawful money of bengal to the said Rupa Beeby monthly & every month & by the month during the term of her natural life … the payment of fifty sicca rupees to be made to the said Rupa Beeby out of my said personal estate & the profits & produce these of on the first day of the month … it being my will and desire & intention that the said Rupa Beeby should whether I die or live continue to receive monthly and every calender (sic) month during the term of natural life, The said monthly sum of 50 sicca rupees without failure or intermission as the same has been heretofore paid and allowed by me to her. And I do hereby will, require and direct the said John Miller, Captain John Reid, and John Shoolbred esquire … and all my trustees and executors … to suffer and permit the said Rupa Beeby during the term of her natural life to inhabit and continue to possess occupying and enjoy the house and premises belonging to my estate which she now occupies and inhabits or if she should choose to reside elsewhere then to take. Enjoy for her own use (torn) during the term of her natural life, the rents and profits of the said house and premises if it being my will desire and intention that the said Rupa Beeby should enjoy a life estate in the said house and premises subject nevertheless/while she continues to hold or enjoy the same/to keep the said house and premises in good and tenantable … and to pay all the taxes imposts and assessments on and for the same out of and from her own proper monies and at her own cost and the charge except

> all such repairs as may become necessary from or by the act of God, floods, earthquakes, lightening, total decay fire or other misfortunes of the like kind without her wilful neglect or default and from immediately after the death of the said Rupa Beeby the said fund set apart for her use and all the profits and produce thereof then unappropriated and unapplied and the said house and premises and the rents thereof them due and outstanding shall sink and fall into the residuum of my estate herein after.

To Remain in India

Not all children were sent back to Europe. From the last decade of the 18th century itself, more and more mixed-race children were made to stay back in India. The development of a wide institutional response to the problem of increasing numbers of Eurasian children was spearheaded by the Company's Armies in Bengal and Madras who established their own orphanages in the 1780s, reflecting the nature of the 'service family' in which the care of the dependants of officers and men was a responsibility accepted by the military community.[46] It is estimated that by the 1830s, there were probably between 2,000 and 3,000 children, many of them Eurasian, in the charitable institutions of the three main Presidency towns and elsewhere in British India, who were fortunate to be there.[47] Even by providing and creating funds for soldiers' widows and children, the Company hoped to secure the loyalty of its subjects while representing itself as a benevolent state; however, the native female partners often received some financial assistance only by championing the cause of their children, and not for themselves.[48] As seen in previous sections, most of the wills that mentioned children in such arrangements, of course mention them in context of a legacy. That is because as records, wills do the job of leaving and distributing property and possessions among the surviving family, friends, servants, and so on. It would not be possible to know exactly how many British men who came to India, had native mistresses, and fathered children, if they did not leave wills mentioning them.

However, there are wills that talk about placing the children in orphanages and schools. Some wills leave detailed instructions for the children's future conduct beyond education. A lot of the time, the role of executors, trustees, and family or friends mentioned as guardians, continued to control the purse strings, and held some moral as well as financial control over the children. Even in the case of *bibis*, the executors often played a similar role.

Lieutenant Colonel Jacob Camac, in his will from 1781, not only made substantial provisions for his natural daughter, but also for his *bibi*. He also provided the native concubine with jewellery, the town of Kadly, and four or five villages with complete rights over them, a yearly 'income' of 900 rupees and left provisions if another child was to be born of their relationship. He expected his natural daughter to obtain the consent of the executors of his will for marriage. He added the condition,

> I give and bequeath to Eliza Mariam Camac, the infant natural daughter of myself and Mariam nissa of Patna the sum of Ten thousand pounds sterling and I beg my friends Turner Camac ... of London and Maean of Armagh will be her guardians and trustees for this her fortune in the following manner. In the first place they are according to their wisdom to secure this money either in landed property or otherwise and settle it upon the said Eliza Mariam Camac at her marriage. In case the said Eliza Mariam Camac shall marry ... without obtaining the consent of one or both of the trustees ... she shall not have more than the interest or produce of this money and principal to be settled on her heirs provided her husband and her heirs take the family name of Camac.[49]

Captain John Williamson, in 1791, left 'to my girl the mother of my natural children (called Mariam) the sum of two thousand sicca rupees.'[50] He then asked for the money from selling his effects to be divided into four equal shares – for his three natural children Eliza Williamson, William Peter Williamson, and Janet Williamson. He left one share to be divided among his five sisters. He emphasized that the legacies for his children were to be spent on their education, till they attained the age of 18.

Another will that talks in greatest detail on this matter and has already been referred to earlier is by Lieutenant Nathaniel Leonard. He mentioned his natural children in his elaborate will, where he explained his circumstances in detail leaving all his property to his natural children and nothing to his relatives. This image of European men who came to India, the land of opulence and decadence, had filled pages of travel literature. After the impeachment of Warren Hastings, the image of those who had gone to India transformed into that of someone with a lot of wealth. Lieutenant Leonard confesses that he does not have sufficient property to support and educate them, and 'with pain and anguish' recommends them to the care of the Orphan Society:[51]

> unto my dear and beloved children Natheniel, Bridget and an infant not at present baptized all of them born of the body of a native of Hindostan called by me Winifred, to be equally divided into them ... As I am not at present possessed of sufficient property to support and educate my children. I feel some consolation at their not becoming a burthen to my friends and that there is some provision for them; though at the same time it is with pain and anguish am obliged to recommend them to the care of the Orphan Society.

Further, he elaborated about his native mistress or the mother of his children that how he would be bequeathing a similar amount of property to both his mother and 'female friend' while leaving nothing to his relatives. He justified that,

> before they pass censure, I hope they will recollect my conduct towards them during life ... The law of nature is the strongest of laws, and as I have the most sincere esteem and affection for my children, I conceive them better entitled to my property than any other human being; and to have bequeathed of it in any other manner than I have done would be acting like an unfeeling monster, and unworthy of all the pardon of the almighty whose forgiveness, for all the offences committed against him I hope to obtain should I be so fortunate as to be possessed of sufficient property to defray the expenses of sending my children to Europe – It is my earnest request that you who I now deem my friends, and appoint their guardians will take the trouble to send them to England to be educated; and should my estate not be sufficient for the purpose I hope you will not forsake those whom I so tenderly love, and who will so much stand in need of your friendship and protection in their infant years, but use your utmost endeavours to have them sent to England for education, they may then be capable of advancing themselves in the world, and have no reasons to curse the author of their existence.

Likewise, John Diehle, who we discussed in the previous chapter, urged his executors to take care of his infant son. In his will, he left instructions that all his effects be sold upon his death and the money from the sale be given to his son Charles, for his maintenance and education. 'I recommend him to executors that they may have compassion on the young babe and take him under their protection, that he may not want for anything.'[52]

Major Andrew Wilson Hearsey, Captain in the Military Service of East India Company – Bengal Establishment mentioned both his family through marriage as well as his natural children. Both set of children were left taken care of. He went on to request his employer, i.e., the East India Company, to protect his illegitimate children too, as they were 'essentially the children of necessity, and alas the Law proves a cruel stepmother to them.' He gave out details of some fascinating political intrigues he was a part of, while not even mentioning the name of his native *bibi*.[53] He wrote,

> In hopes from the services I have performed to the pecuniary interest of my Honourable employers, and the large sum which is due to me for their acknowledged services in the Carnatic on the score of my account whilst Grain keeper to the army in the field, promised me

> by the Lieut. Sir Eyre Coote their commander in chief on the harassing actual service on the behalf of my Honourable Employees, that the Honourable Company of Directors will take these matters into consideration and I trust extend their bounty to the Widow and Orphans of an officer who has served the Honourable company with unremitted assiduity, honor (sic) and zeal for years distress brought on them by my premature death and the small amount of my estate after so long a period of service.

He appointed two different sets of executors for his will, one in England and another in India. His Will also reminded the Company directors of his political role. The political role he was talking about was from the year 1782, when Sir Eyre Coote, appointed Mr J. Erskine to be the grain keeper, who resigned on the grounds that, 'the department in question required a person not only well skilled in the language of the country, but who was also perfectly acquainted with the customs and finesse of the natives.'[54] This was probably part of his duty to defend the Madras Government and support the continuous action against Hyder Ali. Lieutenant-General Coote in a letter to the Governor-General and Council at Fort William, in 1783, praised Captain Hearsay's 'able executions of his arrangements,' which he said exceeded his expectations.[55] He interestingly named his illegitimate son, Hyder Hearsey,[56] who was mentioned in the text of a generational history of Hearseys as his 'near relation,' and not as his natural son.[57]

Lieutenant James Horsburgh, in the Honourable United Company of Merchants of England left all his real and personal estate to his child, Catherine Horsburgh in 1790. He made it very clear, 'it is my desire that no want of law form may occasion this will to be disputed nor attempt made to construe it otherwise than what is meant viz that Catherine Horsburgh is to be my Heir.'[58] Other than that, he left 1,000 rupees to his brother.

Major Samuel Black in 1796 mentioned his 'much beloved wife' whom he left two out of eight shares of his property. Then, to one of his sons a share and three quarters; to two daughters and a son one share each. He then noted about 'three children born of a native woman … named viz. Isabella, Andrew and Samuel one share and a quarter to be divided among them.' He shared that Isabella and Andrew were under the kind care of Miss Helen Bruce of Edinburgh and Samuel was at school with the reverend Mr Brown at Calcutta.[59] James Turnbull of Patna, in the province of Bihar, in 1789, after making all his due payments, wanted his cash from Europe to be also remitted to Calcutta for the use of his children. He then went on to make his legacy where two of his daughters Peggy Turnbull and Amelia Turnbull got 4,000 sicca rupees each. He specified that both were 'under the patronage and in the Orphan Asylum of Lady Campbell at Madras.'[60] He also specified the interest from his estate and any other money in the form of a scheme of survivorship for his sons. He also left money for Sylvia, the mother of his several children and another native woman, Soburney, who was living at the time of writing of his will.

Pierce Cassady, whose will we have discussed earlier, made lengthy provisions for his natural daughter Mary Cassady, leaving her all his property in land, money, houses, and any other kind too. He gives the responsibility of his daughter's education to his executors and wants her to be put in a boarding school at Calcutta until married which is not to do before she is 19 years of age.[61]

In the first quarter of the 19th century, the maximum numbers of illegitimate children of mixed race were children of European soldiers. 'The children of ordinary soldiers were placed in orphanages where they were trained for menial jobs or married off to soldiers who attended the regular match-making dances at the orphanages.'[62] In the words of Captain Thomas Skinner,[63]

> Half-caste women are frequently chosen by the British soldiers for their wives, and I believe they make extremely good ones. In habits and morals, I am sorry to say, they are far before our own country-women of the same class in the East, and the domestic comforts of the two families are not to be compared. Soldiers are sometimes allowed to select them from the Government School in Calcutta, without any previous acquaintance. The blushing maids are drawn out in a favourable light, and formed into 'a line of beauty' ... A tantalizing position, I dare say, they (the young soldiers) find themselves in: they are not long, however, in fixing upon their mates, and the marriages turn out generally well ... for the half-cast women generally behave with great propriety.

L. De Grandpre, an officer in the French Army, wrote in the early 19th century about the mixed race children of the army officers. He also confirms that they were considerably numerous,[64]

> As the children from these alliances have often no fortune, that of their father consisting merely of his commission, which is but a precarious inheritance, they are supported in that case by the English company, which has provided for the purpose an establishment at Calcutta that is honourable to human nature, where the legitimate issue, both male and female, of any of its servants, receive a suitable education, and are taught all the useful accomplishments: the boys are afterwards provided with situations according to their abilities and genius, and the girls settled in life, and sometimes even sent to Europe at the expense of the company, to finish their education. The good order and decency of this institution have obtained it the praise of all who have attended to it.

He then went on to encourage the marriages between the Europeans and women of colour. Highlighting the role of 'English blood,' he believed that it was this group of Anglo-Indians that could be the base for the British political stronghold over India,

> The power of the company depends for its support on a force which is not English: the Company is sensible of this, but it is an evil which cannot be avoided: the hand of time can alone gradually furnish the remedy, by destroying the aversion of Europeans to marriages with women of colour. The marriages should be encouraged, as a generation would thereby be produced which, descending from English blood, would feel towards England a national attachment.[65]

The mixed community flourished initially because they were not treated differently and, therefore, had opportunities to go to England for studies and to settle, without any stigmas. The East India Company even 'granted five rupees per month for the upkeep of children born to British soldiers and Indian women. There were no legal limits on the employment of half-castes in the company or their movement outside India.'[66] However, in 1786, the first of the three orders issued by the Court of Directors stated that 'wards of Upper Orphanage School at Calcutta, which had been established by the Company for orphans of British military officers, were prohibited from proceeding to England to complete their education.'[67] This was the first official step towards discrimination against the Anglo-Indians.

Mixed-Race Unions / Mixed-Race Policy – The Shift

The numbers of mixed-race children had gone up, just as the numbers of lower-ranking military personnel. But now, they were not being sent back 'home,' and were expected to stay in India. Much change may be attributed to the increase of the bourgeois and Christian sentiment generally among the British officials, officers, professionals, and merchants who served in India under the Crown, as well as the laws reflecting these attitudes.[68] In April 1791, the mixed-race offspring were debarred from joining the Company's civil, military, or even marine services. One of the reasons given was that it was the Indian opinion that brought about this measure. The British also went on to claim that it was the Indians who despised the Anglo-Indians. George Spilsbury noted, in 1813, that the polite society or the Europeans were also beginning to reject them.[69] Emma Roberts, who accompanied her sister and brother-in-law, Captain R.A. M'Nahgten, to India in 1828 also echoed similar thoughts. She took on an editorial position at the newspaper, *Oriental Observ*er, and frequently contributed essays on Anglo-Indian life to the widely read *Asiatic Journal*.[70] She published her three-volume travelogue, where she wrote how the 'natives look down, or have at least looked down, with great contempt upon a mixed breed which, upon the maternal side must have sprung from the lowest or the least virtuous class of society.'[71] She went on to discuss the impossibility of the social interaction between the British coming to India and the half-caste children of the soil.

> To be seen in public with, or to be known to be intimate at the houses of Indo-Britons, was fatal to new arrival in Calcutta, there was no emerging from the shade, or of making friends or connections in a higher sphere.

She then goes on to explain her views in a special footnote,[72]

> It cannot be too strongly impressed upon the reader's mind that these exclusions originated in the prejudice of the natives, who while professing their willingness to be governed by Europeans, absolutely refused to submit to persons springing from outcast females. Hence the impossibility of admitting half – castes into the Company's Army.

Between 1785 and 1795, the English East India Company introduced several discriminatory measures restricting the rise of mixed-race children as well as the indigenous population. Eventually, directives were issued prohibiting anyone not having European parentage on both sides from entering the military service except as 'fifers, drummers, bandsmen and farriers.'[73] They were, instead, pushed to other occupations, and were certainly not to be treated at par with the Europeans of 'pure blood.' Regarding whether all east-Indians were subject to the Company's laws in the interiors; it clarified that it included 'the descendants of Europeans, by native mothers as well as the offspring of such individuals are included in the description of persons subject to the jurisdiction of the Zillah and city courts.'[74] It clearly excluded those born of European parents. A government regulation of 1791 defined the subjects of *mofussil* courts as – 'all natives and other persons, not British subjects, are amenable to the jurisdiction of the Zillah and city courts'.

In a document titled 'East-India Pamphlets, 1818–1825,' there was an interesting pamphlet concerning the 'Indo–Britons.' One of the pieces in them was by Mr Kyd, emphasizing the commencement of a plan which will ultimately be the only sure one to raise the Indo–British to a respectable rank in society. He, thereby, suggested certain occupations, making them self-reliant. Amongst others, he also mentioned book-binding.

> The art of bookbinding has, in a few years, been brought to great perfection by the boys of the Free School, much to the credit of its managers: and I am glad to hear, that it has also been a source of profit. This entirely confirms my statement that every and any trade

> if taught to the boys and followed up with European method and industry, will and must succeed. [75]

This document advocated that the 'Indo–Britons,' both men and women, should be engaged in artisanal work. He also added that how it would also be more profitable to engage the mixed-race women in work of this kind, including making hats for ladies, rattan bottoms for chairs and couches, paper and leaf fans, artificial flowers, etc. Then, the pamphlet made its intentions clearer,

> However cheap articles may be brought from abroad, where industry and method have already been established, and however, for a time, the articles produced here might be inferior in quality; yet, eventually, they would not only be equal in quality, but cheaper: first, because, the raw material is at hand, and secondly, because the expense of carriage, insurance etc. will be saved. [76]

There was a concern that was also expressed in it viz, how 'from the rapid increase of the Indo–Britons, they will soon, be unavoidably, become … a dangerous burden to the Government and the country' unless, as suggested in the write-up, the British Government utilized them as industrious labour.[77]

L. De Grandpre, from his voyage to Bengal, recorded in his travelogue that,

> The military officers stationed at Calcutta, or in the neighbourhood, sometimes intermarry with these girls, whose fathers it frequently happens they have been acquainted with. Such marriages are by no means uncommon: all who have acquired any fortune, whether civil officers or others, finding the necessity of a female companion to banish from their minds the remembrance of their country.[78]

There was mention of the same in the will of Captain William Hyde of the 20th Regiment of Sepoy. He mentioned his mistress, who he said was the daughter of a sergeant in the Company's service.

> I will and bequeath unto my girl Mary (the daughter of Bennet, a sergeant in the company's service since either dead or gone to Europe) the sum of one thousand current rupees, as a testimony of my regard and I also leave her wearing apparel, gold and silver ornaments, a silver paundanne and in short whatever may be supposed to belong to a person in her situation, the gold and silver weights about seven hundred rupees.[79]

Here, the native *bibi*'s parentage was known, so it got mentioned. Going by the names of native women in the wills, as discussed earlier, were either women who had been given different names, or part-European and mixed-race women, who often became live-in partners, but there are no other details about them. Some wills do talk about it. Like in the case of Blechynden, he specified when the potential Eurasian *bibi* could speak in excellent English.[80] Some wills also specified if a mistress was Catholic or even mention her Portuguese descent. But often, the term 'native,' as discussed earlier, carries a complex meaning – it was a term used to distinguish them from the women who came from Europe. This will of Captain William Hyde, painstakingly mentioned the details of the parentage of his native mistress, claiming that her father was a European working in the Company's service. This either meant that the Captain was emphasizing her European descent or was just providing details for legal purposes.

Mr Kyd's writing gave different suggestions regarding the unmarried women of mixed parentage, again stressing their need to learn some artisanal work, certainly advising them to stay away from idle life, perhaps implying the 'native' influences.

> From every quarter, then, examples invites the Indo–Briton female to industry – from the Nuns of Catholic countries, down to the Mugs ... whose wives and daughters, spin, weave, and dye the clothing for their families. All are active, industrious and happy: why then should the Indo–Briton females be prey to that monster Ennui? That offspring of idleness, more to be dreaded than direct calamity.[81]

This is also conveyed in the words of Sir John Malcolm, in the 'Selected Documents of Nineteenth Century Bengal.' Here, the bias is apparent, along with a sympathy that had strong racial undertones.

> The half–castes (as they are generally termed,) or children of Europeans from native women, form a considerable class of British subjects in India, who certainly merit more of the attention of the Government, than they have hitherto received. They may be considered a distinct class; and one which is gradually rising into importance, from its increasing numbers. They have not the robust frame of their fathers; but they are in general equal, if not superior, in strength to the natives of those parts of India where they are born. They are remarkable for their docility and intelligence; and only require the care of the state, to become valuable subjects.[82]

On the one hand, this viewpoint tries to sympathize with the mixed-race, while on the other, it tries to define them in relation to their being either European or 'native.' It does talk about the need for the intervention of the

British state to improve their condition, it somewhere also re-establishes the stereotypes by reducing the mixed-race individuals to mere physical terms while explaining this point. The fear of all that miscegenation had come to mean by the mid-19th century, was echoed in these writings quite clearly. Sir John Malcolm also pointed out the need to put more faith on 'this class,' which, according to him, could be turned into a distinct group of corps, a part of the British Army 'on whose fidelity and attachment every reliance might be placed.'[83] This essay was written in 1830.

Another viewpoint, i.e., of the Army, towards the mixed race, is reflected in a document around the same time, 1832. It also presented a feeling of mistrust, a fear of the mixed-race seen as a threat to the British power in India,[84]

> But again, as to Spanish America; does our admixture with the native of India promise a progeny better, if so good? Far be it from me to say, much less insinuate, that there are not many worthy half–castes men as religious, brave and virtuous as their forefathers. Talent or rather cleverness, they are universally allowed to possess; but, in general, there is an instability of character, a violence throughout the race, which it is to be feared, no elevation of condition could eradicate, though hopeless depression must engrain them the more.

Quite a similar opinion was presented in travel writings, where all Indians and natives were seen as a homogenous entity. All the natives and even those of the mixed race were seen as dwelling in the land of 'vices,' as also reflected in another report by Bishop Cotton on the 'Existing Schools for Europeans and Eurasians throughout India,' However, here, more than the emphasis on identity as race, their religion is highlighted, putting them in the same category, as Europeans.

> Whatever may be our hopes of benefitting the natives of India by direct missionary efforts, by education, by good Government, and by contact with European thought, it is quite certain that the conduct and character of the Christians settled among them must have the most direct influence on their estimate of Christianity and Western Civilisation. If a generation calling itself Christian, and descended wholly or partly from European parents, grow up in ignorance and evil habits, the effects of the heathen and Mahomedan population will be most disastrous. But besides this obvious evil, it is nothing less than a national sin to neglect a class who are our fellow Christians and fellow subjects, whose presence in India is due entirely to our occupation of the country, but who, unless real efforts are made for their good, are in great moral and spiritual danger.[85]

This document comes from the late 1880s, but it showed an understanding of the mixed race, as a class which emerged only due to the European occupation of India. However, it is the missionary zeal that hopes to save them from both Hindu as well as Muslim influences.

Considering that the number of Eurasians in the Army was higher, there was a concern about the exclusion. In the *Appendix to the Report from the Select Committee of the House of Commons on the Affairs of the East-India Company*, Major D. Wilson expressed the need to consider raising the troops of Eurasians keeping. This, he said, should be done keeping in mind their 'distinct character,' which would carry the virtues of both races, and 'carefully abstain from doing anything that would risk' bringing in the vices of either.

> It is much to be lamented, that it has been judged advisable to exclude East–Indians as officers, by positive enactment, from the military service of his Majesty and the Company. This has undoubtedly had a great tendency to degrade in the estimation of the world a race sprung from ourselves, and who might have mixed among us without injuring or degrading the services of the State. But this is not the place to discuss the general rights of this depressed race, and the advantages the State might derive from its elevation into a useful and efficient members of a great empire, in which they are born with the rights of British subjects. Their talents, their feelings, and their acquirements can never be fully developed until they have an unrestricted admission into the service of the state, neither can we count on their loyalty and attachment until they possess the full enjoyment of their birth right. [86]

Here is a passage that talks about their inclusion, and deals with the status of the Eurasians with empathy; however, the same document has other opinions too where their increasing numbers is a concern and so is their distinctiveness. Nonetheless, there existed a discourse that continued to talk about, and disagree with the exclusion of mixed races from the Army, that how it may not be the correct way,

> Their admission into the Company's service alone, therefore, would not give them the highest elevation, whilst it would have a tendency to depress that service … men born and educated under the peculiar circumstances of the mixed race in India must have a distinct character, and if we were as anxious to obliterate, as some men are desirous to perpetuate this difference, we should certainly be unsuccessful in attempting to do so. Many of their peculiarities arise out of natural causes, which we cannot control. Our, object, therefore, ought to be to give which is peculiar the most favourable shape and direction.[87]

This viewpoint wants them to be seen as a distinct group and, therefore, be given opportunities that suit them, instead of constantly juxtaposing them against the Europeans. Their distinctiveness is not seen as separate but often the 'native' aspects are what is seen as the problem. That's what makes the British suspicious of the Eurasians.

This is a point that is missed in many other manuals on 'Anglo-Indians' or Eurasians, where the aim is only to achieve all that is 'European.' This was the other end of the spectrum, which over-emphasized the 'native' element in the Eurasians, holding it against them. For example,

> Had their children from their birth been tended by Christian, English–speaking servants, drawn from the lower ranks of their own community, free from the grosser vices of lower-class natives, then it might have been intelligible that to consort with low class Hindoo and Mahomedan lads in schoolwork and school sports would have been a process to which few parents would have cared to subject their children. We are bound to say that many Eurasian lads are in possession of an amount of vernacular abuse and nastiness acquired from the native servants which it would be difficult, if not impossible, for them to acquire either in the upper classes of a well-regulated school, or still less in the classrooms of an efficient college, even though educated side by side with lads of pure birth.[88]

The added emphasis on 'pure birth' along with class was an intersection, where, once again, the influence of 'lower-class natives and their vices' played a role. This is quite like what we have discussed about the figure of the Ayah, who both belonged to a lower class of servants and was also a native woman. The initial acceptance of the mixed race had drastically altered, especially due to the increasing concerns about purity of blood and the fear of miscegenation, and resultant physical distancing (at least in the administrative circles). The changes that started in the last decade of the 18th century, were now consolidating as far as Eurasians were concerned. Their growing numbers were certainly a cause for this acceleration. This, again, points to the fact that it was not as if the native mistress disappeared or that the Memsahib made her disappear. If we are to go by the concern over the increasing number of mixed-race children, one can be sure that the sexual access to native women continued; however, it remained comfortably unmentioned and certainly there in the army. For the sake of internal coherence of the European communities as well as to continue redefining the boundaries of privilege between the colonizer and the colonized, policies towards sexual access and domestic arrangements keep changing.[89] In this case, mix-race children are increasingly becoming a concern, while the native mistress disappears from the conversations of the colonial empire.

A late 19th-century document, 'Collections of the decisions of the High Court and the Privy Council on the Laws of Succession...' from Madras, stated some very important aspects regarding the mixed-race children. Here, Ralph Dodsworth and an Indian Muslim woman Omeda Khanum had a son called Henry Thompson Dodsworth. Ralph Dodsworth had two other mistresses, besides the aforementioned one, with whom he had children who never converted to Christianity. This record says,[90]

> The question was who are the heirs, if any, of the deceased, [Ralph Dodsworth] and by what law is their succession determined, whether if the deceased died without heirs, his estate escheated to the Crown.

The English law of succession ultimately was not applied in this case, as this son (probably the other children too) was accepted as Ralph Dodsworth's rightful heir. But this begged the question as to whether the mixed-race children could be considered heirs or not?

Another case, discussed in the same document, concerned a plaintiff of mixed race, who was born in 1848 and said his great-grandfather was a European 'according to the tradition of the family.' The judge observed that,[91]

> The legitimate descendants of a European British subject retain the law of their ancestor however remote the descent. The case has no analogy to that of descendants of British subjects' residents in a foreign country, who, I believe are generally considered in three generations to lose their nationality, and with their nationality their legal status as subjects of their original country.

This case in the end accepted the plaintiff as a person, subjected to a modified form of English law. However, the usage of the term 'legitimate' and the rights of legitimate British descendants were upheld. Both the abovementioned cases represented a later time but elaborated the ideas that had begun to take root much earlier. The colonial representations, and distancing, did not come at the last minute. There were early influences, that started in previous centuries and were only manifested with a position of power, rule of law, and functioning colonial structure.

The beginnings of the change, vis-à-vis the mixed-race children, had started by the last decade of the 18th century, made visible by restricting their entry into official services or even in sending them to Europe to complete their education. This completely altered the history of the Anglo-Indians (as they came to be known later), who were the progeny of the intimacies that were established between the British men with the native women of India. It reflected a new idea and a new mindset in tandem with the changing political scenario of the times.

Mixed-race unions were encouraged for various reasons by all European trading companies in each of their colonial settlements at some point. The often-gendered language for the empire and colony, was also marked by the mixed-race relationships established by the white men with the native women of the colonies. These relationships were romanticized to portray the homogenous experience of colonialism at the socio-cultural level. However, research focusing on various ways in which the asymmetries of gender, race, class, colour, and knowledge production would have kept these mixed-race unions benefitted the colonial men. The mixed-race policy, however, shifted quite swiftly in the case of South Asia. The changes in attitude and policy were a result of the changing role of the British vis-à-vis the colonized populace. The British had emerged as an unparalleled political power by the close of the 18th century. The children born of interracial relationships were a reminder of a shared social and interpersonal space that was now being frowned upon. This is clear from the official attitudes shared in the last section of this chapter. Over time, the 'half-caste' population did, in fact, come to be seen as a threat to the British in India. The mixed-race population was by no means a new phenomenon, but the social dynamics through which they were earlier accepted and admitted into the European circle had changed. Now, it was the 'native' part of their lineage that was being questioned and completely mistrusted.

Notes

1 'Oriental and India Office Collection: Bengal Wills,' L/AG/34/29/5.
2 'High Court Calcutta – Original Side: Bengal Wills,' 8784.
3 T. Edwards, 'Eurasians and Poor Europeans in India,' *Calcutta Review* 72 (1881): 39–40.
4 Ibid., 39.
5 P. Spear, *The Nabobs: A Study of the Social Life of the English in the Eighteenth Century* (Cambridge: Cambridge University Press, 1963).
6 J.M. Mickelson, *British Women in India, 1757–1857* (Michigan: University of Michigan Press, 1978), 74.
7 N. Chaudhuri, 'Memsahibs and Motherhood in Nineteenth-Century Colonial India,' *Victorian Studies* 31, no. 4 (1988).
8 E. Wald, 'From Begums and Bibis to Abandoned Females and Idle Women: Sexual Relationships, Venereal Disease and the Redefinition of Prostitution in Early Nineteenth-Century India,' *Indian Economic and Social History Review* 46, no. 1 (2009): 8.
9 R. Hyam, *Empire and Sexuality: The British Experience* (Manchester: Manchester University Press, 2017), 120.
10 J. Nair, 'Uncovering the Zenana: Visions of Indian Womanhood in Englishwomen's Writings, 1813–1940,' *Journal of Women's History* 2, no. 1 (1990): 25.
11 A.L. Stoler, *Carnal Knowledge and Imperial Power: Race and the Intimate in Colonial Rule* (Berkeley: University of California Press, 2002), 1.

12 S. Zlotnick, 'Domesticating Imperialism: Curry and Cookbooks in Victorian England,' *Frontiers: A Journal of Women Studies* 16, no. 2/3 (1996).
13 S. Markowitz, 'Pelvic Politics: Sexual Dimorphism and Racial Difference,' *Signs: Journal of Women in Culture and Societ* 26, no. 2 (2001): 399–400.
14 'Oriental and India Office Collection: Bengal Wills,' L/AG/34/29/11
15 Ibid.
16 'Bengal Proceedings,' *India Office Records and Private Papers*, n.d., fol. IOR/P/154/56.
17 'Bengal Proceedings,' in *India Office Records* (London: British Library), IOR/P/154/56.
18 Ibid.
19 Ibid.
20 'Oriental and India Office Collection: Bengal Wills,' L/AG/34/29/5.
21 Ibid.
22 Ibid., L/AG/34/29/6.
23 Ibid., L/AG/34/29/8.
24 Ibid., L/AG/34/29/7.
25 Ibid., L/AG/34/29/11.
26 Ibid., L/AG/34/29/6.
27 Ibid.
28 Ibid., L/AG/34/29/8.
29 Ibid., L/AG/34/29/7.
30 Ibid.
31 'High Court Calcutta – Original Side: Bengal Wills,' 6093.
32 G. Chattopadhyaya, *Awakening in Bengal in Early Nineteenth Century: Selected Documents* (Calcutta: Progressive Publishers, 1965), 8.
33 'Oriental and India Office Collection: Bengal Wills,' L/AG/34/29/8.
34 'High Court Calcutta – Original Side: Bengal Wills,' 7218.
35 'Oriental and India Office Collection: Bengal Wills,' L/AG/34/29/7.
36 'High Court Calcutta – Original Side: Bengal Wills,' 7241.
37 Ibid., 5332.
38 'Oriental and India Office Collection: Bengal Wills,' L/AG/34/29/6.
39 'Oriental and India Office Collection: Bengal Wills,' L/AG/34/29/5.
40 'Oriental and India Office Collection: Bengal Wills,' L/AG/34/29/5.
41 Ibid., L/AG/34/29/6.
42 Ibid., L/AG/34/29/5.
43 Ibid., L/AG/34/29/7.
44 Ibid., L/AG/34/29/13.
45 'High Court Calcutta – Original Side: Bengal Wills,' 5355.
46 C.J. Hawes, *Poor Relations: The Making of a Eurasian Community in British India, 1773–1833* (Surrey: Curzon Press, 1996), 23–24.
47 Ibid., 21–22.
48 D. Ghosh, 'Making and Un-Making Loyal Subjects: Pensioning Widows and Educating Orphans in Early Colonial India,' *The Journal of Imperial and Commonwealth History* 31, no. 1 (2010).
49 'Oriental and India Office Collection: Bengal Wills,' L/AG/34/29/5.
50 Ibid., L/AG/34/29/7.
51 Ibid., L/AG/34/29/8.
52 Ibid., L/AG/34/29/11.
53 'High Court Calcutta – Original Side: Bengal Wills,' 5246.
54 H. Pearse, *The Hearseys: Five Generations of an Anglo-Indian Family* (London: W. Blackwood and Sons, 1905), 20.

55 Ibid., 23.
56 Hawes, *Poor Relations: The Making of a Eurasian Community in British India, 1773–1833*, 163.
57 Pearse, *The Hearseys: Five Generations of an Anglo-Indian Family.*
58 'Oriental and India Office Collection: Bengal Wills,' L/AG/34/29/7.
59 Ibid., L/AG/34/29/11.
60 Ibid., L/AG/34/29/6.
61 'High Court Calcutta – Original Side: Bengal Wills,' 5318.
62 Capt T. Williamson, *The East India Vade-Mecum; or Complete Guide to Gentlemen Intended for the Civil, Military or Naval Service of the East India Company*, 2 vols. (London: Printed for Black, Parry, and Kingsbury, 1810), 216.
63 Capt.T. Skinner, *Excursions in India; Including a Walk over the Himalaya Mountains, to the Sources of the Jumna and the Ganges*, 2 vols. (London: Henry Colburn and Richard Bentley, New Burlington Street, 1832), Vol. 1, 215.
64 L. de Grandpre, *A Voyage in the Indian Ocean and to Bengal Undertaken in the Years 1789 and 1790: Containing an Account of the Sechelles Islands and Trincomale ... To Which Is Added, a Voyage in the Red Sea* (London: Printed for G. and J. Robinson, 1803), Vol. 2, 33.
65 Ibid., Vol. 2, 36.
66 L. Roychowdhury, *The Jadu House: Travels in Anglo-India* (London: Black Swan, 2001), 287.
67 C. Younger, *Anglo-Indians: Neglected Children of the Raj* (Delhi: B.R. Publishing Corp., 1987), 11.
68 P. Robb, *Sentiment and Self: Richard Blechynden's Calcutta Diaries, 1791–1822* (Oxford: Oxford University Press, 2011), 38.
69 E.M. Collingham, *Imperial Bodies: The Physical Experience of the Raj, C. 1800–1947* (Cambridge: Polity Press, 2001), 76.
70 Priya Shah, '"Barbaric Pearl and Gold": Gendered Desires and Colonial Governance in Emma Roberts's Scenes and Characteristics of Hindostan,' *Studies in Travel Writing* 16, no. 1 (2012): 32.
71 E. Roberts, *Scenes and Characteristics of Hindostan with Sketches of Anglo-Indian Society*, 3 vols. (London: W. H. Allen & Co., 1835), Vol. 3, 95.
72 Ibid., Vol. 3, 98.
73 N.P. Gist and R.D. Wright, *Marginality and Identity: Anglo-Indian as a Racially-Mixed Minority in India*, ed. K. Ishwaran, Monographs and Theoretical Studies in Sociology and Anthropology in Honour of Nels Anderson (Leiden: E. J. BRILL, 1973), 12.
74 Chattopadhyaya, *Awakening in Bengal in Early Nineteenth Century: Selected Documents*, 8.
75 'Kyd's Pamphlet,' in *East India Pamplets, 1818–1825* (Calcutta), 29.
76 Ibid., 32–33.
77 Ibid., 33.
78 de Grandpre, *A Voyage in the Indian Ocean and to Bengal Undertaken in the Years 1789 and 1790: Containing an Account of the Sechelles Islands and Trincomale ... To Which Is Added, a Voyage in the Red Sea*, 33.
79 'Oriental and India Office Collection: Bengal Wills,' L/AG/34/29/6.
80 P. Robb, *Sex and Sensibility: Richard Blechynden's Calcutta Diaries, 1791–1822* (New Delhi: Oxford University Press, 2011), 2.
81 'Kyd's Pamphlet,' 30–31.
82 Chattopadhyaya, *Awakening in Bengal in Early Nineteenth Century: Selected Documents*, 89.
83 Ibid.

84 Reply of Capt. J.G. Duff, March 25, 1832, 'Appendix to the Report from the Select Committee of the House of Commons on the Affairs of the East India Company, 16th Aug. 1832 and Minute of Evidence' (London: Select Committee on the House of Lords, 1833), 400.
85 A. J. Lawrence, 'Report on the Existing Schools for Europeans and Eurasians Throughout India,' (Calcutta 1887), 1.
86 Reply of Major D. Wilson 29th March 1832, 'Appendix to the Report from the Select Committee of the House of Commons on the Affairs of the East India Company, 16th Aug. 1832 and Minute of Evidence,' 371.
87 Ibid.
88 Edwards, 'Eurasians and Poor Europeans in India,' 44.
89 A. L. Stoler, 'Making Empire Respectable: The Politics of Race and Sexual Morality in 20th-Century Colonical Cultures,' *American Ethnologist* 16, no. 4 (1989): 651.
90 C. Ramachendrier, *Collections of the Decisions of the High Court and the Privy Council on the Laws of Succession, Maintenance Etc. Applicable to Dancing Girls and Their Issues, Prostitutes Not Belonging to the Dancing Girls' Community, Illegitimate Sons and Bastards, and Illatom Affiliations Upto December 1891* (Madras: Scottish Press, 1892), 64.
91 Ibid., 65.

6

CONCLUDING REMARKS

Domestic and household structures are constantly being reconfigured by the historically changing contours of the political context. Even the interpersonal relationships became more complex with the colonial intervention in most parts of the world. Understanding the personal without the political dynamics of that time, would render our understanding incomplete. To look at domestic arrangements that came into existence as a by-product of commerce and colonization within just the confines of four walls, would rob the individuals of their historical significance. It would relegate the affairs of households to the realm of the private, as opposed to that which was political, economic, and thus, public. The precise purpose with which this research had started off was to bring the history of what the early colonial archive designates as 'the native women' to the forefront. It also undertook to understand the dynamics of her intimacy with the early colonial British men in Bengal, through bequeaths he left for her in his will.

The intersection of race, gender, and law become an interesting meeting point for understanding the rise of colonialism. For the most part, the history of the colonial enterprise remained the history of political negotiations with a purely economic intent. For long, the relationship between the colonizer and the colonized was seen as nothing but two opposites, where anything other than oppression or exploitation, was not possible and there was no scope for any other exchange. The social, personal, and sexual dimensions, where the two may have had a shared experience, were never delegated as historical experiences due to archival shortcomings. The discussions largely revolved around the empire as masculine, and the colony as the controlled, feminized opposite. Such assumptions remained as problematic as the binaries of the colonial and the colonized. While it is true, that there is no dedicated archive where native women exist, that itself proves a gendering of the archive, and not so much the lack of women's history in them. The attempts to go into micro-histories and the native experiences is to reclaim them from the margins of historical enquiry, that is what this book has attempted to do. By going beyond studying native women as a part of a larger structure, it undertook the task of seeing them as historical players, who played a

 DOI: 10.4324/9781003315186-6

role and witnessed the shifts in the historical role of the British East India Company. This is not to deny the asymmetries of interracial intimacies but to find the voices of these women in the everyday aspects, and details that come out in legal papers, mainly the wills. This is to render them visibility, especially for their service, role, and work and see them as an integral part to our understanding of the construct of the early colonial period itself.

Aspects of pre-modern South Asian notions were carried forward by the advent of the Europeans, who donned the mantle of the erstwhile Mughal nobility. During the course of the 18th century, however, there was a plebianization of that lifestyle. Hence, along with the visual, and literary picture of the elite *bibi*, references to native concubines in different ways, such as washerwomen, housekeepers, and so forth, increased in the legal archive. It is essential to go beyond the semantics of these terms and view these terms as the *actual* work these women performed in the course of these interracial connections. By reducing them to euphemisms, it not only undermines all the work the native concubines did but also makes them invisible. The fact that native mistresses were being mentioned for their care work, being long-term companions, faithful servants, mothers of the British men's children, and so on, also points to the number of tasks they were performing and the various roles they undertook in the domestic arrangements with the British men.

These relationships were rarely solemnized into marriages, but it neither stopped nor impacted these arrangements. The moral condemnation of concubinage happened much later, but even then, it was not stopped, except in the higher echelons of the British population in India. The soldiers, and even the British men in the *mofussils* (outskirts) continued to have native companions. Although with the impact of the Evangelicals, there was some emphasis on marriage, especially when the Lord Clive Fund designated for military widows in 1829 began to ask for written confirmation on marital status, it became a difficult document to produce for the non-married women.[1] In fact, the Indian widows of the British Army's European soldiers had only recently been granted similar rights as Anglo-Indian and European women. How does one study these relationships, without looking at the political structures? If the political structures were influencing these mixed-race domesticities, we also have to look at the way mixed-race relationships and these women were considered active participants in the early colonial social space in Bengal.

While studying the wills to understand these interpersonal relationships, one must keep in mind the early colonial, racial as well as personal contexts, because each case was different from the other. However, there were interesting overlaps in these wills. They inadvertently carried information that would leave clues to understand what that relationship may have been like, how would these have been started, what was the relationship of the women with material household objects. They also leave us wondering, where would the women have gone back to, and would they have met their child or children and so on. It is interesting how the emerging colonial consciousness and the social role of the British father separated the child from the mother, almost always. This was not just true of the middle- and lower-class British men but also in the case of the elite in the British social hierarchy as well. Some of these children were sent back home to the person's family or friends. For others, there were orphanages, schools, and other institutions to educate and train the mixed-race children. It increasingly became the responsibility of the emerging colonial state to look after the mixed-race progeny. What comes to the surface while reading documents like travelogues, or even the wills and memorandums is the plight of racialized bias towards an entire community – who were robbed of both their Indian and gradually their European heritage. Which is why it is difficult for me to accept that these native women were all along just mentioned in few words, lines, or as an Indian experience and not as participants, who along with their children, bore the brunt of the growing racial distancing and the fear of miscegenation.

Another important question which arises while working on this theme has been where to situate this work. Does this fall under the category of race, gender, law, women's history, sexuality, or something else? The wills in themselves cannot talk about an entire life, but many of them do leave details, at times entire stories that can conjure up aspects not mentioned elsewhere. Stephanie Jane Appleton in her unpublished thesis on 'Women and Wills in Early Modern England,' argues quite the opposite. She says, it is vital to place as much additional evidence as possible alongside the wills when interpreting them.[2] While I would like to agree that additional information would certainly make for a more rounded historical understanding but in this case, even the intimate partners, i.e., the native women, are rendered nameless, and worse, get named in another language that disassociates them from their social histories. The practice of renaming women and adding the husband's last name is still prevalent in patriarchal practices. However, in these wills, no one else is ever given a name, without their formal name being mentioned alongside, except the native concubine. Wills are serious and sombre documents, written on a person's deathbed or when one is entertaining thoughts about death. But no British family members, no British friends nor even the mixed-race children were mentioned by just their popular names but have their formal names alongside. So, what was it about the native woman and her relationship with the British man, that made her remaining unnamed, or alternatively named, or even to get mentioned merely as a role, possible? Most of the time, it effectively erased any chance of situating her against any religious, social, or regional context? Not that the names are always very clear markers of these, but some wills do provide the geographical, ethnic, or even religious identities of these women. Are they indicative of anything? The wills that go on about the details of native mistresses, are they not submissions on how social relations went about? Details such as native mistresses' names (or lack of them), how they were written about by their British men, the duration of their cohabitation, descriptions about their residence, the material objects like jewels, furniture, clothing, money, and property left for her in different conditions, give us a clear picture about the mixed-race domesticities and the lives they lived together.

The study of the colonial legal archive highlights the different facets of these relationships, it also points out the biases against the natives, the racial physical distancing of the early 19th century, as well as the position of the native woman as the 'colonized' female who was also the sexual partner of the 'colonizer.' On the one hand, the natives as witnesses, plaintiffs, victims, etc. become a crucial part of modern law, but it is ultimately their being native that reigns supreme. The glaring dichotomy between theoretical ideas about egalitarian colonial justice and the way violent Europeans were treated in legal practice is shown in Elizabeth Kolsky's work. She argues that despite a rhetorical stance of legal equality, legal practice and conventions placed most Europeans in India above the law and, in effect, tolerated and condoned widespread physical assault and abuse.[3] It makes the law and legal categories as much influenced by the social idea of the native as what the travel writings had been constructing all along.

The reading of the earliest travel narratives, and its entire focus on the land, custom, and people points to a racial separateness even early on. Hence, this work had started off by taking into consideration not only the work and ideas of the Orientalists but considering it as a building block to a more concrete sense of the 'other.' Again, not to take away the importance of political shifts of the 19th century, but the concept and treatment of natives in India were always a step away from the full-fledged colonial racial hierarchy. The role of the Indian service class, and their structures – caste and otherwise, remain the same. It was the British who came, witnessed, adopted, and interacted with the weather and the existing social norms in India. The relationship that developed between the British man who came to India without a family, and as an individual promoting his personal aspirations and the fortunes of the English East India Company, assimilated into the Indian cultural milieu while understanding it from a position of authority. European explorers and travellers, even during their initial observations of the exotic and its populace, controlled the narrative of their construct for the times to come. The idea of the Nabob was not so much a condemnation of the British man working in India making abundant wealth for himself, but perhaps an enviable caricature of a British man who was redeemed and glorified despite his corruption by portraying him akin to the decadent Indian elite. What better way to do that than anglicizing the term Nawab! The corruption became justifiable the moment an Indian headgear was placed on his head, he was shown growing closer to Indian customs, his belly is shown full of contentment with where he is. These became the tropes of opulence that reflected his being in India, and in effect brought him closer to the natives, their bodies, and their customs. The corruption within the East India Company, despite all the hype around Hasting's trial, was not so much for the system they were creating but the imagined influence that was made out to be the root cause of the 'Nabobery.' It spoiled the goodness of the hard work that the British man was doing and who suddenly transformed as 'indolent,' like the natives. Yet, despite that, the ambition to go out to India grew by leaps and bounds. Hence the glossy image of racial harmony in the early colonial era was still charged with power, hierarchies, and otherness. Material wealth was an easy indicator, even in the wills and writings of the not so well-off British men.

It was in the 18th century when women were largely dependent on the men for economic resources, legal developments, and political modifications of the times. The women were not always victims, but often active participants in these historical processes. If they had any means of recording their past, it would have been a treasure for an alternate understanding of history. But as one reads about their presence, interestingly some of them did have access to resources that even the native men did not. The bequests that were made to the native women often consisted of regular pensions, interest, rights to occupy a house, jewellery, and other material household goods. They were relatively disadvantaged, but many of them, when they got their legacies in the wills, were recognized for their services, and roles assigned to and expected of them. The dynamics of the intimate spaces also made them closer to a familial experience for British men. What a loss not to know of it from the women's perspective. However, it's important to note that the earliest detailed reference of the native women was while they were viewed as an experience of the 'exotic.' They were sexualized, without contextualizing their sexualities. The seclusion of the royal harem, the site of the nautch, women performing mundane tasks like going to the *ghats* – everything was rendered sensual, and for the consumption of the reader. This was an act of power that made both the native women and men, and consequently, the Indian society at large, open to a portrayal from the position of power. The writings of the Orientalists certainly attempted to know India's past but failed to understand the 18th-century political rearrangements that they were in fact bringing in. Their writings engaged with the laws and codes of the past, but not on how India was changing unprecedently. The Orientalist discourse remains silent on the mixed-race relationships because they were relegated to the actual, real background, as useful but ahistorical. Knowledge production and history writing were relegated to men historically, and women were usually excluded from it. Women could be part of a structure, but they are never seen as actual historical actors. Even the Mughals, despite their traditional reverence for the women in their families, never wrote their histories, but simply mentioned them as part of the imperial household and as mothers. Important, but not as historical beings. Likewise, in the writings of extremely learned men, constructing a comprehensive past of India, they do not write about history as they witnessed it, which is where they remain inextricably linked to the way the colonial structure developed, policies were fashioned, and natives remained racially distanced.

This work has attempted to go beyond easy binaries and look at historical events as transformations rather than drastic events. The history of interpersonal relationships cannot be kept away from political changes, that they were impacting and getting influenced. Once it is understood that native women were disadvantaged, under or not represented in history, were renamed and unnamed, they all point to systematic erasures from monumental historical archives. Hence, their histories cannot be seen without the frame of gender. Race, which added to the asymmetry of the relationship, also remains the larger paradigm against which these intimacies need to be studied. The English East India Company may have turned into a colonial enterprise in the latter part of the 18th century, but the racial gaze was set in motion from early on. It started from the task of seeing, observing, and writing about the natives as bodies and themes in the vast travel writing. It was in fact, the first step in constructing a colonized native. The coming face to face, entering the service of the British man, and becoming his native partner, all systematically added to that construct. This work relies almost solely on the colonial archive, and hence the submission, that the mixed race arrangements and individuals, were all constructed in the colonial archive, but they exist there.

The natives, and how they were impacted by colonial policies from the 18th to the early 19th century, are not denied their presence in history, only their version of it. As a woman, and a historian, I cannot emphasize enough how important that distinction is. So is the importance of accepting that these women who entered the European household, did so in the capacity of servants. They were concubines, with no formal contracts, no law protecting them, no legal or even social guarantees, ensuring certain a wage, benefits, or rights. Reading the wills provides ample data on the kind of work these women were expected to do. However, it was also dependent upon the class as well the will of her British 'keeper.' The lower-ranking British individuals or officials may not have had a host of servants in their households. There was certainly a possibility of an overlap between the sexual and domestic service conditions. None of the wills of the rich British men termed the native concubines as housekeepers or washerwomen, probably because this work was not expected from them there. The dimension of class makes a lot of difference through a careful reading of these wills. It is not just a change in the nature and value of the bequeaths, but also the inner workings of intimacies that can be seen as changing too. It changes the work women did or were expected to do in a different class setting. At the same time, in many polygamous households, women were mentioned as hierarchically different from each other. Sexual access to female servants and even the slave women was reflected in these wills. This means, one cannot agree on a single kind of interracial domesticity, for there were several kinds. Each of them can be treated as micro-histories where some details are not recorded, and some details are forever lost. As Durba Ghosh argues that without the complete names of the native women in the men's wills, church records, etc., their archival trail goes cold.[4]

There are more records available concerning the natural children, who were mentioned with their correct names, and then also existed in other records and archives, subsequently. These children were mostly left provided for by their fathers, but otherwise too, the emerging British Empire was fully aware of the mixed-race population and chose to take it into cognizance. The book has discussed how they were sent back to Europe if the British man could afford to, or as long as it was an accepted practice. They were a part of the early modern South Asian mixed-race families, that remained fluid and mobile, especially when juxtaposed with the legitimate families back in Europe. These children were seen as markers of the closeness of the kin networks, as the word 'natural' is used for them frequently, to denote their identity and to also separate them from the legitimate children. There is often no difference between the two in terms of bequeaths, except when one joined the family network and the other, over time got excluded from it. It is also through the birth of these 'natural' children, along with other intimate services offered by the 'native' concubine, that the racial and sexual could be seen as a more structured colonial kinship unit. Within the confines of this familial, and private arrangement, the shifting colonial relations were visible too. The symptoms of the changes, that the heyday of the colonial state was yet to bring in, became visible in the intimate spaces first. Can kinship and familial spaces signify the shifts in social mores, through physical and racial distancing much before they are politically announced and adopted as policies? I would like to argue, that they do, and yet depending on the class affinities, these children were sent back home. It would be quite telling to see how much property the mixed-race children got from their father's side, if they are sent to Britain, these wills do not carry that information. But what their fathers, the British men had made in India during their careers in Bengal, was what was left through heredity to the children, more readily than to the mothers of these children.

That also brings us to the role of marriage and the notion of respectability. Many scholars mention these interracial unions, where marriage or no marriage, does not make a difference. However, the wills always mention marriage, if there was one. The most important change would not have been for the native woman, but the status of the children would have turned legitimate. In the 18th century, in legal parlance, these terms held not just a legal but a social meaning too. It is interesting that it does not mean much to make alternate identities of native women, but the shift in the status of a mixed-race child from the natural to the legitimate becomes an important factor.

Apart from the British Empire, there is pioneering research bringing forth the shared intimate space between the local women and the colonizers elsewhere too. The similarity of the mixed-race conjugal set-ups, the language of serviceability and the work of indigenous women, and the struggle to retrieve their voices, are some of the concerns we come across in almost all these writings. The native women are visible, in almost all colonial records, even when they remain silent and are constructed in the voice and language of the master and emerging colonial structures. The early modern legal archive, where these women exist in substantial numbers, brings us back to the agency and leverage of these women, making scholars rethink their larger categories. A pertinent point of intervening in this intimate connection, in my research is the contentious issue of emoluments and the crucial role that money played in forging and continuing these domesticities. It also renders the generalized romanticization of the mixed-race concubinage problematic, by engaging with the idea, that we could measure intimate labour in an interracial set-up, in purely economic terms. Also, how do we then study these women – as servants, providing sexual as well as reproductive labour, or consider them merely as concubines cohabiting with the colonizers, and in the process 'taking care' of the household matters? We place this intimacy, and look for answers to these questions, against the shifting politics in early colonial India.

This epilogue is just a way to share the ideas that have been running in the back of my mind while writing this book. Engaging with colonial intimacies, right before the colonial structures manifest themselves, is certainly work in retrospect. As a historian, that is a luxury that I have. However, I would like to close this book with more questions, some answered and some purportedly nuanced to think further. It should also be mentioned here that this work started out by teasing out the terms, and their historical meanings, especially in context of the most under-mentioned and unmentioned native women in wills pertaining to early colonial Bengal. This ended up becoming a lot more, with interdisciplinarity and multiple interpretations. As this makes us rethink the categories of constructed native identities, it should also lead us to treat micro-histories, what we hear in them, as more telling by their intent than just the content.

Notes

1 E. Wald, 'From Begums and Bibis to Abandoned Females and Idle Women: Sexual Relationships, Venereal Disease and the Redefinition of Prostitution in Early Nineteenth-Century India,' *Indian Economic and Social History Review* 46, no. 1 (2009): 10–11.

2 S.J. Appleton, 'Women and Wills in Early Modern England: The Community of Stratford-Upon Avon, 1537-1649' (University of Birmingham, 2016).

3 E. Kolsky, *Colonial Justice in British India: White Violence and the Rule of Law* (Cambridge: Cambridge University Press, 2010), 4.

4 D. Ghosh, 'Decoding the Nameless: Gender, Subjectivity, and Historical Methodologies in Reading the Archives of Colonial India,' in *A New Imperial History: Culture, Identity and Modernity in Britain and the Empire*, ed. Kathleen Wilson (Cambridge: Cambridge University Press, 2004), 315.

BIBLIOGRAPHY

Primary Sources - Unpublished

"Bengal Proceedings." In *India Office Records*. London: British Library.

"Hicky's Bengal Gazette." Calcutta.

"High Court Calcutta – Original Side: Bengal Wills."

"Hyde Books." 1777–1798, https://hydebooks.njit.edu/.

"The Hyde Papers and Hyde Reports." Calcutta: National Library Calcutta.

"Kyd's Pamphlet." In *East India Pamplets, 1818–1825*. Calcutta.

"Oriental and India Office Collection: Bengal Wills."

Primary Sources - Published

"Appendix to the Report from the Select Committee of the House of Commons on the Affairs of the East India Company, 16th Aug. 1832 and Minute of Evidence." London: Select Committee on the House of Lords, 1833.

Bacon, Lieut T. First Impressions and Studies from Nature in Hindostan; embracing an outline of the voyage to Calcutta, and five year's residence in Bengal and Doab, London, 1837.

Briggs, Lieut Col J. *Letters Addressed to a Young Person in India Calculated to Afford Instructions for His Conduct in General and More Especially in His Intercourse with the Natives*. London: John Murray, Albemarle Street, 1828.

Burton, I. *The Life of Captain Sir Richard Burton, with Numerous Portraits, Illustrations and Maps*. 2 vols. Vol. 1. London: Chapman & Hall, Ltd., 1893.

Caunter, Rev. H. *The Oriental Annual or Scenes in India*. London: Charles Tilt, 86, Fleet Street, 1838.

Constable, A., ed. *Travels in the Mogul Empire, A.D. 1656–1668 by Francois Bernier*. London: Archibald Constable and Co., 1891.

Cruise, W. *A Digest of the Laws of England Respecting Real Property*. London: Printed for J. Butterworth & Sons, 1818.

Daniell, W., and Rev. H. Caunter. *The Oriental Annual or Scenes in India Comprising Twenty Two Engravings from Original Drawings by William Daniell and a Descriptive Account by the Rev. Hobart Caunter*. London: Charles Tilt, 86, Fleet Street, 1838.

de Grandpre, L. *A Voyage in the Indian Ocean and to Bengal Undertaken in the Years 1789 and 1790: Containing an Account of the Sechelles Islands and Trincomale...To Which Is Added, a Voyage in the Red Sea*. London: Printed for G. and J. Robinson, 1803.

Dow, A. *The History of Hindostan from the Death of Akbar to the Complete Settlement of the Empire under Aurangzebe, to Which Are Prefixed; I. A Dissertation on the Origin and Nature of Despotism in Hindostan; Ii. An Enquiry into the State of Bengal; with a Plan for Restoring That Kingdom to Its Former Prosperity and Splendor*. 3 vols. Vol. 3. London: Printed for John Murray, No. 32, Fleet-Street, 1792.

———. *The History of Hindostan; Translated from the Persian, to Which Are Prefixed Two Dissertations; the First Concerning the Hindoos and the Second on the Origin and Nature of Despotism in India*. 3 vols. London: Printed for J. Walker, 1812.

Dubois, Abbe J. A. *Description of the Character, Manners, and Customs of the People of India; and of Their Institutions, Religious and Civil*. London: Printed for Longman, Hurst, Rees, Orme, and Brown, 1817.

Eden, E. *'Up the Country' Letter Written to Her Sister from the Upper Provinces of India*. London: Richard Bentley, New Burlington Street, 1867.

Edwards, T. "Eurasians and Poor Europeans in India." *Calcutta Review* 72, no. 143–144 (1881): 38–56.

Fawcett, C. *The Travels of Abbe Carre in India and the Near East, 1672–1674*. Translated by Lady Fawcett. Works Issued by Hakluyt Society. 2 vols. London: The Hakluyt Society, 1947.

Fay, E. *Original Letters from India Containing a Narrative of a Journey Though Egypt and the Author's Imprisonment at Calicut by Hydor Ally. To Which Is Added an Abstract of Three Subsequent Voyages to India*. Calcutta: Messrs. Thacker, Spink & Co., 1789.

Fenn, V. *Sex and Sexuality in Victorian Britain*. Philadelphia, PA: Pen and Sword Books, 2020.

Fenton. *The Journal of Mrs. Fenton: A Narrative of Her Life in India; the Isle of Franoe (Mauritius) and Tasmania During the Years 1826-1830*. London: Edward Arnold, publisher to the India Office, 1901.

Foote, S. *The Dramatic Works of Samuel Foote, Esq., in Four Volumes, Vol. 4: Containing Maid of Bath, Nabob, Trip to Calais and Capuchin*. London: Printed for P. Vaillant, J. Rivington, T. Cadell, W. Nnicoll, and S. Bladon, 1781.

Forbes, J. *Oriental Memoirs: Selected and Abridged from a Series of Familiar Letters Written During Seventeen Years Residence in India...And Narrative of Occurrences in Four India Voyages. In 4 Volumes*. London: Printed for the author by T. Bensley, Bolt Court, 1813.

Forrest, G. W., ed. *The State Papers of the Governor General of India, Vol. 2: Warren Hastings Documents*. Oxford: B. H. Blackwell, Broad Street, 1910.

Foster, W. *Early Travels in India, 1583–1690*. London: Humphrey Milford, 1921.

———, ed. *The Embassy of Sir Thomas Roe to India, 1615–1619, as Narrated in His Journal and Correspondence*. 2 vols. London: Printed for Hakluyt Society, 1899.

Fryer, J. *A New Account of East India and Persia, Being Nine Years' Travels, 1672–1681*. 3 vols. Edited by William Crooke, First Published. London, 1909. Reprint, Asian Educational Services, New Delhi, 1992.

Graham, M. *Journal of a Residence in India*. Edinburgh: Archibald Constable & Company, 1812.

Grant, C. *Anglo Indian Domestic Life: A Letter from an Artist in India to His Mother in England*. London: W. Thacker, 1862.

———. *Observations on the State of Society among the Asiatic Subjects of Great Britain, Particularly with Respect to Morals; and on the Means of Improving It; Written Chiefly in Year 1792*. London: House of Commons, 1813.

Hamilton, A. *A New Account of the East Indies, being the Observations and Remarks of Capt. Alexander Hamilton from the Year 1688–1723, Trading and Travelling, by Sea and Land to Most of the Countries and Islands of Commerce and Navigation between the Cape of Good Hope and the Island of Japan*. 2 vols. London: Published by Red Lion, 1739.

Heber, R. *A Narrative of a Journey from the Upper Provinces of India from Calcutta to Bombay, 1824–1835*. 3 vols. Vol. 1. London: John Murray, Albemarle Street, 1827.

Hodges, W. *Travels in India During the Years 1780, 1781, 1782, & 1783*. London: J. Edwards, Pall-Mall, 1793.

Huggins, W. *Sketches in India, Treating on Subjects Connected with the Government Civil and Military Establishments; Characters of the European, and Customs of the Native Inhabitants*. London: John Letts, Cornhill, 1824.

Irvine, W., ed. *Storio Do Mogor or Mogul India, 1653–1708 by Niccalao Manucci Venetian*. 4 vols., Indian Texts Series. London: John Murray, 1907.

Johnson, J. *Influence of Tropical Climates on European Constitutions: Being a Treatise on the Principal Diseases Incidental to Europeans in the East and West Indies, Mediterranean, and Coast of Africa*. New York: W. E. Dean, Printer, no. 3 Wall Street, 1826.

Kelly, S. *The Life of Mrs. Sherwood, Chiefly Autobiographical, with Extracts from Mr. Sherwood's Journal During His Imprisonment in France and Residence in India*. London: Darton & Co., 1857.

Kindersley, N. *Letters from the Island of Teneriffe, Brazil, the Cape of Good Hope, and the East Indies*. London: Printed for J. Nourse, in the Strand, 1777.

Lawrence, A. J. "Report on the Existing Schools for Europeans and Eurasians Throughout India." Calcutta, 1887.

Mayne, J. D. *A Treatise on Hindu Law and Usage*. London: Stevens and Haynes, 1878.

Moore, T., Lord Jeffrey, Sir W. Scott, B. Heber, S. Rogers, Prof. Wilson, J. G. Lockhart, L. Broughton, T. Campbell, and W. Gifford. *The Poetical Works of Lord Byron, Complete in One Volume, Collected and Arranged with Illustrated Notes*. London: John Murray, 1866.

Mundy, G. C. *Pen and Pencil Sketches in India. Journal of a Tour in India*. 2 vols. London: John Murray, Albemarle Street, 1832.

Nugent, Maria. *A Journal from the Year 1811 Till the Year 1815, Including a Voyage to and Residence in India, with a Tour to the North-Western Parts of the British Possessions in That Country under the Bengal Government, in Two Volumes*. London: T. and W. Boone, 1839.

Orme, R. *Historical Fragments of the Mogul Empire, of the Morattoes, and of the Concerns in Indostant; from the Year 1659*. London: Printed for F. Wingrave, 1805.

Ovington, J. *A Voyage to Surat in the Year1689*. Edited by H. G. Rawlinson. London: Oxford University Press, 1929.

Parkes, F. *Wanderings of a Pilgrim in Search of the Picturesque, During Four and Twenty Years in the East with Revelations of Life in the Zenana, Illustrated with Sketches from Nature*. London: Pelham Richardson, 23, Cornhill, 1850.

Pearse, H. *The Hearseys: Five Generations of an Anglo-Indian Family*. London: W. Blackwood and Sons, 1905.

(Pseudonym), Boxwallah. *An Eastern Backwater*. London: Andrew Melrose, Ltd., 1916.

Ramachendrier, C. *Collections of the Decisions of the High Court and the Privy Council on the Laws of Succession, Maintenance Etc. Applicable to Dancing Girls and Their Issues, Prostitutes Not Belonging to the Dancing Girls' Community, Illegitimate Sons and Bastards, and Illatom Affiliations Upto December 1891*. Madras: Scottish Press, 1892.

Roberts, E. *Scenes and Characteristics of Hindostan with Sketches of Anglo-Indian Society*. 3 vols. London: W. H. Allen & Co., 1835.

Sitaram. *From Sepoy to Subadar: Being the Life and Adventures of a Native Officer of the Bengal Army Written and Related by Himself*. Translated by Lieut.-Col. Norgate. Edited by D. C. Philott. Calcutta: Baptist Mission, 1911.

Sherwood, M. M. *The Ayah and Lady: An Indian Story*. New York: John P. Haven, 1822.

Skinner, Capt. T. *Excursions in India, Including a Walk over the Himalaya Mountains, to the Sources of the Jumna and the Ganges*. 2 vols. London: Henry Colburn and Richard Bentley, New Burlington Street, 1832.

Spencer, A., ed. *Memoirs of William Hickey (1749–1792)*. 4 vols. London: Hurst & Blackett, Ltd., 1923.

Stanhope, P. D. *Genuine Memomirs of Asiaticus, in a Series of Letters to a Friend, During Five Year Residence in Different Parts of India...In the Service of the Nawab of Arcot*. London: J. Debrett, opposite Burlington House, Piccadilly, 1785.

Stavornius, J. S. *Voyages to the East Indies, Translated from the Original Dutch by Samuel Hull Wilcocke, with Notes and Additions by the Translator*. 3 vols. London: Printed for G. G. & J. Robinson, Paternoster-Row, 1798.

Stuart, C. *The Ladies Monitor, Being a Series of Letters, First Published in Bengal, on the Subject of Female Apparel, Tending to Favour a Regulated Adoption of Indian Costume; and a Rejection of Superfluous Vesture by the Ladies of This Country*. London: J. Bodwell, 344, near Catherine-Street, Strand, 1809.

Tennant, Rev. W. *India Recreations: Consisting of Thoughts on the Effects of the British Government on the State of India, Accompanied with Hints Concerning the Means of Improving the Condition of the Natives of That Country*. 2nd ed. 3 vols. Vol. 3. Edinburgh: University Press, 1808.

Williamson, Capt T. *The East India Vade-Mecum; or Complete Guide to Gentlemen Intended for the Civil, Military or Naval Service of the East India Company*. 2 vols. London: Printed for Black, Parry, and Kingsbury, 1810.

Williamson, Capt T., and F. W. Blagdon. *The Europeans in India; from a Collection of Drawings by Charles Doyley Esq...Accompanied by a Brief History of Ancient and Modern India from the Earliest Periods of Antiquity to the Termination of the Late Maharatta War*. London: Edward Orme, Bond Street, 1813.

Secondary Sources

Alam, M. *The Crisis of Empire in Mughal North India*. Delhi: Oxford University Press, 1986.

Alam, M., and S. Subrahmanyam, eds. *The Mughal State, 1526–1750*. New Delhi: Oxford University Press, 1998.

Alavi, S., ed. *The Eighteenth Century in India*. New Delhi: Oxford University Press, 2002.

Alloula, M. *Colonial Harem*. Translated by M. Godzich. Edited by W. Godzich. Manchester: Manchester University Press, 1986.

Appleton, S. J. "Women and Wills in Early Modern England: The Community of Stratford-Upon Avon, 1537–1649." University of Birmingham, 2016.

Auerbach, J. "The Picturesque and the Homogenisation of Empire." *The British Art Journal* 5, no. 1 (2004): 47–54.

Ballhatchet, K. *Race, Sex and Class under the Raj: Imperial Attitudes and Policies and Their Critics 1793–1905*. London: Weidenfeld and Nicolson, 1980.

Banerjee, S. *Dangerous Outcast: The Prostitute in Nineteenth Century Bengal*. Calcutta: Seagull Books, 1998.

Banerji, B. *Begum Samru*. Calcutta: Mittal Publications, 1989.

Banerji, H. *Inventing Subjects: Studies in Hegemony, Patriarchy and Colonialism*. New Delhi: Tulika, 2001.

Baxi, U. "People's Law in India, the Hindu Society." In *Asian Indigenous Law in Interaction with Received Law*, edited by Masaji Chiba, 216–65. London: Kegan Paul International, 1986.

Bayly, C. A. *Empire and Information: Intelligence Gathering and Social Communication in India, 1780–1870*. Cambridge Studies in Indian History and Society. Cambridge: Cambridge University Press, 1996.

———. *Indian Society and the Making of the British Empire*. The New Cambridge History of India. Cambridge: Cambridge University Press, 1990.

———. *Rulers, Townsmen and Bazaars: North Indian Society in the Age of British Expansion, 1770–1870*. 3rd ed. Oxford: Oxford University Press, 1983. 2012.

Benton, L. *Law and Colonial Cultures: Legal Regimes in World History, 1400–1900*. Cambridge: Cambridge University Press, 2001.

Bhattacharya, N. *Reading the Splendid Body: Gender and Consumerism in Eighteenth Century British Writings on India*. Newark, NJ: University of Delaware Press, 1998.

Bird, D. *Travelling in Different Skins: Gender Identity in European Women's Oriental Travelogues, 1850–1950*. Oxford Modern Languages and Literature Monographs. Oxford: Oxford University Press, 2012.

Blake, S. P. "Courtly Culture under Babur and the Early Mughals." *Journal of Asian History* 20, no. 2 (1986): 193–214.

———. "The Patrimonial-Bureaucratic Empire of the Mughals." *The Journal of Asian Studies* 39, no. 1 (1979): 77–94.

———. "Returning the Household to the Patrimonial-Bureaucratic Empire – Gender, Succession, and Ritual in the Mughal, Safavid and Ottoman Empires." In *Tributary Empires in World History*, edited by P. F. Bang and C. A. Bayly, 214–26. New York: Palgrave Macmillan, 2011.

Blunt, A. "Imperial Geographies of Home: British Domesticity in India, 1886–1925." *Transactions of the Institute of British Geographers* 24 (1999): 421–40.

Bowen, H. V. "Investment and Empire in the Later Eighteenth Century: East India Stockholding, 1756–1791." *Economic History Review, 2nd Series* 42, no. 2 (1989): 186–206.

Boxer, C. R. *Mary and Misogyny: Women in Iberian Expansion Overseas, 1414–1815: Some Facts, Fancies and Personalities*. London: Duckworth, 1975.

———. *Race Relations in the Portuguese Colonial Empire, 1415–1825*. Oxford: Clarendon Press, 1963.

Cassels, N. G. "Social Legislation under the Company Raj: The Abolition of Slavery Act V 1843." *South Asia: Journal of South Asian Studies* 11, no. 1 (1988): 59–87.

Chatterjee, I. "Colouring Subalternity: Slaves, Concubines and Social Orphans in Early Colonial India." In *Subaltern Studies*, edited by G. Bhadra, G. Prakash and S. Tharu. Delhi: Oxford University Press, 1999.

———. "Testing the Local against the Colonial Archive." *History Workshop Journal*, no. 44 (1997): 215–24.

_____, ed. *Unfamiliar Relations: Family and History in South Asia*. New Delhi: Permanent Black, 2004.

Chattopadhyaya, G. *Awakening in Bengal in Early Nineteenth Century: Selected Documents*. Calcutta: Progressive Publishers, 1965.

Chaudhuri, N. "Memsahibs and Motherhood in Nineteenth-Century Colonial India." *Victorian Studies* 31, no. 4 (1988): 517–35.

Chenoy, S. M. *The Mughal Capital in Time of Muhammad Shah or Murraqqa-I-Dehli of Dargah Quli Khan*. New Delhi: Deputy Publication, 1989.

Cohn, B. S. "The British in Benares: A Nineteenth Century Colonial Society." *Comparative Studies in Society and History* 4, no. 2 (1962): 169–99.

Collingham, E. M. *Imperial Bodies: The Physical Experience of the Raj, C. 1800–1947*. Cambridge: Polity Press, 2001.

Dalrymple, W. *The Anarchy: The East India Company, Corporate Violence, and the Pillage of an Empire*. New York: Bloomsbury Publishing USA, 2019.

———. *White Mughals: Love and Betrayal in Eighteenth Century India*. New Delhi: Penguin Books, 2002.

Datta, R. "Commercialisation, Tribute, and the Transition from Late Mughal to Early Colonial in India." *The Medieval History Journal* 6, no. 2 (2003): 259–91.

———. "The Making of the Eighteenth Century in India: Some Reflections on Its Political and Economic Processes." In *Sir J. N. Sarkar Memorial Lecture*. Kolkata: Bangiya Itihas Samiti, 2019.

Delgoda, S. T. "'Nabob, Historian and Orientalist.' Robert Orme: The Life and Career of an East India Company Servant (1728–1801)." *Journal of the Royal Asiatic Society* 2, no. 3 (1992): 363–76.

Dirks, N. B. "Castes of Mind." *Representations* 37: Special Issue: Imperial Fantasies and Postcolonial Histories (1992): 56–78.

———. *The Scandal of Empire – India and the Creation of Imperial Britain*. Cambridge, MA: The Belknap Press of Harvard University Press, 2008.

Dyson, K. K. *A Various Universe: A Study of the Journals and Memoirs of British Men and Women in the Indian Subcontinent, 1765–1856*. Oxford: Oxford University Press, 2002.

Eaton, N. "Nostagia for the Exotic: Creating an Imperial Art in London, 1750–1793." *Eighteenth-Century Studies* 39, no. 2 (2006): 227–50.

Ferguson, N. *Empire. How Britain Made the Modern World*. New Delhi: Allen Lane, 2004.

Finn, M. "Slaves out of Context: Domestic Slavery and the Anglo-Indian Family, C. 1780–1830." *Transactions of the Royal Historical Society*, Sixth Series 19 (2009): 181–203.

Fisch, J. "Solitary Vindicator the Hindus: The Life and Writings of General Charles Stuart (1757/8-1828)." *Journal of the Royal Asiatic Society of Great Britain and Ireland*, 117, no. 1 (1985): 35–57.

Fischer-Tine, H., and M. Mann. *Colonialism and Civilizing Mission: Cultural Ideology in British India*. London: Anthem Press, 2004.

Franklin, M. J. *Orientalist Jones: Sir William Jones, Poet, Lawyer, and Linguist, 1746–1794*. Oxford: Oxford University Press, 2011.

Furber, H. *John Company at Work: A Study of European Expansion in India in the Late Eighteenth Century*. Cambridge, MA: Harvard University Press, 1948.

Garg, S. *Monetary Foundations of the Raj*. New York: Routledge, 2019.

Ghose, I. *Travels, Explorations and Empires: Writings from the Era of Imperial Expansion, 1770–1835*. London: Pickering & Chatto, 2001.

Ghosh, D. "Decoding the Nameless: Gender, Subjectivity, and Historical Methodologies in Reading the Archives of Colonial India." In *A New Imperial History: Culture, Identity and Modernity in Britain and the Empire*, edited by Kathleen Wilson, 297–316. Cambridge: Cambridge University Press, 2004.

———. "Household Crimes and Domestic Order: Keeping the Peace in Colonial Calcutta, C. 1770–C. 1840." *Modern Asian Studies* 38, no. 3 (2004): 599–623.

———. "Making and Un-Making Loyal Subjects. Pensioning Widows and Educating Orphans in Early Colonial India." *The Journal of Imperial and Commonwealth History* 31, no. 1 (2010): 1–28.

———. *Sex and Family in Colonial India: The Making of Empire*. Cambridge: Cambridge University Press, 2008.

———. ""Who Counts as 'Native?': Gender, Race, and Subjectivity in Colonial India"." *Journal of Colonialism and Colonial History* 6, no. 3 (2005)). Project MUSE. https://doi.org/10.1353/cch.2006.0007.

Ghosh, S. C. *The Social Condition of the British Community in Bengal: 1757–1800*. Lieden: BRILL, 1970.

Gist, N. P., and R. D. Wright. *Marginality and Identity: Anglo-Indian as a Racially-Mixed Minority in India*. Monographs and Theoretical Studies in Sociology and Anthropology in Honour of Nels Anderson. Edited by K. Ishwaran. Leiden: E. J. BRILL, 1973.

Green, W. A., and J. P. Deasy Jr. "Unifying Themes in the History of British India, 1757–1857: An Historiographical Analysis." *Albion: A Quarterly Journal Concerned with British Studies* 17, no. 1 (1985): 15–45.

Hall, Catherine, and Sonya O. Rose. *At Home with the Empire – Metropolitan Culture and the Imperial World*. Cambridge: Cambridge University Press, 2006.

Harley, D. "Provincial Midwives in England: Lancashire and Chechire, 1660–1760." In *The Art of Midwifery: Early Modern Midwives in Europe*, edited by H. Marland, 27–48. London: Routledge, 1993.

Harlow, B., and M. Carter, eds. *Imperialism and Orientalism. A Documentary Sourcebook*. Oxford: Blackwell, 1999.

Harvey, K. "Sexuality and the Body." In *Women's History in Britain, 1700–1850: An Introduction*, edited by Hannah Barker and Elaine Chalus. Women's and Gender History, 78–99. London: Routledge, 2005.

Hasan, F. *State and Locality in Mughal India: Power Relations in Western India, C. 1572–1730*. Cambridge: Cambridge University Press, 2006.

Hawes, C. J. *Poor Relations: The Making of a Eurasian Community in British India, 1773–1833*. Surrey: Curzon Press, 1996.

Holden, Livia, ed. *Legal Pluralism and Governance in South Asia and Diasporas*. London: Routledge, 2015.

Hutchins, F. G. *The Illusion of Permanence: British Imperialism in India*. Princeton, NJ: Princeton University Press, 1967.

Hyam, R. "The Primacy of Geopolitcs: The Dynamics of British Imperial Policy, 1763–1963." In *The Statecraft of British Imperialism: Essays in Honour of Wm. Roger Louis*, edited by R. D. King and R. Kilson. London: Frank Cass, 1999.

———. *Empire and Sexuality: The British Experience*. Manchester: Manchester University Press, 2017.

James, S. E. *Women's Voices in Tudor Wills, 1485–1603: Authority, Influence and Material Culture*. Surrey: Ashgate, 2015.

Joseph, B. *Reading the East India Company, 1720–1840: Colonial Currencies of Gender*. Chicago, IL: University of Chicago Press, 2004.

Juneja, R. "The Native and the Nabob: Representations of the Indian Experience in Eighteenth Century English Literature." *Journal of Commonwealth Literature* 27, no. 1 (1992): 183–98.

Kabbani, R. *Europe's Myth of Orient: Device and Rule*. London: Macmillan, 1986.

Karras, R. M. *Sexuality in Medieval Europe: Doing Unto Others*. London: Routledge, 2017.

Kaul, H. K., ed. *Travellers' India: An Anthology*. New Delhi: Oxford University Press, 1997.

Kermode, J., and G. Walker, eds. *Women, Crime and the Courts in Early Modern England*. London: University College London Press, 1994. Reprint, Taylor & Francis e-Library, 2005.

Kerr, H. *A Few Words of Advice to Cadets, and Other Young Persons Proceeding to India*. London: Munro and Congreve, 1839.

Keymer, T., and J. Mee, eds. *The Cambridge Companion to English Literature, 1740–1830*. Cambridge: Cambridge University Press, 2004.

Kincaid, D. *British Social Life in India upto 1938*. London: Routledge, 1939.

Kolsky, E. *Colonial Justice in British India: White Violence and the Rule of Law*. Cambridge: Cambridge University Press, 2010.

———. "The Rule of Colonial Indifference: Rape on Trial in Early Colonial India, 1805–57." *The Journal of Asian Studies* 69, no. 4 (2010): 1093–117.

Kowaleski, M., and P. J. P. Goldberg, eds. *Medieval Domesticity: Home, Housing, and Household in Medieval England*. Cambridge: Cambridge University Press, 2009.

Kreps, B. I. "The Paradox of Women: The Legal Position of Early Modern Wives and Thomas Dekker's the Honest Whore." *ELH* 69, no. 1 (2002): 83–102.

Lafond, Jean-Pierre, ed. *Indika: Essays in Indo-French Relations, 1630–1976*. New Delhi: Manohar, 2000.
Lacqueur, T. *Making Sex: Body and Gender from the Greeks to Freud*. Cambridge, MA: Harvard University Press, 1990.
Lal, R. *Domesticity and Power in the Early Mughal World*. Cambridge: Cambridge University Press, 2005.
Laughlin, J. L. "Indian Monetary History." *Journal of Political Economy* 1, no. 4 (1893): 593–95.
Leask, N. *British Romantic Writers and the East: Anxieties of Empire*. Cambridge: Cambridge University Press, 1992.
Llewellyn-Jones, R., ed. *A Man of the Enlightenment in Eighteenth-Century India: The Letters of Claude Martin, 1766–1800*. Delhi: Permanent Black [in association with] The Embassy of France in India, 2003.
———. *A Very Ingenious Man: Claude Martin in Early Colonial India*. New Delhi: Oxford University Press, 1999.
Leonard, K. "Indigenous Banking Firms in Mughal India: A Reply." *Comparative Studies in Society and History* 23, no. 2 (1981): 309–13.
Leonard, Karen. "The 'Great Firm' Theory of the Decline of the Mughal Empire." *Comparative Studies in Society and History* 21, no. 2 (1979): 151–67.
Levine, P. "Venereal Disease, Prostitution, and the Politics of Empire: The Case of British India." *Journal of the History of Sexuality* 4, no. 4 (1994): 579–602.
Lewis, R. *Gendering Orientalism: Race, Femininity and Representation*. Gender, Racism, Ethnicity. Edited by Kum-Kum Bhamani. London: Routledge, 1996.
Loizides, A. *James Mill's Utilitarian Logic and Politics*. New York: Routledge, 2019.
Long, Rev. J. *Calcutta in the Olden Time: Its Localities & Its People*. Calcutta: Granthan & Sanskrit Pustak Bhandar, 1974.
Madar, H. "Before the Odalisque: Renaissance Representations of Elite Ottoman Women." *Early Modern Women: An Interdisciplinary Journal* 6 (2011): 1–42.
Mani, L. "Contentious Traditions: The Debate on Sati in Colonial India." *Cultural Critique*, no. 7 (1987): 119–56.
Markowitz, S. "Pelvic Politics: Sexual Dimorphism and Racial Difference." *Signs: Journal of Women in Culture and Societ* 26, no. 2 (2001): 389–414.
Marshall, P. J. *Bengal – the British Bridgehead – Eastern India, 1740–1828*. The New Cambridge History of India. Cambridge: Cambridge University Press, 1987.
———, ed. *The Eighteenth Century*. Edited by William Roger Louis, The Oxford History of the British Empire, vol. 2. Oxford: Oxford University Press, 1998.
———. *The New Cambridge History of India, Bengal: The British Bridgehead, Eastern India, 1740–1828*. Cambridge: Cambridge University Press, 1987.
Martin, R. M. *History of the Colonies of the British Empire in the West Indies, South America, North America, Austral-Asia, Africa and Europe: From the Official Records of the Colonial Office*. London: W. H. Allen, 1843.
McClintock, A. *Imperial Leather: Race, Gender and Sexuality in the Colonial Contest*. London: Routledge, 1995.
Mickelson, J. M. *British Women in India, 1757–1857*. Michigan: University of Michigan Press, 1978.
Morgan, J. "'Some Could Suckle over Their Shoulder': Male Travelers, Female Bodies, and the Gendering of Racial Ideology, 1500-1770." *William and Mary Quarterly* 54, no. 1 (1997): 167–92.

Mukherjee, S. N. *Sir William Jones: A Study in 18th Century British Attitudes to India*. Cambridge: Cambridge University Press, 1968.

Mukhia, H. *The Mughals of India*. Oxford: Blackwell Publishing, 2004.

Nair, J. "Uncovering the Zenana: Visions of Indian Womanhood in Englishwomen's Writings, 1813–1940." *Journal of Women's History* 2, no. 1 (1990): 8–34.

———. *Women and Law in Colonial India: A Social History*. Bangalore: Kali for Women, 1996.

Narayan, U. "Colonialism and Its Others: Considerations on Rights and Care Discourses." *Hypatia* 10, no. 2 (1995): 133–40.

Nayar, P. K. "The Rhetoric of Ruin: William Hodges' India." *1650–1850: Ideas, Aesthetics, and Inquiries in the Early Modern Era* 12 (2008): 75–106.

Nevile, P. *Beyond the Veil: Indian Women in the Raj*. New Delhi: Nevile Books, 2000.

Nijhar, P. *Law and Imperialism: Criminality and Constitution in Colonial India and Victorian England*. London: Pickering & Chatto Ltd., 2009.

Nussbaum, F. A. *The Brink of All We Hate: English Satires on Women, 1660–1750*. Kentucky: The University Press of Kentucky, 1984.

Oldenburg, V. T. "Lifestyle as Resistance: The Case of the Courtesans of Lucknow." *India Feminist Studies* 16, no. 2 (1990): 259–87.

Olivelle, P., and D. R. Davis Jr., eds. *The Oxford History of Hinduism: Hindu Law – a New History of Dharmaśāstra*. Oxford: Oxford University Press, 2018.

Osborn, J. *India and the Company in the Public Sphere*. Edited by H. V. Bowen, M. Lincoln and N. Rigby. Suffolk: The Boydell Press, 2002.

Pearse, H. *The Hearseys: Five Generations of an Anglo-Indian Family*. London: W. Blackwood and Sons, 1905.

Pettigrew, W. A., and M. Gopalan, eds. *The East India Company, 1600–1857: Essays in Anglo-Indian Connection*. London: Routledge, 2017.

Phillips, K. M. *Before Orientalism: Asian Peoples and Cultures in European Travel Writing, 1245 – 1510*. Philadelphia, PA: University of Pennsylvania Press, 2014.

Prakash, O. *European Commercial Enterprise in Pre-Colonial India, The New Cambridge History of India*. Cambridge: Cambridge University Press, 1998.

Rajan, R. S. *Real and Imagined Women: Gender, Culture and Postcolonialism*. New York: Routledge, 1995.

Riddy, F. "'Burgeis' Domesticity in Late Medieval England." In *Medieval Domesticity: Home, Housing and Household in Medieval England*, edited by Maryanne Kowaleski and P. J. P. Goldberg, 14–36. Cambridge: Cambridge University Press, 2009.

Ridley, H. *Images of Imperial Rule*. Routledge Library Editions: World Empires. London: Routledge, 2018.

Robb, P. "Clash of Cultures? An Englishman in Calcutta in the 1790s. An Inaugural Lecture Given on 12 March 1998." London: School of Oriental and African Studies, University of London, 1998.

———. *Sentiment and Self: Richard Blechynden's Calcutta Diaries, 1791–1822*. Oxford: Oxford University Press, 2011.

———. *Sex and Sensibility: Richard Blechynden's Calcutta Diaries, 1791–1822*. New Delhi: Oxford University Press, 2011.

Rosenberg, C. M. *Losing America, Conquering India: Lord Cornwallis and the Remaking of the British Empire*. Jefferson, NC: McFarland & Company, Inc., Publishers, 2017

Roy, T., and A. V. Swamy. *Law and Economy in Colonial India*. Chicago, IL: University of Chicago Press, 2016.

Roychowdhury, L. *The Jadu House: Travels in Anglo-India*. London: Black Swan, 2001.

Rubiés, Joan Pau. "Race, Climate and Civilization in the Works of François Bernier". Fourcade, Marie, and Ines G Županov. In *L'Inde des Lumières: Discours, histoire, savoirs (XVIIe-XIXe siècle)*, 53–78. Paris: Éditions de l'École des hautes études en sciences sociales, 2013. http://books.openedition.org/editionsehess/22612.

Said, E. W. *Orientalism*. New York: Vintage Books, 1979.

Sawyer, S., and A. Agarwal. "Environmental Orientalisms." *Cultural Critique* 45, no. Spring (2000): 71–108.

Schofield, K. B. "The Courtesan Tale: Female Musicians and Dancers in Mughal Historical Chronicles, C. 1556–1748." *Gender & History* 24, no. 1 (2012): 150–71.

Sen, I. *Women and Empire, Representations in the Writings of British India (1858–1900)*. New Delhi: Orient Longman, 2002.

Shah, Priya. "'Barbaric Pearl and Gold': Gendered Desires and Colonial Governance in Emma Roberts's Scenes and Characteristics of Hindostan." *Studies in Travel Writing* 16, no. 1 (2012): 31–46.

Shah, S. "In the Business of Kama: Prostitution in Classical Sanskrit Literature from the Seventh to the Thirteenth Centuries." *Medieval History Journal* 5, no. 1 (2002): 121–56.

Sharafi, Mitra. "South Asian Legal History." *Annual Review of Law and Social Science* 11, no. 1 (2015): 309–36.

Sharma, R. "The Indian Nautch Girl in Early Colonial Travel Writing." Edited by Mythili Anoop and Varun Gulati. Lanham, MD: Lexington Books, Rowman and Littlefield, 2016.

Singh, J. G. *Colonial Narratives Cultural Dialogues: 'Discoveries' of India in the Language of Colonialism*. London: Routledge, 1996.

Singha, R. "Colonial Law and Infrastructural Power: Reconstructing Community, Locating the Female Subject." *Studies in History* 19, no. 1 (2003): 87–126.

———. *Despotism of Law: Crime and Justice in Early Colonial India*. Delhi: Oxford University Press, 1998.

———. "Making the Domestic More Domestic: Criminal Law and the Head of the Household, 1772–1843." *Indian Economic & Social History Review* 33, no. 3 (1996): 309–43.

Sinha, C. "Doctrinal Influences on the Judicial Policy of the East India Company's Administration in Bengal, 1772–1833." *The Historical Journal* 12, no. 2 (1969): 240–48.

Sinha, N. "Who Is (Not) a Servant, Anyway? Domestic Servants and Service in Early Colonial India." *Modern Asian Studies* 54, no. 3 (2020): 1–55.

Sinha, P. *Calcutta in Urban History*. Calcutta: Firma KLM Pvt. Ltd., 1978.

Spear, P. *The Nabobs: A Study of the Social Life of the English in the Eighteenth Century*. Cambridge: Cambridge University Press, 1963.

Standford, J. K. *Ladies in the Sun. The Memsahibs' India 1790–1860*. London: Gallery Press, 1962.

Stoler, A. L. *Carnal Knowledge and Imperial Power: Race and the Intimate in Colonial Rule*. Berkeley, CA: University of California Press, 2002.

———. "Making Empire Respectable: The Politics of Race and Sexual Morality in 20th-Century Colonical Cultures." *American Ethnologist* 16, no. 4 (1989): 634–60.

———. "Matters of Intimacy as Matters of State: A Response." *The Journal of American History* 88, no. 3 (2001): 893–97.

———. "Rethinking Colonial Categories: European Communities and the Boundaries of Rule." *Comparative Studies in Society and History* 31, no. 1 (Jan., 1989): 134–61.

———. "Sexual Affronts and Racial Frontiers: European Identities and the Cultural Politics of Exclusion in Colonial Southeast Asia." *Comparative Studies in Society and History* 34, no. 3 (1992): 514–51.

Stone, L. *The Family, Sex and Marriage: England, 1500–1800*. London: Harper & Row, 1977.

Stuurman, S. "François Bernier and the Invention of Racial Classification." *History Workshop Journal* 50 (2000): 1–21.

Subrahmanyam, S. *Europe's India: Words, People, Empires, 1500–1800*. Cambridge, MA: Harvard University Press, 2017.

Teltscher, K. *India Inscribed: European and British Writing on India, 1600–1800*. New York: Oxford University Press, 1995

Thirsk, J. *The Rural Economy of England: Collected Essays*. London: The Hambledon Press, 1984.

Tobin, B. F. *Picturing Imperial Power: Colonial Subjects in 18th Century British Paintings*. Durham: Duke University Press, 1999

Verma, N. "The Many Lives of Ayah: Life Trajectories of Female Servants in Early Nineteenth-Century India." In *Servants' Pasts: Late Eighteenth to Twentieth Century South Asia*, edited by Nitin Sinha and Nitin Verma, 73–107. New Delhi: Orient Blackswan, 2019.

Verma, S. P., and A. J. Qaiser. *Art and Culture: Painting and Perspective*. Vol. 2, New Delhi: Abhinav Publications, 2002.

Wald, E. "From Begums and Bibis to Abandoned Females and Idle Women: Sexual Relationships, Venereal Disease and the Redefinition of Prostitution in Early Nineteenth-Century India." *Indian Economic and Social History Review* 46, no. 1 (2009): 5–25.

Walker, M. E. "The 'Nautch' Reclaimed: Women's Performance Practice in Nineteenth- Century North India." *South Asia: Journal of South Asia Studies* 37, no. 4 (2014): 551–67.

Wilkinson, T. *Two Monsoons*. London: Duckworth, 1976.

Wilson, K., ed. *A New Imperial History: Culture, Identity and Modernity in Britain and the Empire, 1660–1840*. Cambridge: Cambridge University Press, 2004.

Winks, R. W., The Oxford History of the British Empire. In *Historiography*. Vol. 5. Oxford: Oxford University Press, 2001.

Younger, C. *Anglo-Indians: Neglected Children of the Raj*. Delhi: B.R. Publishing Corp., 1987.

Zlotnick, S. "Domesticating Imperialism: Curry and Cookbooks in Victorian England." *Frontiers: A Journal of Women Studies* 16, no. 2/3 (1996): 51–68.

Paintings

"An Englishman Sits Smoking a Hookah as an Asian Man Approaches Making a Salaam. Engraving by W. Humphrys, C. 1834, after W. Daniell. Wellcome Collection. Public Domain Mark." One print: engraving; image 9.8 x 14.6 cm. London (26 Holles Street, Cavendish Square): Bull & Co. – Wellcome Library no. 24879i; https://wellcomecollection.org/works/vvhtrpx4.

"Ayah, or Female Attendant for European and Indian Women, Calcutta, West Bengal. Coloured Etching by Francois Balthazar Solvyns, Ca. 1808–1812." London: Wellcome Collection. - https://wellcomecollection.org/works/t5edz8r3.

"Female Attendants, Undated, by Sir Charles D'oyly, 1781–1845, Printed by the Behar Amateur Lithographic Press, 1781–1845." New Haven, CT: Yale Centre for British Art, Paul Mellon Collection. - http://collections.britishart.yale.edu/vufind/Record/3623224.

"George Morland, 1763–1804, British, Indian Girl, Oil on Canvas, Mounted on Panel." Oil on canvas mounted on panel. New Haven, CT: Yale Center for British Art, Paul Mellon Collection, 1793. - https://collections.britishart.yale.edu/catalog/tms:939.

"Grinding Corn, between 1792 and 1795, by Arthur William Devis, 1762–1822, Oil on Canvas." New Haven, CT: Yale Center for British Art, Paul Mellon Collection. - https://collections.britishart.yale.edu/catalog/tms:1199.

"Muslim Lady Reclining, 1789 (Probably a Bibi of a British Man, in Dacca), by Francesco Renaldi, 1755 after 1798, Oil on Canvas." New haven, CT: Yale Centre for British Art, Paul Mellon Collection. - http://collections.britishart.yale.edu/vufind/Record/1665157

"Tilly Kettle, 1735–1786, British, Active in India (1769–76), Dancing Girl, 1772, Oil on Canvas." New Haven, CT: Yale Centre for British Art, Paul Mellon Collection. - http://collections.britishart.yale.edu/vufind/Record/1671353.

"William Hodges, 1744–1797, British, the Marmalong Bridge, Ca. 1783, Oil on Canvas, Yale Center for British Art, Paul Mellon Collection, B1974.3.8." New Haven, CT: Yale Center for British Art, Paul Mellon Collection, 1783. - https://collections.britishart.yale.edu/catalog/tms:169.

INDEX

Printed in the United States
by Baker & Taylor Publisher Services